GLIMPSES OF THE NEW CREATION

Glimpses of the New Creation

Worship and the Formative Power of the Arts

W. David O. Taylor

WILLIAM B. EERDMANS PUBLISHING COMPANY
GRAND RAPIDS, MICHIGAN

Wm. B. Eerdmans Publishing Co.
4035 Park East Court SE, Grand Rapids, Michigan 49546
www.eerdmans.com

26 25 24 23   4 5 6 7

ISBN 978-0-8028-7609-6

Library of Congress Cataloging-in-Publication Data

Names: Taylor, W. David O., 1972- author. | Begbie, Jeremy.
Title: Glimpses of the New Creation : worship and the formative power of the
     arts / W. David O. Taylor.
Description: Grand Rapids, Michigan : Wm. B. Eerdmans Publishing Co., 2019. |
     Includes bibliographical references and index.
Identifiers: LCCN 2019011905 | ISBN 9780802876096 (paperback)
Subjects: LCSH: Christianity and the arts. | Aesthetics—Religious
     aspects—Christianity. | Public worship. | BISAC: RELIGION / Christian
     Rituals & Practice / Worship & Liturgy. | RELIGION / Christian Ministry /
     Pastoral Resources. | RELIGION / Christianity / Literature & the Arts.
Classification: LCC BR115.A8 T395 2019 | DDC 261.5/7—dc23
     LC record available at https://lccn.loc.gov/2019011905

To my friends,
who bear all things, believe all things,
hope all things, endure all things

Contents

Foreword

A scholar once wrote on the back of a book: "This book fills a much-needed gap in the market." In other words, it should never have been written.

In this case, the opposite is true. There are numerous books now available on the arts in worship—and rightly so. But few are needed as much as *Glimpses of the New Creation*. And for a number of reasons.

First, David Taylor presses us to ask: What do the arts actually *do* when employed in worship? This is quite different from asking: "Is this good art?" Or: "Is it appropriate?" Or: "Does it work?" Taylor wants to probe how the arts get inside us, how they shape the way we think, the way we sense the world around us as bodily creatures, the way we imagine the future, and the way we live once we've left the worship sanctuary. The arts, he reminds us, have the capacity to form (and de-form) us, and that has immense consequences for how they are drawn into the praise of God.

Second, Taylor is not bewitched by a generic concept of "art." He attends to the *distinctive* capacities of different artistic media. This is rare today, when one art medium is often treated as a kind of paradigm (and that usually means music or visual imagery), and everything else gets shoehorned into that category. Taylor presses us to ponder carefully the "singular powers" of diverse art forms.

Third and most important, although Taylor is very down-to-earth (he has always been an "on-the-ground" man), from the first page to the last, the book is theologically charged. Sadly, the arts in many churches are in danger of taking on an inflated life of their own. But in this book, the bottom line is always theological. As Taylor puts it, "the arts in worship ought to be freed to form the church in their own ways *though not on their own terms*." And what are the terms of worship? For this author, they cohere around the one true worshiper, Jesus Christ, and the conviction that our worship is a sharing by the Spirit in his supreme (and supremely human) worship.

David Taylor has established himself as one of the leading voices in theology and the arts today. He brings years of real-world wisdom to his writing, gleaned from hundreds of conversations with artists, worship leaders, and academic theologians from a multitude of different traditions. It is hard to imagine anyone not being enriched by this book. Indeed, you are likely to be given manifold glimpses of the New Creation to come.

JEREMY BEGBIE
Duke University

Acknowledgments

Similar to the work of artists, the work of writing a book often involves an element of discovery. While I have taught several courses on the topic of the arts in worship, it was not until I began writing this book that I discovered what it needed to be. But I could not have discovered its best shape apart from the help of good friends and colleagues.

Heartfelt thanks go to the following individuals who provided invaluable feedback on drafts of chapters: Peter Coehlo, Matt Dampier, Noel Snyder, Greg Scheer, Kevin Twit, Brian Turnbow, Lester Ruth, Wen Reagan, Daniel Campbell, Noel Snyder, Brian Moss, John Witvliet, and Jeremy Begbie. Special thanks go to Victoria Emily Jones for her incisive and timely comments. I am immensely grateful to my students at Fuller Seminary and Regent College for their lively engagement of the material and their helpful questions and suggestions.

I'm likewise grateful to the Laity Lodge retreat center for the opportunity to see how both pastors and laypersons might respond to ideas that I have developed in this book. Thanks to Blockhouse Coffee Shop for its provision of good coffee and to The Guild (and to Emily Scherer in particular) for its gift of a beautiful space in which to write the final drafts of the manuscript. To Christi Wells I owe double thanks: for creating the index to my first book with Eerdmans, *The Theater of God's World*, and for doing the same with this book—such an extraordinary gift. To Michael Thomson I owe particular thanks for his unwavering confidence in the success of the book; the same goes for James Ernest. And to Jenny Hoffman, my sincerest gratitude for shepherding this book to its final form.

To my children, Blythe and Sebastian, who bore patiently (and, justly enough, impatiently!) all the times that I had to excuse myself from the dinner table in order to complete the work of this book: a father's love from here to the moon and back. To my wife, Phaedra, who has borne all things, believed all things, hoped all things, and endured all things, I owe an incalculable debt of gratitude.

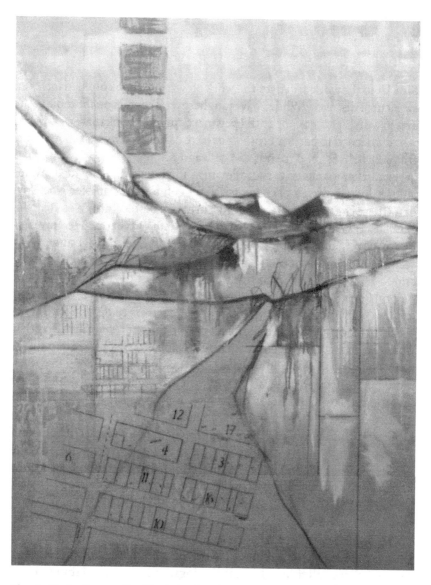

Phaedra Taylor, *Pentecost* (detail), Christ Church Anglican, Austin, Texas (2015)

Introduction

We have indeed been right to stress the priority of "being the Church" over "going to church." But we are now being reminded that the church people go to has an immensely powerful psychological effect on their vision of the Church they are meant to be. The church building is a prime aid, or a prime hindrance, to the building up of the Body of Christ. And what the building says so often shouts something entirely contrary to all that we are seeking to express through the liturgy. And the building will always win—unless and until we can make it say something else.

Bishop John A. T. Robinson,
preface to *Making the Building Serve the Liturgy*

To starve the eye, the ear, the skin, the nose is just as much to court death as to withhold food from the stomach.

Lewis Mumford, *The City in History*

The work of art is a "something"—a "reality" with powers of its own.

Michael Polanyi, *Meaning*

This book is about how the arts form the church in worship. The argument of this book is that every choice of art in corporate worship, what we might call liturgical art, both opens up and closes down possibilities for the formation of our humanity. This is another way of saying that no instance of art in worship is neutral. Each instance is potent—each in its own way. Each practice of, say, liturgical music or liturgical architecture, whether modern or folk, has its own singular powers.[1] It forms our desires; it shapes our capacities to imagine the world; it confirms and disturbs our emotional

---

1. This is language that I have borrowed from Jeremy Begbie, which he uses in *Resounding Truth: Christian Wisdom in the World of Music* (Grand Rapids: Baker Academic, 2007), ch. 11, to describe the unique capacities or characteristics of music to do its own work in its own kinds of ways.

instincts, while also activating the faculties of the physical body or muting them, as the case may be; and it solidifies and reconfigures identity and over time generates a certain way of being in the world.

Gesture in worship, for instance, forms us in its own ways. It does so by training Christlikeness in *sensory, bodily* manner. When hands are raised upward, this is a way for physical bodies to acquire a "feel for the game," to use a common sports metaphor. Hands raised upward engender at their best a feel for a life that is habitually oriented to the things "that are above." Hands raised "heavenward" express *and* train the heart to yearn for the things that characterize the life of God. Whether this hand raising is done in exclusively spontaneous or prescriptive fashion, with understanding or apart from it, in close quarters or in an expansive space, in a way that is familiar or strange to the congregation—all of these contextual aspects significantly determine how it will form a people. Context, one might say, is everything.

However the art is experienced, the presumption of this book is that the arts in worship ought to be freed to form the church in their own ways, though not on their own terms. The arts form us in their own ways by bringing us into intentional and intensive participation in the aesthetic aspect of our humanity—that is, our physical, emotional, imaginative, and metaphorical capacities. In doing so, they invite us to participate in the praise of the truly Human One, the Firstborn of creation, and in the praise of all creatures great and small, animate and inanimate, which by the Spirit's power raise their peculiar voices to our heavenly Father. If the arts are capable of becoming effective servants of the church at worship, I argue, it is only because they have been caught up in the life of the Triune Creator.

To say that the liturgical arts ought not to form us on their own terms is to say that they ought to form us on the terms of corporate worship, whatever they may be for a given congregation, whether Baptist or Lutheran, Presbyterian or Pentecostal.[2] Liturgical art serves worship—not the other way around. Poetry, for example, serves preaching. Architecture serves prayer. Music serves confession. Dance serves praise. Stained glass serves communion. Story serves reconciliation. Rhetoric serves testimony. Drama serves baptism. Video serves offertory. Whatever the art medium or mode of use, art's best service to the church's worship is by serving the purposes of the gathered assembly with its own "native tongue."

---

2. This is a point that several authors persuasively argue, among them Nicholas Wolterstorff, *Art in Action: Toward a Christian Aesthetic* (Grand Rapids: Eerdmans, 1980), who writes, "good liturgical art is art that serves effectively the actions of the liturgy and which we find generally good and satisfying to use in this way" (185).

If the argument of the book is right, the question then is this: How do our community's practices of art in worship form us in the triune life? Or more pointedly: how *might* they form us in the triune life? In this introduction I wish briefly to unpack some of the basic features of the book's argument. What do we mean by "singular powers"? How do we understand the aesthetic dimension of our humanity? How is the Triune God already at work in this dimension of our life? And how does context, in all its manifold aspects, open up and close down possibilities for the formation of a human life?

The Singular Powers of the Arts in Worship

To argue that the medium of visual art, for example, should be allowed to serve corporate worship in its own way is to recognize a distinctive power that visual art possesses—a power that must be understood and respected before it can be used well in a liturgical space with any hope of a fruitful outcome. Far too often advocates of art in worship rush headlong into superlatives—*Art is spiritual! It ushers the transcendent! It makes the invisible, visible!* That may be so, and fine as far as it goes, but it begs the question: Do the visual arts reveal something of the knowledge of God or the world or ourselves in a *unique* way? If so, how might the "logic" of visual art, in contrast to, say, the "logic" of music, open up an opportunity to form a people at worship?

A painting, for instance, does not unfold over time like a song does. A linen banner does not expire in the way that a musical note does. A cast-iron sculpture does not bend to the subjectivity of a particular audience as in the case of an anthem, which is sung one way by a professional choir and in a rather different manner by untrained folk. A two- or three-dimensional work of visual art, like John Nava's tapestries, featuring saints of all ages, races, and occupations across church history, hanging in the Cathedral of Our Lady of the Angels in Los Angeles, or the neo-Gothic architecture of St. John the Divine in New York City, built on high ground in cruciform shape, is *static*, insistently and visually *there*, and *indifferent* at some level to its audience.[3] These, among others, are art's singular powers.[4]

3. See http://www.johnnava.com/COLA/COS.html; http://www.olacathedral.org/cathedral/art/tapestries.html; and http://www.stjohndivine.org/about/architecture/cathedral-concrete.

4. On this point, see my essay in *Contemporary Art and the Church: A Conversation between Two Worlds*, ed. W. David O. Taylor and Taylor Worley (Downers Grove, IL: IVP Academic, 2017), ch. 10; and Katie Kresser, "Contemporary Art and Worship: *Imago Dei* in the Twenty-First Century," in *Contemporary Art and the Church*, ch. 9.

As it relates to the other media of art, how does poetry "work"? What does dance enable us to "say" to God that we could not say otherwise? What is the unique power of a live dramatic performance? How does story shape identity? How do spaces "learn" their inhabitants? How do color, stone, wood, metal, glass, and wind praise God in their own ways? How do different forms of music—Lutheran cantatas or rock-and-roll anthems or improvised spirituals—enable us to be in the world in irreducibly particular ways? And how might the singular powers of film and the oratorical arts overlap? These are the sorts of questions that require a careful, clear-headed answer if we wish to discern the ways in which the arts form our humanity in worship.

An Aesthetic Way of Knowing the World

To say that the arts afford us a distinctive way of being in the world is to say, as I will argue more fully in chapter 3, that *they bring us into intentional and intensive participation in the aesthetic aspect of our humanity.* By this I mean that the arts engender a way to grasp the world through our physical bodies, they afford us a unique way to be emotionally attuned to others, they enable us to imagine what, at first glance, may seem improbable or even impossible, and they immerse us in a sphere of metaphors by which human beings make sense of their personal and social lives.

Art and the Senses

What most of us know at a general, if only subconscious, level, artists know firsthand: that our physical bodies afford us an irreducible sense of the world.[5] Mark Johnson, in his book *The Meaning of the Body: Aesthetics of Hu-*

---

5. Maurice Merleau-Ponty, *Phenomenology of Perception,* trans. Colin Smith (London: Routledge, 1962), 162. He adds this: "The body is the vehicle of being in the world, and to have a body is, for a living creature, to be intervolved in a definite environment, to identify oneself with certain projects and be continually committed to them" (94). The bodily basis of meaning is explored variously by Mark Johnson, *The Meaning of the Body: Aesthetics of Human Understanding* (Chicago: University of Chicago Press, 2007), x; Michael Polanyi, *The Tacit Dimension* (Chicago: University of Chicago Press, 1966), 2–25; James K. A. Smith, *Imagining the Kingdom: How Worship Works* (Grand Rapids: Baker Academic, 2013), 29–100; Tony Clark, *Divine Revelation and Human Participation: Responsive and Imaginative*

man Understanding, writes, "what and how anything is meaningful to us is shaped by our specific form of incarnation."[6] David Abram adds that, for human beings, meaning "sprouts in the very depths of the sensory world."[7] Humans make sense of their worlds by "coming to their senses."[8] Their sense of awe before God, their sense of delight in the details of life, their sense of truth in reality and of hope for the future—these are all bodily rooted senses.[9]

The ballet dancer, for example, knows the properties of velocity rather differently than a non-dancing physicist. The dancer knows them tactilely; the physicist knows them theoretically.[10] Misty Copeland, a principal dancer with the American Ballet Theater, describes her earliest experience of dance this way. After only a few weeks of dance classes, at the rather late age of thirteen, Copeland was able to perform pirouettes and renversés. As she explains in her memoir, *Life in Motion*, "My body knew what my mind didn't yet comprehend."[11] Her body possessed an intuitive knowledge of dance long before she acquired knowledge about dance.

What is true of the art of ballet is also true of the kinetic arts of corporate worship. What a ballet dancer knows kinetically, a worshiper will also know kinetically—that is, through the physical body in motion. A mature worshiper acquires a *know-how* of a Christlike life by way of the physically constitutive practices of corporate worship—through embodied practices of prayer and of reconciliation, practices of Communion and of singing and of confession, for instance. It is the liturgical arts, at their best, that train our bodies in intentional and intensive ways to become, say, *confessionally* faithful or *eucharistically* faithful Christ-shaped persons.

Participation (Eugene, OR: Cascade, 2008), ch. 5; Iain McGilchrist, *The Master and His Emissary: The Divided Brain and the Making of the Western World* (New Haven: Yale University Press, 2009), esp. ch. 3.

6. Johnson, *The Meaning of the Body*, ix.

7. David Abram, *The Spell of the Sensuous: Perception and Language in a More-Than-Human World* (New York: Vintage Books, 1996), 75.

8. Morris Berman, *Coming to Our Senses: Body and Spirit in the Hidden History of the West* (New York: Simon and Schuster, 1989).

9. Don E. Saliers, *Worship Come to Its Senses* (Nashville: Abingdon, 1996).

10. While both knowledge *of* and knowledge *about* matter, they matter differently. On this point, see Howard Gardner, *Frames of Mind: The Theory of Multiple Intelligences* (New York: Basic Books, 2011), ch. 4. Witness also the short documentary "The Art of Flight," https://www.youtube.com/watch?v=kh29_SERH0Y.

11. Misty Copeland, *Life in Motion: An Unlikely Ballerina* (New York: Touchstone, 2014), 21.

Art and Emotion

As with the physical senses, so with the emotions: the arts foreground them.[12] In *Last Night a DJ Saved My Life*, Bill Brewster and Frank Broughton write, "DJing is not just about choosing a few tunes. It is about generating shared moods; it's about understanding the feelings of a group of people and directing them to a better place."[13] "What's important," argues the illustrator Christoph Niemman, "is the story, the message, the feeling, the connection."[14] "You have to feel the emotion of what you're seeing," the choreographer Benjamin Milliped remarks in the film documentary "Reset."[15] As the English and quintessentially Romantic poet William Wordsworth puts it: "all good poetry is the spontaneous overflow of powerful feelings."[16]

As these comments illustrate, for artists the emotions play a significant and constitutive role in the experience of making and sharing art. Alex Neill puts the general point this way: "The thought that art is in one way or another profoundly connected with human emotion . . . is one that has run very deep for a very long time."[17] For Leo Tolstoy, an artist seeks to convey his emotion to the reader so that the reader might experience that same emotion;[18] or as philosopher R. G. Collingwood sees it, making art is a process that enables the artist to clarify her emotion.[19] Whatever the view, the relation between art and emotion is an integral one.

An exuberantly joyful liturgical dance in response to the miraculous

12. Aware of the complex and contested territory that characterizes the scholarly study of emotions, and of the careful distinctions that scientists and philosophers draw between ideas of emotion, feeling, affect, affection, mood, and passion, in this book I will use the terms "emotions," "feelings," and "affections" interchangeably. Cf. Helena Wulff, ed., *The Emotions: A Cultural Reader* (Oxford: Berg, 2007).

13. Cited in Amena Brown, *Breaking Old Rhythms: Answering the Call of a Creative God* (Downers Grove, IL: IVP, 2013), 47.

14. In "Abstract: The Art of Design," https://youtu.be/DYaq2sWTWAA.

15. See https://www.youtube.com/watch?v=NTkpb2Uqxp8.

16. William Wordsworth, in "Preface to Lyrical Ballads," in *English Literature and Its Backgrounds*, vol. 2, *From the Forerunners of Romanticism to the Present*, ed. Bernard D. Grebanier et al., rev. ed. (New York: Dryden Press, 1949), 336.

17. Alex Neill, "Art and Emotion," in *Oxford Handbook of Aesthetics*, ed. Jerrold Levinson (Oxford: Oxford University Press, 2005), 421. Tiger C. Roholt says, "If we construe emotion broadly to include not only the full-blown variety such as sadness and elation but also feelings such as pleasure, then we find emotion to be ubiquitous in the philosophy of art." *Key Terms in Philosophy of Art* (London: Bloomsbury Academic, 2013), 26.

18. Leo Tolstoy, *What Is Art?*, trans. Aylmer Maude (New York: Thomas Y. Crowell, 1898), 43.

19. Roholt, *Key Terms in Philosophy of Art*, 28.

deliverance of God may befit one occasion, while a quiet, more contemplative movement may befit another occasion. A church graveyard, as a work of sculptural art, physically confronts a congregation with an image of death. It may evoke in members of the congregation hopeful or fearful emotions as they are reminded weekly of their own mortality. And a short film shown during the sermon that depicts the tragic effects of the sex trade may provoke deep sadness in the worshiper, while a spoken word about the systemic damage of racism, performed during the prayers of the people, may provoke a righteous anger in a congregation.

Art and the Imagination

As with the physical body and the emotions, so with the imagination: it, too, is a fundamental way to know the world and to discover our place in it. Garrett Green, in his book *Imagining God*, writes that the "imagination is the means by which we are able to represent anything not directly accessible, including *both* the world of the imaginary *and* recalcitrant aspects of the real world; it is a medium of fiction as well as fact."[20] Such is the case, for example, with both Orthodox and Amish worship.

Worship in an Eastern Orthodox congregation correlates faithful worship with a sensory richness. Old Order Amish worship, on the other hand, ties worthy praise to an artistically spare arrangement. With Orthodox worship, an Amazon rainforest–like fecundity of aesthetic data functions as entry point to see the world as God sees it. With Amish worship, a Sahara-like austerity serves as the suitable medium for the exchange of nonphysical "spirit" with immaterial "Spirit." With the former, the presence of God is refracted *through* physical and artistic artifacts. With the latter, the presence of God is perceived *beyond* the physical creation, which in turn points beyond itself to the Creator, immortal, invisible.

The "festal muchness" that characterizes the aesthetic shape of Orthodox worship is not necessarily better, one might argue, than the "cleansing simplicity" that marks the aesthetic condition of Amish worship.[21] Both

20. Garrett Green, *Imagining God: Theology and the Religious Imagination* (Grand Rapids: Eerdmans, 1998), 66.

21. This is language that I use in the essay "The Dangers," in *For the Beauty of the Church: Casting a Vision for the Arts*, ed. W. David O. Taylor (Grand Rapids: Baker Books, 2010), 159–62. While Wolterstorff's point is well taken, in *Art in Action*, 185, that liturgical art should generally aim at "simplicity," in order for it to serve the actions of the liturgy with clarity and

imagine something true about God's world. But they also imagine the God-world relation in radically different ways. The liturgical context, for each, becomes a microcosm of the world at large. To perceive the aesthetic data of corporate worship is to imagine, consciously or not, something true about the cosmos. Each practice of liturgical arts, moreover, inscribes a social imaginary, for the media of art that bind an Orthodox congregation together will be seen, as likely as not, to separate an Amish congregation from each other, and vice versa.[22]

Art and Metaphor

The last element that comprises an aesthetic understanding of the world as well as a fundamental characteristic of the arts is metaphor.[23] A metaphor is the understanding of one kind of thing in terms of an unexpected other. *Jesus is a vine. The church is a temple. Miles Davis is the Picasso of jazz.*[24] Take the use of the physical body in corporate worship, for example. The energetic movement that characterizes electronic dance music (EDM) worship engenders a particular way of praising God. The worship of God here occurs through "ecstatic" means: as a medium to get outside herself (*ek + stasis*), EDM's expressive physical movement enables the worshiper to get over herself in order to give herself utterly over to God. EDM worship, in its (artificial) fusion of *these* particular musical sounds, with *those* physical movements, in *this* particular context, functions as a kind of metaphor. To praise God *wholly* in this way is akin to the kinesthetically maximal register of Psalm 150, with its summons of the whole self to the praise of God. The experience also becomes a metaphor to view all of life as an act of *un-selfing*.[25]

But this is not the only way to give oneself wholly to God in praise. The

---

without distraction, I might wish to add that simplicity is a culturally contextual virtue and that what is felt to be "simple" for one congregation is felt differently for another.

22. Cf. Charles Taylor, *Modern Social Imaginaries* (Durham, NC: Duke University Press, 2004), 23.

23. This is a key argument for Jeremy Begbie in his book *Voicing Creation's Praise: Towards a Theology of the Arts* (Edinburgh: T&T Clark, 1991), 233.

24. George Lakoff and Mark Johnson, *Metaphors We Live By* (Chicago: University of Chicago Press, 1980), 5.

25. This is a term that Hans Urs von Balthasar uses to describe the work of the Spirit to conform us to Christ's life in his book *Theo-Drama*, trans. Graham Harrison (San Francisco: Ignatius Press, 1992), 5:334. This term also appears throughout Eugene Peterson's book *Where Your Treasure Is: Psalms That Summon You from Self to Community* (Grand Rapids: Eerdmans, 1993).

extensive use of silence and stillness that marks Taizé-style prayer services engenders a different set of bodily instincts, which, in turn, invite a profound surrender of the whole self to God.[26] In quieting the operations of the body—by being physically silent, in respect of Psalm 46 perhaps—the worshiper seeks to quiet her whole self in order to attend wholly to God. This is of course what happens when the body becomes still: things slow down. In slowing down, the worshiper is given a chance to re-collect all the parts of herself as a way to center herself, so that all of it can be yielded to God in worship. This kind of experience also opens up the possibility of seeing all of life, metaphorically speaking, as a quieted attention to God.

Although one might say that the basic goal is the same—a whole offering of self to God—the kind of knowledge that each liturgical practice affords is distinct; and depending on one's theological conviction, it is also distinctly good or to be avoided altogether.

The Liturgical Arts in the Economy of the Triune God

To inquire after the role of the arts in corporate worship also requires us to ask a fundamental theological question: What role do these aesthetic artifacts of human manufacture play in the economy of the Trinity? What are the triune purposes of the physical creation? What specifically is the imagination for—*in Christ*? How does the Holy Spirit enable the liturgical arts like Messianic Jewish circle dances or digital projections to become signs of the good news and foretastes of the new creation? And in what ways might this same Spirit make use of hip-hop poetry or rich expanses of silence to counter the idols of the mind, to repair forgetful memories, to rectify a will that is warped, to heal the disorder of broken bodies and dysfunctional affections, and to illumine the imagination to see the world as God sees it?[27]

The key question is not simply how the arts can lead to the faithful praise of God and the edification of the church. The key question, more crucially and far more interestingly, is how the Triune God is *already* active in creation. In Christ, the physical, affective, imaginative, and metaphoric aspects of our humanity are *already* being transformed. The Father is *already* liberating the cosmos from its bondage to decay. The Spirit is *already* en-

26. See https://www.youtube.com/watch?v=j4ukgp1YAr0 and https://www.youtube .com/watch?v=645lh5xmYo4.

27. I develop these ideas at length in *The Theater of God's Glory: Calvin, Creation, and the Liturgical Arts* (Grand Rapids: Eerdmans, 2017).

abling the stuff of heaven and earth to resound with the glory of God. Said otherwise, hue and texture, decibels and rhythm and metaphoric speech are *already* being loved, named, judged, redeemed, and rightly oriented by the Triune God before humans enter the scene.

In concrete terms, while creation bears witness to God "in its own ways," praising God by being fully itself, creation is also put to artistic and symbolic uses in a liturgical context. Wind, flesh, and stone praise God in their *wind-y, flesh-y, stone-y* ways; they also praise God in humanly devised musical, dancerly, and architectural ways. In the end, the purpose of the arts in theological terms is not to "get out of the way" of worship. The purpose of the arts is to *fittingly* serve the respective activities of the church's liturgy, whether praise, thanksgiving, confession, proclamation, or otherwise.

When this is done, I wish to propose that the church at worship, helped along by the diligent labors of liturgical artists, becomes a *partner* of Christ's praise and a *poet* to creation's praise: on the one hand joining Christ's praise for all of the Father's marvelous works as well as offering praise of and through Christ, while, on the other, joining the praise of the cosmos but also, by the Spirit's power, translating and transposing that praise through the metaphorical and material language of the arts. It is in this sense that one might speak of the church's praise as a symbolic prelude to the restoration of creation's perfect praise.

Context Is Everything

The manner in which a work of liturgical art forms the church at worship is contextually based. This is perhaps to state the obvious, but it bears stating nonetheless. The formative powers of the arts are inevitably conditioned by social, cultural, and linguistic factors, among others. Chant in Latin means one thing for the Roman Catholic brothers at Pluscarden Abbey in Moray, Scotland. It means quite a different thing to an Anglican couple (like myself and my wife) whose grasp of Latin is academic at best and at worst a barrier to meaningful participation in worship. How a black Baptist choir *feels* a gospel song, such as "Take My Hand, Precious Lord," written by former bluesman Thomas A. Dorsey in 1932, is markedly different than how a traditional Korean Presbyterian choir *feels* that same song and all of its sociocultural associations.

When the Presbyterian Charles G. Finney (1792–1875) imported certain features from camp meetings, such as the style of singing, into public worship, this transfer of music from one context to another, as Tim Dowley explains, introduced "customs that have exercised a lasting effect on American worship practice."[28] The same can be said about the music of Youth for Christ in the mid-twentieth century and the music of John and Charles Wesley in the eighteenth century.[29] Singing a particular music at summer camp and in the open fields is one thing; singing that same music in corporate worship is another. And while certain concert-goers may feel inspired to pray while listening to a performance of Rachmaninov's *Liturgy of St. John Chrysostom* (1910), many Orthodox believers find it too operatic for liturgical use.

My point here is not simply that one kind of art in worship is different from another kind. The point is that each instance of liturgical art possesses inherent powers, capable of forming a particular people in a particular context. In the process, liturgical identity is reinforced, making certain practices of art more or less viable in that same context. Whatever is "orderly," "participatory," "respectful," "holy," "sacred," "reverential," "cool," "grave," "missional," or capable of "touching the Father-heart of God"—none of these liturgical priorities are self-evident, contextless things. As they relate to the arts in worship, they are even less so. While biblical and theological ideas play a determinative role in whether a specific work of art in worship is considered "decent" or "authentic," contextual matters play an equally decisive role.

This is another way of reiterating what I stated at the beginning, that each instance of liturgical art opens up and closes down possibilities for the formation of a human life in the particular contexts of corporate worship.

Opening Up and Closing Down the Formation of a Human Life

The loss of songbooks, for certain congregations, has involved a lost opportunity to teach people how to read music or to sing four-part harmony. The inclusion of floodlights—by which mood can be modulated, visibility restricted, the perception of worship leaders altered, and a videographic scenery superimposed on the chancel or stage—may, for other congregations, stimulate theater-like desires that are at odds with the intentions of specific liturgical activities. The replacement of in-person testimonies with videoed testimonies undoubtedly secures a well-spoken word and keeps

28. Tim Dowley, *Christian Music: A Global History* (Minneapolis: Fortress, 2011), 180.
29. See *Wonderful Words of Life: Hymns in American Protestant History and Theology*, ed. Richard J. Mouw and Mark A. Noll (Grand Rapids: Eerdmans, 2004).

the worship on time. Yet it may likewise increase a sense of inadequacy in parishioners who witness these precisely edited, pre-produced testimonies, set to an evocative soundtrack, and find that their own unedited, inarticulate, unscored lives cannot measure up to the lives of their brethren played out on the silver screen.

This is simply to say that every practice of art in worship opens up and closes down possibilities to form a congregation. At its best, the use of a songbook, which includes the willingness to learn the scored music and to sing four-part harmony, invites a congregation to attend to each other's voices and to inhabit a pattern of textured sound. In precisely this way, they are able to experience a sense of aurally tethered, physically resonant *togetherness*, what Alfred Schutz calls a "mutual tuning-in relationship."[30] Conversely, the use of a video projector, at its best, enables a congregation to attend to each other visually, if only peripherally, as they look up rather than down. It allows them to take advantage of the kinetic power of the hands: to respond freely to the music and to give a visible sign of the church's unity (Ps. 134:2; 1 Tim. 2:8). In this way, with holy hands, wholly raised, in all shapes and sizes, the congregation is united.[31]

There is, of course, no practice of art in worship that forms a congregation comprehensively. Each practice does some things but not others to form our knowledge and love of God in worship. Each practice of liturgical art activates the imagination, the emotions, and the senses in unique ways. Each practice of liturgical art, alternatively, mutes the aesthetic dimension of our humanity. So the question for any given congregation is how its practices of art in worship over time might more richly form them in the triune life in a way that remains integral to their context and their tradition. This is both the promise and the challenge of every decision about the arts in worship.

What This Book Is Not

Having looked at what this book aims to accomplish, I would like to clearly state what this book is not. This book is not a biblical argument for the arts in

---

30. In Mary E. McGann, *Exploring Music as Worship and Theology: Research in Liturgical Practice* (Collegeville, MN: Liturgical Press, 2002), 25.

31. It is of course possible to imagine a congregation so musically capable that it could sing four-part harmonies by memory, without the aid of a hymnbook, even as they raised their hands in one accord, and thereby remained richly together. But this would be a rare case. It is more usual that congregations will be one or the other or a mix of some sort.

worship, even if we might argue that Holy Scripture supplies a fundamental grammar to think about them.[32] Nor is this book a history of the worship arts. History offers us insight into the ways in which our particular tradition shapes us, for better or for worse.[33] But this book does not engage in extensive historical analysis. And while a Trinitarian theology orients the project throughout, a theology of art does not exhaust the interests of the book. The driving interest of this book is with the formative powers of the arts in a corporate worship context.[34] How do music, visual art, story, poetry, dance, and drama *work*? What are their *powers*? And how might they *form* the people of God at worship in their own ways but not on their own terms?[35]

It is impossible, of course, to write a book on art in worship without raising normative questions in the mind of the reader. What ought we to be doing with the arts in worship? How should we remain faithful to Scripture or to our particular context? How do we remain truthful to the God whom we worship? These are important questions. But while I touch on normative issues throughout, I choose to hold lightly certain *oughts* and

32. Helpful resources here include Michael A. Farley, "What Is 'Biblical' Worship? Biblical Hermeneutics and Evangelical Theologies of Worship," *Journal of the Evangelical Theological Society* 51 (Sept. 2008): 591–613; Begbie, *Resounding Truth*, ch. 2; Peter J. Leithart, "Synagogue or Temple? Models for the Christian Worship," *Westminster Theological Journal* 63 (2002): 119–33; N. T. Wright, "Freedom and Framework, Spirit and Truth: Recovering Biblical Worship," *Studia Liturgica* 32, no. 2 (2002): 176–95; William A. Dyrness, *Visual Faith: Art, Theology, and Worship in Dialogue* (Grand Rapids: Baker Academic, 2001), chs. 1 and 3.

33. A few good resources include Peter Auksi, "Simplicity and Silence: The Influence of Scripture on the Aesthetic Thought of the Major Reformers," *Journal of Religious History* 10, no. 4 (1979): 343–64; Wladyslaw Tatarkiewicz, "The Great Theory of Beauty and Its Decline," *Journal of Aesthetics and Art Criticism* 31 (1972): 165–80; William L. Holladay, *The Psalms through Three Thousand Years: Prayerbook of a Cloud of Witnesses* (Minneapolis: Fortress, 1993); Paul Westermeyer, *Te Deum: The Church and Music* (Minneapolis: Fortress, 1998).

34. It is hopefully obvious by now that my use of the phrase "worship art" is meant to include all media of art, not only the visual arts. The latter is the presumption of books like Janet R. Walton, *Art and Worship: A Vital Connection* (Collegeville, MN: Liturgical Press, 1998); Christopher Irvine and Anne Dawtry, *Art and Worship* (Collegeville, MN: Liturgical Press, 2002); Albert Rouet, *Liturgy and the Arts*, trans. Paul Philibert (Collegeville, MN: Liturgical Press, 1997).

35. John D. Witvliet has played a significant role in the contemporary shift of attention in worship studies from the "expressive" view of corporate worship to a "formative" view. See, for example, his essay, "Liturgy as God's Language School," *Pastoral Music* 31, no. 4 (2007): 19–23; and "What to Do with Our Renewed Trinitarian Enthusiasm: Forming Trinitarian Piety and Imagination through Worship and Catechesis," in *Trinitarian Theology for the Church: Scripture, Community, Worship*, ed. Daniel L. Treier and David Lauber (Downers Grove, IL: IVP Academic, 2009), 237–53.

shoulds. I do this so that readers, occupying all points along the ecclesial and liturgical spectrum, will be able to clarify their own convictions. I trust that they also will discover something useful in these pages: new insights to inform their own practices of art in worship; exposure to the practices of other congregations as a way to engender sympathetic understanding; careful language to describe the media of art; theological ideas to underscore present uses of art in worship or even to push against them; and the opportunity to love God and neighbor *through* the liturgical arts.[36]

It goes without saying that this book does not pretend to say everything that could be said about the arts in worship. It is *far* from exhaustive. In some cases the treatment of the topic will be cursory instead of substantive, as with the chapter on the meanings of art.[37] In other cases, it will be selective rather than comprehensive, as with the exploration of architecture and the exclusion of film.[38] The use of illustrations often represents personal experiences, and the case studies will vary in length and focus. My hope nonetheless is that teachers and students, along with pastors, worship leaders, and artists, will find the contents of the book helpful in some manner to their work. My aim in the end is to present a vision for the arts in worship as instruments of the Trinity—and as glimpses of the new creation—to form and feed the people of God. My hope is that such a vision may be seen as good news for the church at worship, whether of the "traditional" or "contemporary" sort, whether of the majority or minority world, and that such a vision might be seen, on its best days, as good news for a watching world, too.

A Chapter-by-Chapter Summary of the Book

Without becoming derailed by the near-infinite concerns a reader may bring to the question of worship, I offer a working definition and a general

36. Frank Burch Brown says it well, in *Inclusive Yet Discerning: Navigating Worship Artfully* (Grand Rapids: Eerdmans, 2009), 20: "Hospitality does not mean accepting every kind of music and art that others like, without question or criticism. Instead, as an extension of the will and habit of love, it means learning more about what others care for, and finding a middle ground where, with patience and practice, we can transcend initial reactions of distaste or even revulsion."

37. For a near-exhaustive collection of essays on the topic of the arts in worship, see Robert E. Webber, ed., *The Complete Library of Christian Worship*, vol. 4: *Music and the Arts in Christian Worship, Book 2* (Nashville: Star Song, 1994).

38. I explore some of the issues related to the videographic arts in the appendix.

vision for faithful worship in chapter 1. In chapter 2 I define what I mean by art. A wide range of meanings marks discussions of art both within a common culture (such as the contemporary art scene of New York City or Mexico City) and across cultures (say, predominantly European and Asian, urban and rural). The visceral feeling and heightened rhetoric that mark discussions of the arts in worship only underscore the need for a careful use of terms.

In any discussion of the arts in worship, normative concerns inevitably come into play. What *ought* we do with the arts in corporate worship? What *could* we do better? And what *might* we do that we have yet to try? Chapter 3 focuses on the theological dimension of the liturgical arts. It does so by advancing a Trinitarian vision for the arts that stresses the goodness of creation and the goodness of culture as an expression of the work of the Father, the Son, and the Spirit to enable these things to become good for human beings within a context of worship.

In chapters 4 through 9, I ask the same basic question of each medium of art. What does music "do"? What do the visual arts "do"? What do the poetic and narrative arts, along with the dramatic and kinetic arts, "do"? What are their respective singular powers? How might they serve corporate worship? And how do specific practices of art enable the faithful to be in the world in irreducibly particular ways? These six chapters also explore ways in which the different uses of liturgical art open up and close down possibilities for the formation of our humanity at worship.

If we can assume that public worship is a primary place for the discipleship of God's people, what does it mean for a congregation to use art in worship with its "mother tongue," as a way to be true to itself, while also being open to new practices of art in worship, to worship with "adjectival tongues"? Chapter 10 addresses the question of tradition and innovation as it relates to practices of liturgical art. In chapter 11 I explore ways in which the arts within a liturgical context might serve the mission of God in the world. And I conclude the book with an invitation to the reader to consider ways in which the liturgical arts might become instruments of love, for God's sake, and for the sake of the world that God so loves.

Gustave Doré, *Paradiso, Canto XXXI* (ca. 1868)

CHAPTER 1

The Meanings of Worship

Worship is a journey—a journey into God's presence (gathering), of hearing from God (Word), that celebrates Christ (Table), and that sends us into the world changed by our encounter with God (sending).

Constance Cherry, *The Worship Architect*

In God's Home there is an everlasting party. What is celebrated there is not some occasion that passes; the choirs of angels keep eternal festival, for the eternally present face of God is joy never diminished.

Saint Augustine, *Expositions of the Psalms*

The liturgical environment isn't the artistic playground for even the most gifted of artisans. It is the sacred space in which liturgy is celebrated so that the paschal mystery of Jesus Christ unfolds.

Joyce Ann Zimmerman,
The Ministry of Liturgical Environment

The basic presumption of this book is that the arts ought to serve the worship of the church in their own ways but not on their own terms. The arts should always serve the church on the terms of corporate worship, whatever they may be for a given congregation. Art will not serve worship best, I argue, when it is done "for art's sake." Within a liturgical context, it is art not for experts' but for worshipers' eyes; it is art that aims not to draw attention to itself but "to impart the urge to pray."[1] Only on these terms will the arts render their best service. In order for us to have a fruitful discussion about the ways in which art might serve corporate worship, however, we need first to be clear what we mean by worship and what we believe its

1. Cited in Robert Marteau, *The Stained-Glass Windows of Chagall 1957–1970* (New York: Tudor, 1973), 17. See also http://www.artway.eu/content.php?id=1960&lang=en&action=show.

purposes are (and are not).[2] Like much that is central to the Christian faith, of course, this is easier said than done. But the way we define the nature and purposes of worship directly informs how we integrate the arts in our liturgical contexts.

I should state up front that the goal of this chapter is not to recommend a single definition of worship; others have done that task already and their work deserves careful study.[3] Nor is my goal to propose a normative order of worship that aims to be conclusive. This is not because I lack opinions or convictions on the matter—both will become evident throughout the chapter. I avoid an exclusive understanding of corporate worship, in part, because I assume a broad readership for the book and my aim is to offer readers a lens that might help inform decisions to include or exclude any one practice of art in their corporate worship. As such, this chapter is less of a constructive exercise than a diagnostic one, less a prescription for one form of worship than an interpretive frame. While the immediate goal of this chapter is greater clarity in our respective practices of liturgical art, the ultimate goal is more meaningful, vital, wholehearted worship that forms a congregation in the triune life.

The invitation of this chapter, then, is for readers to discover ways in which their understandings and practices of worship might support or hinder this formative work. More particularly, the invitation is for readers to discern how the arts might serve the actions and purposes of corporate worship in a manner that honors their congregation's unique identity as a member of Christ's worshiping body.[4] For the sake of clarity I will be using

---

2. While it is necessary in a book like this to define the explicit purposes of corporate worship, it also needs to be said that there is a certain "purposelessness" to worship, that our worship is *for God's sake alone* and thus perhaps, in the end, a "royal waste of time," as Marva J. Dawn puts it in her book *A Royal Waste of Time: The Splendor of Worshiping God and Being Church for the World* (Grand Rapids: Eerdmans, 1999).

3. For a particularly helpful introduction to distinctly Protestant understandings of worship, see James F. White, *Protestant Worship: Traditions in Transition* (Louisville: Westminster John Knox, 1989). For a brief overview of Christian worship throughout history, see James F. White, *A Brief History of Christian Worship* (Nashville: Abingdon, 1993). For a more thorough introduction, see *The Oxford History of Christian Worship*, ed. Geoffrey Wainwright and Karen Westerfield Tucker (New York: Oxford University Press, 2006).

4. This idea draws on Nicholas Wolterstorff's essay on church music, "Thinking about Church Music," in *Hearing the Call: Liturgy, Justice, Church and World*, ed. Mark R. Gornik and Gregory Thompson (Grand Rapids: Eerdmans, 2011), 262–66. Wolterstorff writes that any action of the liturgy can be enhanced by artistic action and that the character of the artistic action must fit the liturgical action it serves.

the language of "corporate worship" interchangeably with the language of "liturgy." On this reasoning all congregations have an identifiable liturgy: a way in which they order their public worship. *Liturgical art*, on these terms, is simply another way of saying *art in corporate worship*. Liturgical art is not to be reduced to visual art in worship; nor is liturgical art something only so-called liturgical churches do. Liturgical art identifies any practice of art in any church's experience of corporate worship.[5]

The Determinative Patterns of Worship

With these definitions in mind, I wish to suggest that our understanding of corporate worship is informed by a series of determinative patterns that, in turn, generate a set of expectations and plausible applications for art in corporate worship. What is a pattern? A pattern involves the repetition of things that over time engender an identifiable character. This would include, for example, patterns of economic behavior, patterns of speech, or patterns in the weather. In the case of Holy Scripture, as the fundamental grammar for Christian worship, we discover, for instance, a pattern of language about the physical world. While any one passage may leave in doubt the goodness of the materiality of creation, the pattern of language in Scripture involves a consistently positive estimation of the physical cosmos.

Robert Webber argues, rightly I believe, that a theologian's task is "to think about the biblical narrative and teachings and then to systematize these materials into a coherent whole."[6] A coherent picture is the ultimate goal. Jeremy Begbie elaborates on this basic task when he urges theologians "to live inside the world of these texts and inhabit them so deeply that we begin to recognize links, lines of association, and webs of meaning that may not always be laid out explicitly or at any length but that nevertheless give Scripture its coherence, contours, and overall directions."[7] Faithful

---

5. On purpose I avoid the language of "sacred art," "religious art," and "spiritual art" because such terms are far too ambiguous and therefore unhelpful to the task of describing what Christians do when they practice art in a context of corporate worship.

6. Robert E. Webber, *Worship Old and New: A Biblical, Historical, and Practical Introduction* (Grand Rapids: Zondervan, 1994), 65. From his own reading of the patterns of Scripture, he concludes that worship is the gospel in motion and the gospel enacted through forms and signs.

7. Jeremy Begbie, *Resounding Truth: Christian Wisdom in the World of Music* (Grand Rapids: Baker Academic, 2007), 188.

ideas for corporate worship will not, I suggest, come by piling biblical texts one on top of the other. Nor will they come by simply collating all the prescriptive and proscriptive statements in Scripture.[8]

They will come, rather, by a judicious reading of the broad patterns and unifying threads in Scripture, as Begbie writes, and by being "alert to the themes and counterthemes that crisscross its pages" in order to discern the proper shape of the church's liturgical life. To argue that patterns play a determinative role in our conception of true worship, then, is to argue that, while both prescriptive and proscriptive statements about worship are to be carefully heeded, along with any number of principles, they should also be interpreted in relation to relevant patterns that run throughout Scripture. It is also to argue that these patterns will suggest inertias and trajectories for practices of the arts in worship, rather than self-evident plans or formulae.

What specific patterns are determinative for Christian worship? Allow me to suggest the following patterns and to relate each one to the arts in corporate worship.

A Pattern of Starting Points

Where we begin to answer our definition of corporate worship is key. Do we begin with specific biblical texts? Do we begin with theological ideas? Do we begin with the priorities that characterize our ecclesial tradition or with the experiences that, like those of the disciples at Pentecost, fundamentally orient our sense of God? Departure points are always consequential. How a departure point issues in a series of methodical steps, informed by signature vocabulary, undergirded by basic assumptions and resulting in determined convictions—this also is key. For certain communities within the global church, Scripture will be regarded as the proper starting point for the discovery of the faithful use of art in worship.

If we choose to start with the Bible, however, where exactly do we begin? In Exodus 24? In Isaiah 6? In John 4 or Acts 2? With Romans or with Revelation? But how ought we to relate one passage to another—to *weigh* one over the other? And how exactly ought passages in Scripture serve to

---

8. Prescriptive statements would include these texts: 1 Cor. 11:25–26 and Luke 22:19 ("Do this in remembrance of me"); John 4:23–24; 1 Cor. 14:26–40; Col. 3:16. Examples of proscriptions might be these: 1 Cor. 11:27–32 ("Do not eat unworthily"); Deut. 5; 12:31–32.

authorize a practice of liturgical art? The answer is rarely self-evident. If we build our idea of worship on the basis of key Bible terms, such as *proskuneo* or *hishtahavah*, worship might be viewed as a matter of kneeling in submission before God, which could be seen to undergird Anglican and charismatic practices of the body.[9] Or if worship is perceived chiefly as a matter of reverence to a holy Sovereign who is "worth" such *weorth-scipe*, then practices of art may be restricted to solemn activities that befit a solemn encounter.[10]

It involves all such things, no doubt, but how we actually *do* worship does not simply result from an aggregation of terms. How Old Order Mennonites or Pentecostals do reverence is not merely a result of good exegesis. One could appeal to the words of Proverbs 1:7 (NIV), that "the fear of the LORD is the beginning of knowledge," but other factors inevitably come into play to determine whether our fear-full, awe-filled worship is marked by "dignified" musical practices, drawing inspiration perhaps from Isaiah 6, or whether the fear of the Lord includes notions of familiarity, as the disciples repeatedly experienced with Jesus, and suggest more "homey" musical practices, oriented around intimately relational experiences.[11]

The point is this: starting points in Scripture are never neutral; terms are never neutral; exegesis is never neutral. And to say that worship must be in "accord" with Scripture is far from self-explanatory. One is hard-pressed, in fact, to find any normative models for expressly corporate worship in the New Testament. Theological ideas always come into play. Why John Calvin

---

9. Worship may also be regarded as sung praise (*halal*) to God, which is why charismatic Christians may say things like "Worship was good today" to signify the musical portion of corporate worship. Worship may further be seen to require humble prayer to God (*proseuchomai*) and an earnest supplication of God (*deomai + palal*). The German word *Gottesdienst* foregrounds the idea of worship as service (*latreuo; abad*) to God, and it represents the term that many free-church congregations commonly use to describe their experience on Sunday mornings: "a service." This term includes the twin idea of our service to God and God's service to us. All these terms tend to point congregations in particular liturgical directions.

10. John Goldingay, summarizing the dominant worship-related verbs in the psalms, says this: "These terms combine body words, sound words, attitude words, and words for the purpose expressed in the praise. They are notably short on references to feelings; the feelings come out in the actions." *Psalms*, vol. 1: *Psalms 1–41* (Grand Rapids: Baker Academic, 2006), 50.

11. John 15:15; Heb. 2:11–12; and Ps. 84:2 are representative texts that function as focal points for this approach to God in worship. Also Ps. 73:28: "But as for me, it is good to be near God" (NIV).

parts ways with Martin Luther, for instance, on practices of public worship cannot be accounted for on strictly exegetical terms.[12] The fact that angels in heaven repeatedly blow trumpets, as we see in the book of Revelation, fails to factor in Calvin's understanding of the eschatological dimension of worship.[13] This is in contrast to Luther, who believed that the music of heaven directly influenced the music of the church on earth.[14]

In the sixteenth century, for example, the Anglican divine Richard Hooker argued that because God was spiritually excellent, the visible church ought to be sensibly excellent.[15] To make his case, Hooker appealed to Scripture. Hooker's argument rested, however, on a very particular reading of Psalm 96:9. Hooker linked the phrase "beauty of holiness" (KJV) to a theological emphasis on the royalty of God. Just as the Queen of England occupied a majestic house from which she governed the realm, he argued, so God must occupy a majestic house from which to govern the world. In short: the "beauty of holiness" was equated to a palatial church building befitting a heavenly monarch.

Whereas Anglo-Catholics today may continue to resonate with Hooker's theologically and culturally inflected reading of the psalms, Pentecostal Christians take the same biblical text and draw from it a theologically different conclusion. The beauty of holiness matters, they might argue, but that beauty describes a singularly internal, rather than external, reality. To offer worship "in the beauty of holiness" requires no sumptuous architecture. It requires only a humble heart, as the human spirit enters into concourse with the unseen spirit of God. For both Anglo-Catholics and Pentecostals, a theological tradition represents a powerful inertia.

A congregation's tradition includes a host of things that are assumed without question. *Of course*, the Episcopalian says, the "beauty of holiness"

12. With Zwingli, John Calvin stressed the importance of rational understanding in the people's praise. Unlike the Zurich pastor, however, who insisted that Saint Paul's meaning in Colossians argued for a voiceless singing of the heart, Calvin believed that the mind, heart, and voice could sing to God in one accord. See Charles Garside Jr., *Zwingli and the Arts* (New Haven: Yale University Press, 1966), 37, 45, 53.

13. See John Calvin, "Foreword to the Genevan Psalter," in *John Calvin: Writings on Pastoral Piety*, ed. Elsie A. McKee (New York: Paulist Press, 2001), 94–97.

14. Andreas Loewe, "'Musica est Optimum': Martin Luther's Theory of Music," *Academia*, https://www.academia.edu/1028886/Musica_est_optimum_Martin_Luthers_Theory _of_Music. Accessed August 17, 2012.

15. *Richard Hooker: Of the Laws of Ecclesiastical Polity*, ed. A. S. McGrade and Brian Vickers, abridged ed. (New York: St. Martin's, 1975), 33.

leads to resplendent buildings, even if, in actual fact, the Hebrew of Psalm 96:9 is more accurately translated as "holy splendor," relating in no direct way to church architecture. Or *of course*, the Baptist says, worship "in spirit and in truth" emphasizes the sincerity of our heart's worship, the internal over the external, the invisible above the visible, even if the context for Jesus's exchange with the woman at the well argues the exact opposite—not for the spirit of the worshiper but for the worship that the Spirit of Christ makes possible.[16]

The inertia of a tradition of worship may make it nearly impossible to perceive biblical texts related to worship in any other way than the way they've always been perceived. For the charismatic believer, for instance, the experience of God as living and active, dynamically here and now, becomes a controlling factor in how biblical texts are related to worship. For the Holy Spirit to make worship faithful, so the charismatic reasons, the order must be easily interruptible so that it can remain "living and active." But, from Scripture, one could argue an opposite conclusion, too: that the Spirit is the author of organization, stability, and standards of worship as much as of non-order, extemporaneity, and improvisatory worship.

In short, how we authorize particular biblical texts on behalf of our practices of worship will always be theologically colored, framed by the lens of our tradition, and oriented by the experiences that have defined our knowledge and love of God. How then do we not become paralyzed by all the complex decisions that can and should be made? While no departure point is neutral, I suggest that certain departure points are more plausible than others. I argue here that a right understanding of corporate worship, and the role that the arts might play in this aspect of the church's life, begins with a clear understanding of the role of the Trinity in worship.

16. Marianne Meye Thompson persuasively argues this case from the logic of the narrative: "Both [the narrative of Nicodemus and of the woman] point the reader away from the human being as self-sufficient actor to the human being as recipient of the activity and Spirit of God. It would then seem odd if in conversation with the Samaritan woman Jesus were to urge her to 'look within,' as it were, for the strength and capacity to offer true worship. Quite the contrary, one is brought into the eschatological hour by God's caring activity in Jesus and by the divinely sent Spirit of God." *The God of the Gospel of John* (Grand Rapids: Eerdmans, 2001), 215.

The Pattern of Triune Activity

To identify this pattern at the beginning of our list is to give the Trinity a priority of place in any practice of art in public worship.[17] It is the conviction that the Triune God should inform all our experiences of the arts in corporate worship. In saying this we insist that before human beings do anything with the arts in worship, the Father, Son, and Holy Spirit are doing things that make such faithful worship possible. They are not only spectators to human worship; they are also active agents in the work of the people to offer up to God all their artistic labors in corporate worship.

To confess this is to confess that the encounter of worship always begins with the initiative of the Father. The worship that the Father seeks, Jesus tells us in John 4, is worship that the Father makes possible. Faithful worship originates with the work of the Father and returns ultimately to the Father. To confess this is likewise to assert that Christ is not only the object of worship; he is the Chief Worshiper. "Whatever else our worship is," writes James Torrance, "it is our liturgical amen to the worship of Christ."[18] To confess this, finally, is to believe that such worship is possible only and always because of the Spirit's mediating work in every aspect of corporate worship (Rom. 8; 2 Cor. 3).[19]

To start with this pattern is to argue that the arts in corporate worship accomplish their best service to the church because the Father, Son, and Holy Spirit are intimately at work in creation and culture, in art and artistry, in worship and the worship arts.[20] As aesthetic artifacts of human making, the liturgical arts can become fitting instruments of the Spirit's work to conform us to the life of God in Christ, because fundamentally they are gifts of the Father, by way of the Son, the Firstborn of creation, and they are animated and perfected by the Spirit.

The Pattern of Christ's Worship

A second determinative pattern is the pattern of Christ's worship. In his book *Two Ways of Praying*, Paul Bradshaw writes that Christians "pray both

17. For a concentrated study of the Trinity in musical worship, see Robin A. Parry, *Worshipping Trinity: Coming Back to the Heart of Worship* (Eugene, OR: Cascade, 2012).

18. James B. Torrance, *Worship, Community and the Triune God of Grace* (Downers Grove, IL: IVP Academic, 1996), 14.

19. Torrance, *Worship, Community and the Triune God of Grace*, 88.

20. I elaborate on this idea in chapter 3.

through Christ and with Christ and in Christ, and Christ prays for us and with us and in us, so that, through the work of the Holy Spirit, our prayer becomes Christ's prayer and his prayer becomes our prayer."[21] Saint Augustine says something similar when he writes that "Christ prays for us as our Priest, he prays in us as our Head, he is prayed to by us as our God."[22] It is not simply, then, about what we do *for* God in worship. It is not merely what we say *to* God in worship. It is about how we have entered into the rhythms of *Christ's* own liturgical life.[23]

In Christ, the chief *Leitourgos*, we glimpse the doxological *telos* of the universe, its true end and purpose. In Christ we perceive how the physical world itself is always at praise because of the power of the Spirit to enable it to fulfill its praise-filled and praiseworthy vocation. In Christ we discover how the world of human making, including the worlds of art making, can participate in the faithful praise of all of creation. And in Christ we see how the praise of God's people, from every tongue, tribe, and nation, along with the whole of creation, in all its detailed and ornamented glory, have been summoned to the praise of God in anticipation of the eschatological banquet.

A Pattern of Dialogue

Reading Scripture closely, we also observe a pattern of God speaking and of human beings responding. The self-disclosure of God, on the one hand, occurs in the burning bush; in the plagues of Egypt; in the parting of the Red Sea; in the lives of Noah and Abraham, Deborah and David, Jeremiah and Jonah; on Mount Nebo and Mount Tabor; at Pentecost; and on the road to Damascus. Human beings respond variously to these acts of self-revelation—in acts of prostration, repentance, reverence, prescribed ritual sacrifice, spontaneous praise, or table fellowship. Such responses may be faithful or otherwise, in word, action, or symbols, but they always follow the original initiative of God.

God gets the first word; human beings get the next word. God reveals; humans respond. This is the nature of personal communion with the Tri-

---

21. Paul Bradshaw, *Two Ways of Praying* (Nashville: Abingdon, 1995), 64.

22. Cited in Bradshaw, *Two Ways of Praying*, 64.

23. "When the narrative of the person and work of Jesus Christ permeates worship consistently, worship itself becomes the message." Constance M. Cherry, *The Worship Architect: A Blueprint for Designing Culturally Relevant and Biblically Faithful Services* (Grand Rapids: Baker Academic, 2010), 25.

une God. For human beings it is the invitation to enter into fellowship and partnership with the God who initiates and sustains and brings to completion all good things in our acts of worship. It is an invitation to enter into communion with the God who has already been at work in the world, enabling it to fulfill its doxological vocation, long before humanity arrives on the liturgical scene.[24]

There are many ways in which the liturgical arts can serve this pattern of revelation and response. This might include a response of silence to the God who speaks in a gentle whisper. It could include a response of instrumental music as a sonic space in which to appropriate the word that God has spoken through the preacher. It could include the presentation of the elements of the Lord's Supper by dancers who symbolize, on the congregation's behalf, the reception of these gracious gifts. Or it could include invitations to repentance through the use of visual art or a summons to action by way of a spoken-word performance.

A Pattern of Things That the Psalter Invites Us to Say to God in Worship

A fourth determinative pattern is the pattern of psalmic speech. Inferring the shape of corporate worship from the Psalter has been a habit of the church from the start.[25] But how the form and content of the psalms ought to shape the artistic activities of corporate worship has rarely been a straightforward affair. For example, while the things that the psalmist says to God throughout the Psalter are diverse and wide-ranging, not all these statements result in liturgical practices for certain congregations. The kind of language that we find in the psalms includes such things:

- We come to your presence (Ps. 95)
- I come to your house (Ps. 5)
- You are holy (Ps. 22:3)
- You are worthy (Ps. 18:3)
- We rejoice (Ps. 9:2)

24. Exod. 3:1–2; Neh. 8; Pss. 105–6; Isa. 6:1–8; Luke 1:26–38; 24:13–35; Acts 2; Rom. 9–11; Col. 2; Rev. 5.

25. See William L. Holladay, *The Psalms through Three Thousand Years: Prayerbook of a Cloud of Witnesses* (Minneapolis: Augsburg Fortress, 1993).

- We love you (Ps. 31:23)
- Help us (Ps. 12:1)
- I have sinned and am sorry (Ps. 51)
- Forgive me (Ps. 25)
- Why? (Ps. 22)
- How long? (Ps. 13)
- I am in pain and afraid (Ps. 130)
- I am alone (Ps. 88)
- Defend me; defend others (Ps. 43)
- Have mercy (Ps. 57)
- We thank you (Ps. 100)
- You are good (Ps. 100:5)
- We shout for joy (Ps. 98)
- Speak (Ps. 50)
- Remember what you've done (Ps. 105)
- We meditate on your Word (Ps. 1)
- Your Word is true (Ps. 33)
- Come again (Ps. 6:4)
- Be gracious (123)
- Feed us (Ps. 81)
- We are yours (Ps. 95:7)
- We pray (Ps. 5:2–3)
- Be the God that you say you are (Pss. 4:1; 5:2; 7:1; 8:1; 28:1; 65:5; 80:1; 94:1–2; 99:4)
- We praise you (Ps. 66)
- Bless us (Ps. 67)
- Lead me (Ps. 31)[26]

The entire Psalter is called the *Tehillim*, the "Book of Praise," for a reason. It is here that we are shown what praise looks like, what praise sounds like, what praise says to God—and it says quite a lot. It says what needs saying. As the Psalter sees it, this includes the praise of God in history and the God of creation. It involves praise of God's cosmic redemption and the praise of God's local, personal work. It embraces the praise of saints and sinners. It names the joy of good news in full-throated and wholehearted

---

26. I am grateful to John Witvliet for drawing my attention to this list of statements on the psalms. John D. Witvliet, "Liturgy as God's Language School," *Pastoral Music* 31.4 (2007): 19–23.

ways; and it names, with full-gutted, wholly honest confession, the sorrow and loss that accompany our pilgrimage on earth.

In view of the decisive role that the psalms play in the New Testament and in church history, I would argue that the language of the Psalter ought to inform all of the church's practices of art in worship.[27] To give preference to certain statements over others is to rob congregations of vocabulary to say to God all of the things that the heart wants—and *needs*—to say to God. The arts, in turn, can help these statements take on flesh or definition—jubilant dances, songs of lament, stained glass windows that recount the history of God's deeds, films that bear witness to God's goodness, poems that give voice to injustices in the world, stories that heal, or dramatic enactments of the faithful presence of God in all times and places.

A Pattern of Things That the Psalter Invites Us to Do before God in Worship

It is not just a pattern of psalmic language that ought to form our practices of corporate worship. It is also a pattern of things that the psalms invite us to do. For example, throughout the psalms the worshiper is invited to "shout," "burst," "clap," "thunder," "cry out," "exult," and "dance." One of the peculiar characteristics of contemporary worship music, especially in the genres of pop-rock, folk-rock, hip-hop, and R&B, is an affinity for these psalmic activities. "Applause, everyone," says Psalm 47:1 in *The Message*, "Bravo, bravissimo! Shout God-songs at the top of your lungs!" Indeed, we must.

When Psalm 98:4 charges "all the earth" to shout for joy to the Lord, songwriters like Israel Houghton or Kari Jobe do not read the injunction in a figurative way. Unlike those congregations who shout only tepidly or resist the invitation to dance with timbrels, churches like Bethel in Redding, California, or Holy Trinity Brompton in London actually shout. They revel, clap, thunder, and exult. With the best of contemporary worship music, then, songwriters provide a medium for these heightened emotions to respond to God in fitting ways—energetic emotions corresponding to the expansive laudability of God.

Less commendable perhaps is the habit of such congregations to exclude other subject matter or practices of worship. This would include, for

---

27. James L. Mays, *The Lord Reigns: A Theological Handbook to the Psalms* (Louisville: Westminster John Knox, 1994), 62: "By its movement, conclusion, and title the book in its shape defines all its contents, the prayers and instruction, as the praise of the Lord."

instance, themes related to lament, silence, justice, mission, evil, and the human call to bear out the image of God in all stations of life.[28] Contemporary worship songwriters will nourish the church with better musical foods if they learn to balance emotions that turn inward with emotions that turn outward. As it is, too many songs that typically appear on Christian radio stations exhibit an excessive first-person singular "I" that looks inward, to the exclusion of a biblical emphasis on the first-person plural "we" that looks outward.[29]

What is needed, then, are practices of liturgical art that explore the psalmist's concern for joy *and* sadness, gratitude *and* protest, intimacy *and* reverence, loudness *and* stillness, in a way that articulates both the personal and the public dimension of Christian worship. Congregations will be well served by songs that name both personal tragedy and global tragedy. Congregations will be rightly formed by songs that give affective voice to the small, "grasslike" quality of human life alongside the cosmic splendor of heaven and earth. And it is in doing such things that the church begins to sing as the psalmist sings.

A Pattern of Contexts

Worship takes place in four specific contexts.[30] The first context of worship is creation. Before human beings arrive on the scene, the physical cosmos is already at praise. Whether humanity praises God or not, the rocks and mountains and stars are busy praising God both day and night (cf. Gen. 1; Pss. 19; 104; Rev. 4–5). The second context of worship is "all of life." When life is lived in a God-oriented, God-pleasing way, we can say that such a life fulfills its calling and thereby worships God (cf. Rom. 12).

---

28. On the topic of lament psalms, see the following resources: Claus Westermann, "The Structure and History of the Lament in the Old Testament," in *Praise and Lament in the Psalms*, trans. Keith R. Crim and Richard N. Soulen (Atlanta: John Knox, 1981), 165–213; Walter Brueggemann, *The Psalms and the Life of Faith* (Minneapolis: Fortress, 1995).

29. Hillsong United (http://www.hillsongunited.com/) and Jesus Culture (http://www.jesusculture.com/) music might very well be guilty of this tendency.

30. I owe a considerable debt to John Witvliet for pointing out to me these four contexts long before I ever thought I'd find myself in the world of liturgical studies. Cf. John D. Witvliet, "On Three Meanings of the Term Worship," https://worship.calvin.edu/resources/resource-library/on-three-meanings-of-the-term-worship. Accessed October 5, 2018.

A third context is what we might call a particular context. This involves experiences of worship that take place outside of the strictly regulated context of corporate worship. This would include personal worship, family worship, a midweek worship service, and worship during a retreat or a conference. A fourth context is corporate worship. This is what Christians do when they gather in an intentional, routinized, regulated way to worship God "on the Lord's Day." While each of these contexts has its own integrity and its own purposes, they overlap and mutually inform each other.

In AD 1225 Saint Francis wrote a poem in praise of creation. Drawing inspiration from the words of Psalms 145 and 148, the poem gave voice to the song of all creatures. Nearly seven hundred years later, around 1910, William Draper, an Anglican priest, paraphrased the text for a children's Whitsuntide (Pentecost) Festival in Leeds, England. From one context of worship (creation) to another (personal), from one setting (generally communal) to a different setting (specifically liturgical), the hymn "All Creatures of Our God and King" has become an example of how contexts overlap and mutually inform the artful worship of the church.[31]

The Pattern of New Testament Worship

While it is difficult to discover in the New Testament a clear distinction between what we understand as "corporate worship" and worship that takes place when the disciples gather for any given reason to pray or praise God, we can identify a pattern of worship-related activities that might, in turn, inform the shape of public worship and therefore also liturgical art practices.[32] This would include:

1. Reading of Scripture (1 Tim. 4:13; 1 Thess. 5:27; Col. 4:15, 16)
2. Preaching and teaching of Scripture (Acts 2:42; 20:25; 1 Tim. 4:13; 2 Tim. 4:1–5; cf. Luke 4:20)
3. Prayer (Acts 2:42; 4:23–31; 1 Cor. 11; 14; 1 Tim. 2:1–8)
   a. Sung (Col. 3:16; Eph. 5:19; 1 Cor. 14:26; Rev. 5:9–13; 14:2–3; 15:3–4)
   b. Postures: standing (Matt. 6:5; Mark 11:25; Luke 18:11, 13); kneeling/

31. Cf. Job 38:7; 12:7–10; Luke 19:40.

32. I owe thanks to Michael A. Farley for letting me make use of this list from his own lecture material.

prostration (Acts 20:36; 21:5; Rev. 4:10; 5:8; 7:11; 11:16); hands raised (1 Tim. 2:8)

   c. Unison (Acts 4:24–30; Rev. 4:8–11; 5:9–13; 7:10–12; 11:17–18; 15:3–4; 19:1–8)

   d. Accompanied by musical instruments: trumpets (Rev. 11:15); harps (Rev. 14:3; 15:2)

   e. Loud volume (Rev. 5:12; 7:10; 11:15; 19:1, 6)

   f. Corporate amen: The people respond to prayer with the saying of "Amen" (1 Cor. 14:16; Rev. 5:14; cf. Rom. 1:25; 9:5; Eph. 3:21)

4. Confession of faith (1 Tim. 6:12; 1 Pet. 3:21; cf. 1 Cor. 15:1–3; 1 Tim. 3:16)
5. Offerings to the poor (1 Cor. 16:1–22; 2 Cor. 9:11–15; Phil. 4:18; Heb. 13:16)
6. Celebration of the Lord's Supper (Matt. 26:26–28/Mark 14:22–25/Luke 22:14–23; Acts 2:42; 20:7; 1 Cor 10:16–18; 11:17–34)
7. Blessing of God's people (2 Cor. 13:14; Luke 24:50)
8. Holy kiss of greeting (Rom. 16:16; 1 Cor. 16:20; 2 Cor. 13:12; 1 Thess. 5:26; 1 Pet. 5:14)
9. Gathering on the first day of the week, the Lord's Day (Acts 20:7; 1 Cor. 16:2; Rev. 1:10)
10. Washing of feet (John 13:1–17)
11. Gathering in specific spaces for worship and prayer: temple (Acts 2:46; 3:1); synagogue (Acts 9:20); homes (Acts 2:2; 5:42; 12:12); official public spaces (Acts 17); open fields (Acts 8:26)

As I seek to show throughout this book, the arts can serve any one of these activities of worship in a way that enriches or clarifies or concretizes those liturgical activities.

A Pattern of Slogans

A pattern of slogans often functions as an ordering principle for present activities of worship or for future revisions to worship. For example, certain traditions may argue that worship ought to be done "decently and orderly," drawing from the words of 1 Corinthians 14:40. This language will be understood in a particular way: *decently* correlated to culturally specific notions of "dignified" or "tasteful"; *orderly* matched to the prescriptions of a prayer book or related analogously to the order that marks a military parade. To wonder what "fitting" worship might mean, as a replacement for "decent," may call into question the whole system of worship, or parts of it.

This is as true of the slogan "decently and in order" as it is of other slogans:

- Worship ought to be articulate (1 Cor. 14)
- Worship ought to be "in spirit and truth" (John 4:23–24)
- Worship ought to be "in the beauty of holiness" (Ps. 96:9 KJV)
- Worship ought to include "psalms and hymns and spiritual songs" (Eph. 5:19)
- Worship ought to be from "every tribe and language and people and nation" (Rev. 5:9)
- Worship ought to be an experience where God is "enthroned on" our praises (Ps. 22:3)
- Worship ought to be a covenantal exchange with God (Exod. 24)
- Worship ought to be a sacramental encounter with God (1 Cor. 5:7; Heb. 10:12; 13:15)
- Worship ought to be an act of table fellowship with God (Matt. 26; Mark 14; 1 Cor. 11)

A slogan functions like a de facto law of worship. A slogan is unquestioned, serving as both badge of identity and gatekeeper. Whatever pattern of slogans functions most determinatively for a congregation will in turn lead that congregation to welcome certain practices of art and to resist or exclude other practices. To overcome the inertia and to think beyond the terms of the slogan requires near-herculean effort or the interruption from an outside force.

A Pattern of Fourfold Worship

The church historically has recognized an implicit fourfold pattern of worship in the New Testament. Constance Cherry frames her book *The Worship Architect* by this order and argues that the church should model its worship on this fourfold frame.[33] Cherry argues that this pattern is grounded in a pattern of God's work. It is also grounded in the work of Christ himself, the true human Worshiper. In the Gospels we see this pattern at work:

33. "Worship is a journey—a journey into God's presence (gathering), of hearing from God (Word), that celebrates Christ (Table), and that sends us into the world changed by our encounter with God (sending)." Cherry, *Worship Architect*, 47.

(1) Jesus is called (Luke 1:32); (2) Jesus is spoken to (John 12:49); (3) Jesus is nourished (John 4:32–34; 17:21); (4) Jesus is sent (John 12:49; 17:3, 18). Jesus also stands before humanity on behalf of God: (1) Jesus calls (Matt. 4:21); (2) Jesus speaks (John 12:49); (3) Jesus nourishes (Luke 22:19–20); (4) Jesus sends (John 17:18).

If Jesus is indeed the Chief Worshiper, then it stands to reason that followers of Jesus would in some fashion wish to imitate this pattern within their liturgical contexts. We do not simply arrive at worship; we are gathered *by* God to worship. We speak words—but only by the Spirit's power. We receive real nourishment for life *in* Christ, not just ideas about Christ. And we do not merely "leave" worship; we instead are blessed and sent by God. But we are not left on our own to figure out how to do this work faithfully. Jesus shows us how, and by the Spirit of God, enables us to do these things. Jesus shows us how to be rightly gathered to the Father by the Spirit, and it is Jesus who enables us to gather others in his name. It is Jesus who shows us how to speak and to be spoken to; to be nourished and to nourish; to be sent and to send.[34]

The arts serve these four movements in a host of ways. With the words of the psalmist vividly represented on a screen, for instance, God may get the first word through a short film. In a sermon preached in the voice of a biblical character, the arts can enable a congregation to hear the Word afresh. In response to this Word, a congregation might take a moment of silent contemplation, or a prophetic word might be given through a "spoken word," or intercessory prayer that includes the use of multiple languages might occur. In the final movement, the faithful might bear witness to the recession of the cross as a visual symbol of the promise that Christ goes before his people to their places of home and work.

A Pattern of Priorities

Liturgical binaries frequently characterize the church's worship. These binaries describe not just opposite tendencies but dynamic tensions that a congregation may seek to hold together. These binaries include worship

---

34. Cf. Cherry, *Worship Architect*, 54, 86, 112. Benedictions drawn from Scripture might include Num. 6:22–26; Matt. 28:19–20; Luke 24:50; Lev. 9:22–23; 1 Thess. 3:11–13; Ps. 121:7–8; Rom. 15:5–6; 15:13; Ps. 29:11; Phil. 4:7; 4:19–20; 4:23; 2 Pet. 1:2–3; Jude 24–25; Heb. 13:20–21; 2 Thess. 2:16–17; Eph. 6:24; 2 Cor. 13:14; 9:8; 13:11; Num. 6:24–26; Rom. 12:2.

that is both personal *and* communal, both silent *and* vocal, both simple *and* complex, both accessible *and* difficult, both written *and* spontaneous, both personal *and* communal, both local *and* global, both ascetic *and* festal. It may be worship that is done with full understanding of the mystery of the Trinity as well as beyond our capacity exhaustively to understand this divine mystery.

The arts are often conscripted to stress one side of the binary over the other, or they will be enlisted to resolve the tension in a way that satisfies the requirements of faithful worship. In the Psalter, for example, we have poems by David and in the spirit of David. We have poems by the guild of temple musicians—the Korahites, for instance. And we have poems by individuals who remain anonymous. In the psalms we witness a way in which both sides of the binary make it into the people's prayer. As with the psalms, the hope is that the liturgical arts might enable God's people to worship with both a hospitable "I" and a richly warm "we," in both simple and complex ways, and so on.

Whatever side of these liturgical binaries is given preference in a congregation's worship will determine, in the end, what arts are more readily welcomed or consistently resisted and rejected in a liturgical context.

A Pattern of Participation

A final determinative pattern is a pattern of participation. This involves two parts: what it means for the faithful to *actively* participate in corporate worship and how our liturgical activities give expression to our *togetherness* as Christ's body.[35] The arts inevitably find themselves at the center of controversy surrounding this double question. In Romans 15:6 (NASB), for instance, the apostle Paul prays that the church might be of one mind so that "with one accord" they may "with one voice" praise God. How "one voice" sounds, however, depends on the way in which participation is construed. Is monophonic plainchant the way to achieve "one voice," as the church of the early Middle Ages believed? Or might the oratorios of Bach, involving orchestral instruments, vocalists, and choirs, signify the church's "one voice"?[36]

35. Cf. Alan Rathe, *Evangelicals, Worship and Participation: Taking a Twenty-First Century Reading* (London: Routledge, 2014).

36. It is possible that the congregation played an active role in Bach's oratorios, but

What worship in "one accord" means is far from self-evident, moreover.[37] Historically the church has appealed to different models of harmony in order to establish a particular notion of togetherness in corporate worship. This has included the harmony of the celestial spheres or of things on earth, the harmony of human activities, or the harmony of the Godhead. The advice of the fourth-century bishop of Remesiana will seem obvious to most of us: "No one should sing unbecomingly louder or slower than the rest."[38] To do so, he argues, is to fall out of musical concord with others. Less obvious is whether singing in a foreign language, or extemporaneous shouting, or contemporary architectural idioms contravene the harmony of the church at worship.

In the aftermath of the Second Vatican Council in the early 1960s, the Roman Catholic bishops charged the clergy to foster the "full, conscious and active participation" of the laity in the liturgy. This was done to counter what the laity had experienced for centuries: partial, half-ignorant, passive participation in the liturgical celebrations. But is "passive" participation only one thing—a defect? Or can passive participation involve an alert and attentive dynamic? Might Mary's language of "let it be to me" in Luke 1:38 become a way to construe the nature of "active passivity"? Might this involve, for instance, an active listening to another who sings, an active contemplation of an image, an active posture of physical stillness, or an active reception of the Lord's Supper?

The practice of visual art in worship, to put it sharply, does not automatically generate "mere" spectators of worship, as if the experience of being a spectator were an intrinsic problem.[39] In fact, at a sporting event the experience of spectating is, for many, a richly *active* one.[40] To watch a

---

this is a contested matter. When early Christians spoke in tongues, this was an aural sign of the church's pneumatologically constituted unity (Acts 2:4). When Pentecostals sing in tongues, each in their own way, accompanied perhaps by the improvisations of musicians, this too might signify the unity of God's people.

37. Eusebius of Caesarea writes, "The unison voices of Christians would be more acceptable to God than any musical instrument. Accordingly in all the churches of God, united in soul and attitude, with one mind and in agreement of faith and piety, we send up a unison melody in the words of the Psalms." Cited in Everett Ferguson, "Toward a Patristic Theology of Music," *Studia Patristica* 24 (1993): 278.

38. Ferguson, "Toward a Patristic Theology of Music," 278.

39. The practice of congregational hymnody, conversely, does not by itself generate active worshipers. One could sing the "good ol' hymns" while simultaneously thinking about grocery lists, unrequited love, or television shows.

40. What exactly is spectating? Eric Rothenbuhler, in *Ritual Communication: From*

football game or tennis match is to enter vicariously and thereby affectively and imaginatively into the dramatic activities of the athletes. The spectator participates in the actions of athletes in a way that fully consumes him or her. For some, the experience of watching a sporting event spills over into the rest of the week, driving them crazy at times, imagining all the "what ifs" of a dramatic loss. There is nothing docile or detached about their experience.[41]

This describes, I would argue, a similar experience for Christians in both Western and Eastern liturgical traditions. For them, the experience of visual art is, at its best, far from dispassionate; it is a dynamically involved one. For the Orthodox Christian, to contemplate an icon is to give oneself wholly to Jesus, the Icon of God. For a Roman Catholic Christian, to contemplate a mosaic that represents Christ's passion is to enter vicariously into all that belongs to the passion of Christ.[42] How a congregation construes the nature of participation in corporate worship, then, will inevitably shape how the arts are employed in that context.

And however it is that the arts form us in worship, positively or negatively, will be directly informed by our response to the above determinative patterns.

Conclusion

As a working definition for worship in this book, I would like to propose, finally, that in worship the faithful bring their whole humanity, alongside the whole people of God, in proclamation, prayer, and praise, before the presence of the whole Godhead for the sake of the whole world. This is the

---

Everyday Conversation to Mediated Ceremony (Thousand Oaks, CA: Sage Publications, 1998), 219, answers this way: "spectating is a mode of access. It has limits, so if one's participation goes no further than spectating, then the meaning of the ritual will probably be thin and its effectiveness small. But spectating can provide access to other modes of participating; it can recruit viewers to engagement of festival, ritual, and other social forms."

41. Eileen Crowley, *Liturgical Art for a Media Culture* (Collegeville, MN: Liturgical Press, 2007), 38: "When media and media art are included in worship, only the spectator can really say the degree to which she or he is actively engaged in a ritual moment. Contemplation, a very active internal form of participation, has a time-honored role in Christian tradition."

42. Cf. David Freedberg, *The Power of Images: Studies in the History and Theory of Response* (Chicago: University of Chicago Press, 1989), 179.

opposite of worship that is all brain and no heart or all heart and no body. This is the opposite, too, of worship that is mindlessly rote or mindlessly spontaneous; of worship that is ignorant of the practices of the historic church or that is culturally tone-deaf; and of worship that remains disconnected from the realities of the world. In Trinitarian terms, more positively, it is worship that participates "through the Spirit in the Son's communion with the Father, in his vicarious life of worship and intercession."[43]

If the general presumption of this book is correct—that the arts serve the worship of the church best when they are allowed to serve in their own ways but not on their own terms—how might we understand the nature and power of the arts within a liturgical context? How might the arts enable us to articulate Christian worship in fresh, memorable ways? Assuming a variety of priorities within our respective contexts of congregational worship, how might the arts fittingly serve the things that we do and say in worship? And how might the arts kindle affection for God, foster wisdom, reimagine the reign of God on earth, or inspire a vision of faithful life in the world at large? It is to these questions that we now turn.

43. Torrance, *Worship, Community and the Triune God of Grace*, 15.

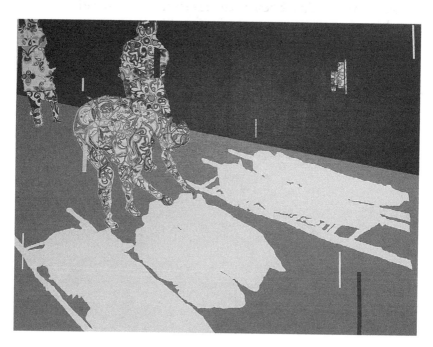

Laura Jennings, *Touched #1* (2007)

CHAPTER 2

The Meanings of Art

For either all works of visual art have some common quality, or when we speak of "works of art" we gibber.

Clive Bell, *Art*

The interesting thing about metaphor, or at least about some metaphors, is that they are used not to redescribe but to disclose for the first time. The metaphor has to be used because something new is being talked about.

Janet Soskice, *Metaphor and Religious Language*

An achieved work of art combines an extraordinary hardiness of form with an exquisite emotional sense.

Jeannette Winterson, "What Is Art For?"

In the previous chapter, we explored the meanings of worship. In this chapter we seek to make sense of the meanings of art. We do so in order to get clarity about the way in which Christians across ecclesial and theological traditions have understood the role of the arts in corporate worship. The question, "What is art?" has bedeviled philosophers and artists for centuries. The answer unfortunately is far from self-evident. Depending on the context, the term, deriving from the Latin, *arti-* or *ars*, or from the Greek, *techne*, could mean *poiesis* (as in "creative making"), *skill* (as in "the art of war"), *craft* (as in "blacksmith"), *fine art* (as in "classical ballet"), *visual art* (as in "I went to art school"), or the *liberal arts* (as in grammar, logic, and rhetoric).[1]

---

1. Specifically philosophical issues inevitably come into play. Is art primarily a matter of imitation, as Plato believed? Is it chiefly concerned with expression, as the Romantics supposed? Is it distinguished by its formal qualities or by a unique social practice or by its relation to beauty? These are issues helpfully discussed at length in *The Oxford Handbook of Aesthetics*, ed. Jerrold Levinson (Oxford: Oxford University Press, 2003).

An additional difficulty with the term is a normative one. When people say, "That's not art," as it relates to "practical art" or the "craft arts," for example, what exactly do they mean? When others say, "Everything is art," what do they have in mind? What makes one artist a "mere artisan" and another artist a "seer, genius, and prophet"? Is it possible to point to a thing and say, "That's good art"? Or must one say, "That's a particular kind of art, with a particular meaning, fulfilling its good purpose within a particular context"?[2] And in what ways are our ideas about art in a liturgical context conditioned by our sociocultural settings—whether ancient or modern, whether Western or Eastern?

Without a shared understanding of art we inevitably experience miscommunication, which, in turn, leads to a breakdown of communion.[3] What I would like to argue in this chapter is two things: one, that a work of art is characterized by a family resemblance rather than by a single trait;[4] and, two, that the arts bring us into an intentional and intensive participation in the physical, emotional, and imaginative aspect of our humanity

2. While I do not directly address the question of bad art in this book, one cannot altogether escape the matter of criteria for art and the practices that inform the production of good/excellent/fitting/beautiful art. Frank Burch Brown, in *Inclusive Yet Discerning: Navigating Worship Artfully* (Grand Rapids: Eerdmans, 2009), 28, rightly argues, "unless aesthetic enjoyment in worship does in fact have some perceptible relation to trustworthy discernments that are both artistic and religious, we have no business employing art in worship." The hyperbole in his assertion notwithstanding, and assuming that such "discernments" will be contextually and culturally conditioned, Brown's point deserves careful consideration. Both elitist and anything-goes-idiosyncratic attitudes to art should be equally rejected. While the way forward may be complicated, we are not without helpful guides. See, for example, Brown, *Good Taste, Bad Taste, and Christian Taste: Aesthetics in Religious Life* (Oxford: Oxford University Press, 2003), chs. 1 and 9; Taylor, "The Dangers," in *For the Beauty of the Church: Casting a Vision for the Arts*, ed. W. David O. Taylor (Grand Rapids: Baker Books, 2010), ch. 7; Nicholas Wolterstorff, *Art in Action: Toward a Christian Aesthetic* (Grand Rapids: Eerdmans, 1980); Jeremy Begbie, *Voicing Creation's Praise: Towards a Theology of the Arts* (Edinburgh: T&T Clark, 1991), chs. 4–5.

3. Like the arts, the subject of aesthetics, by itself and as it relates to art, is a contested one. The aim of this chapter is a modest one. It is to suggest a working, rather than comprehensive and absolute, definition of art, art making, artworks, and aesthetics that will enable us to talk about the arts in corporate worship in a clear and cogent way. Cf. Robert Stecker, "Definition of Art," in *The Oxford Handbook of Aesthetics*, 136–54.

4. I take my cue here from Ludwig Wittgenstein but follow more directly the basic instincts of two mid-twentieth-century essays: Morris Weitz, "The Role of Theory in Aesthetics," *Journal of Aesthetics and Art Criticism* 15 (1956): 27–35; and Maurice Mandelbaum, "Family Resemblances and Generalization concerning the Arts," *American Philosophical Quarterly* 2, no. 3 (1965): 219–28.

and that metaphor is a defining feature of works of art.[5] To understand art as a matter of "family resemblance" is to get a clearer idea of the nature, power, and purposes of artworks. To understand the aesthetic character of art is to understand more fully how the arts form us in a liturgical context.

A Work of Art as a Matter of Family Resemblance

Art and Aesthetics

First, works of art involve an intentional and intensive participation in the physical, emotional, and imaginative features of our creaturehood, that is to say, the aesthetic dimension of our humanity. When a priest of Israel stands in the temple, for example, surrounded by gold-enameled artworks, he *imagines* the world a certain way: as a sign of God's as-yet-unfulfilled promises for creation. With the poetry of the psalmists on her lips, the Benedictine nun comes to grips with the *emotional* contours of a life before God. For a Lutheran pastor to vest in the colors of the liturgical calendar is to get a *physical* feel for the christomorphic shape of time. With Hillsong United's song "Oceans," a cinematic swell of sound matches a lyrical development in order to become a musical *metaphor* for the experience of intimacy with Christ.

"The church is a house where people meet God" represents a common idea in Christian thinking about the church. If God is primarily regarded as a host, then a "homey" church building, a *domus ecclesiae*, marked by intimate spaces, favoring richly relational exchanges, may become the architectural vehicle for a congregation to imagine such a "house" and to feel like a family of God. On the other hand, if God is primarily regarded as a king, a majestic structure, a *domus regis*, marked by royal features befitting a monarch, may become the architectural vehicle for a congregation to imagine such a "house" and to feel like the faithful subjects of God. The particular form of church architecture foregrounds the sensory, imaginative, and affective dimension of the governing idea of God.

---

5. Cf. Rowan Williams, *Grace and Necessity: Reflections on Art and Love* (Harrisburg, PA: Morehouse, 2005), 140. See also Nicholas Cook, *Music, Imagination and Culture* (Oxford: Oxford University Press, 1990), 4–5: "In this way the idea that to perceive something aesthetically is to perceive it as an integrated whole is axiomatic to the entire enterprise of aesthetics."

Art and Metaphor

Second, works of art traffic in metaphor, some more richly than others. A metaphor is a figure of speech whereby we speak of one thing in terms of another—the church is a temple or God is our shepherd, for instance. As a metaphor, it is irreducible: "it cannot be translated into another form of language without loss of meaning."[6] A metaphor also involves a surplus of meaning. To say that Jesus is the bread of life, for example, is to say far more than that he nourishes. The metaphor evokes all sorts of images, feelings, and associations for the hearer, not just one thing: bread as elemental food, bread as political reality, bread as the work of Yahweh, bread as that which Satan tempts Jesus to misuse, bread as Christ's body, bread as eucharistic sign. The metaphor of bread in this sense is richly suggestive or allusive.

Although it is irreducible, a metaphor *can* be elucidated and assessed. To say otherwise is to rob the metaphor of its capacity for significance. Furthermore, metaphors offer actual epistemic access to the world and to the nature and character of God, as the Bible repeatedly shows us. They help us name reality and to experience it accordingly—for example, that the church, in some fundamentally real way, *is* a temple, and we ought to live *as if* we were temple people. As it relates to works of art, metaphor is a defining feature. Within a liturgical setting, a sculpture of a lion can function as a metaphor for Jesus or for Satan, depending on the context. A gold-enameled chalice can serve, for some, as a metaphor of God's abundance or, for others, of ecclesial corruption.

The Logic and Language of Art

Third, the different media of art are constituted by a kind of logic and language that together establish their respective "singular powers." Understanding the logic and language of a medium of art, like poetry or like architecture, enables us to apprehend its power to shape our humanity. The singular powers of music, for instance, include such things as silence, time, pitch, rhythm, meter, tempo, repetition, and so on. To understand how music forms us—how it exercises a singular power over

6. Jeremy Begbie, *Resounding Truth: Christian Wisdom in the World of Music* (Grand Rapids: Baker Academic, 2007), 50.

us—requires that we understand how a particular work of music employs its various singular powers, like the 4/4 time signature common to many Western hymns that moves us in a "regular" fashion or the polyrhythmic time of typically African worship music that moves us in an "irregular" manner.[7]

If we were to ask how stones praise God, we might say that they praise God in distinctly *stony* ways. That is to say, they praise God according to the "logic and language" of their peculiar physical, chemical qualities. Sandstone, for instance, praises God in a "warm and grainy" fashion, while marble does so in its own "cold and crystalline" ways. Both have a logic that makes certain kinds of architectural construction possible and other kinds impossible. Both types of stone generate a "feel" for a space—how people perceive a space and how they move within a space. Whatever the choice of stone in church architecture, it will form how a congregation occupies a space and how a people relate to each other in that space. With their long memories, stones will also recount multigenerational stories, and, while resisting change, they will communicate solidity rather than transience.[8] This, we might say, is the language of stones.

Art and Context

Fourth, the meaning of a work of art is discerned by its context. The contemporary architectural idiom of the Cathedral of Our Lady of the Angels in Los Angeles, for instance, means one thing to Catholics within the multiethnic, polyglot urban context of Los Angeles, for whom a sanctuary space rightly reflects its own time and place, in a way that speaks in a missionally persuasive manner to twenty-first-century Angelenos.[9] It means another

---

7. Cf. Mark Taylor, "Polyrhythm in Worship: Caribbean Keys to an Effective Word of God," in *Making Room at the Table: An Invitation to Multicultural Worship*, ed. Brian K. Blount and Leonora Tubbs Tisdale (Louisville: Westminster John Knox, 2000), 108–28.

8. The writer Ursula K. Le Guin, in her poem "A Meditation in the Desert," describes a stone being "full of slower, longer thoughts than mind can have." In *Out Here: Poems and Images from Steens Mountain Country* (Astoria, OR: Raven Studios, 2010), 102.

9. The Constitution on the Sacred Liturgy, chapter 7, "Sacred Art and Sacred Furnishings," from December 4, 1963, says this: "The Church has not adopted any particular style of art as her very own; she has admitted styles from every period according to the natural

thing altogether to Catholics who find the cathedral's style inimical to "Catholic architecture." For such Catholics, the architecture of a "proper" cathedral resembles the tradition of cathedral building established by medieval and Renaissance European history. For such Catholics, the Los Angeles cathedral fails to be beautiful. To many Angelenos, in contrast, it will feel profoundly beautiful.

The spiritual "Swing Low, Sweet Chariot," to use an example from music, could mean any number of things depending on the context in which it is sung. Originally a work song employed by slaves in the cotton fields, it means one thing when sung by an African Methodist Episcopal congregation in Philadelphia in the early nineteenth century. It means another thing when sung by Dolly Parton at the Grand Ole Opry and a third thing altogether when sung at an English rugby match. A Russian Orthodox icon will mean one thing at the Cathedral of Christ the Saviour in Moscow, but it will mean a radically different thing when hanging in the Metropolitan Museum of Art in New York City. An artwork's power—what it "says," what it can "do," and how it can "form" a person—is directly related to the context in which it is experienced and to the expectations that a viewer brings to it.[10]

---

talents and circumstances of peoples, and the needs of the various rites," http://www.vati can.va/archive/hist_councils/ii_vatican_council/documents/vat-ii_const_19631204_sacro sanctum-concilium_en.html. Accessed August 5, 2018. Likewise, the Diocesan Liturgical Commission, meeting in Superior, Wisconsin, in 1957, offered this observation: "The church edifice is constructed to serve men of our age. Its architectural language should not be foreign or archaic, but contemporary and genuine in expression. True Christian tradition accepts the true, good, and beautiful in each age and culture." Cited in Mark A. Torgerson, *An Architecture of Immanence: Architecture for Worship and Ministry Today* (Grand Rapids: Eerdmans, 2007), 69.

10. As I suggest throughout the book, a work of art is fully meaningful only within the complex of contexts in which it is found. George Dickie asks how we recognize a thing as "art." What is the "leanest possible description of the essential framework of art"? Dickie suggests it involves the following five definitions: (1) An artist is a person who participates with understanding in the making of a work of art; (2) A work of art is an artifact of a kind created to be presented to an artworld public; (3) A public is a set of persons the members of which are prepared in some degree to understand an object which is presented to them; (4) The artworld is the totality of all artworld systems; (5) An artworld system is a framework for the presentation of a work of art by an artist to an artworld public. "Defining Art: Intension and Extension," in *The Blackwell Guide to Aesthetics*, ed. Peter Kivy (Oxford: Blackwell, 2004), 58.

The Conversations of Art

Fifth, the meaning of a work of art is discerned by the "conversation" in which it finds itself. T. S. Eliot famously remarked that "No poet, no artist of any art, has his complete meaning alone. His significance, his appreciation is the appreciation of his relation to the dead poets and artists."[11] Eliot's remark draws attention to the fact that artists and artworks cannot be understood apart from the things that have preceded them. Surrealism does not make sense apart from Cubism and the events of World War I. Baroque music makes sense only in relation to both Renaissance music (the era that preceded it) and Classical music (which negatively nicknamed it after the fact). More to our purposes here, all works of art derive their meaning from the "conversation" in which they find themselves: a conversation with people and movements in both the past and present.[12] This is a helpful reminder as it relates with innovations in the liturgical arts or with uses of liturgical art that may seem strange to a congregation.

Is the architecture of the Cathedral of Our Lady of the Angels, for instance, *good* art—good artistically, good aesthetically, good for liturgical purposes? Yes, I might argue. When the aims of the architect (informed by his conversation with contemporary architecture) and the hopes of multi-ethnic Angelenos and the Catholic diocese (informed by their conversation with the local culture and the longstanding history of Catholics in southern California) are understood, as echoes of Vatican II's proposals for renewal in the sacred arts (which, for contemporary Catholics, informs all conversations about the visual and architectural arts in worship), then the architectural decisions of the cathedral make good sense.[13] Whether we like them or not is another matter. But before we get to issue a judgment about the artistic value of the cathedral or pronounce a personal opinion about our enjoyment

---

11. T. S. Eliot, "Tradition and the Individual Talent," in *Selected Essays: New Edition* (New York: Harcourt, Brace, 1932), 4.

12. Nicholas Wolterstorff distinguishes between two sorts of social-practice meaning: on the one hand, the meaning a work of art has for the person who engages it in accord with a specific social practice (say, museum art or liturgical art), and on the other, the meaning a work of art has in relation to a particular art history. The first sense of meaning includes the meaning that the artist invests in the work and the meaning that an audience invests in it. The second meaning involves the meaning that art historians identify for the work. See Wolterstorff, *Art Rethought: The Social Practices of Art* (Oxford: Oxford University Press, 2015), 116.

13. Cf. the Constitution on the Sacred Liturgy, chapter 7, "Sacred Art and Sacred Furnishings." See also http://www.olacathedral.org.

of its architecture, we do well to understand where it fits in the conversation that Catholics of the late twentieth and early twenty-first century have entertained about church buildings that honor God and serve the worship of God.

The Meaning-Making Power of Art

Sixth, works of art engage us in focused meaning-making activities. Works of art are not only a means by which artists express themselves; they are also a way for artists to interpret the times in which they live. Works of art both express and shape a particular people in a particular time and place. Church architecture is, again, a good example of this. Take the idea that "the church is a place to learn about God." This idea alone does not tell us what church buildings should look like and what kind of learning should take place when a congregation gathers for worship. Because ideas are always theologically inflected, church buildings will concretize the idea that a particular congregation holds about the kind of learning that ought to take place in corporate worship.

Learning, for some, is what happens in a lecture hall, where information is acquired. On this understanding, church architecture will look like a lecture auditorium, a place suited to the transfer of ideas between a teacher-speaker and learner-listeners. Presbyterian or Baptist church buildings often represent such an approach. For others, learning is what happens in shop class or out in the field, where habits are acquired and where skills need to be practiced. On this understanding, church architecture will look like a know-how space, a place suited to movement and the use of designated settings for *doing* things. Catholic and Pentecostal church buildings often represent this approach.

Whatever the design of the building, it will give people a "feel" for things by inviting them to imagine how one ought to learn about God. The building will speak—and it will often speak louder than certain words may wish.

Art: Simple and Complex, Accessible and Difficult

Seventh, works of art may be simple or complex, and they may be accessible or difficult. While "simple and complex" usually describes the composition of a work of art or its aesthetic qualities, "accessible and difficult" will describe people's psychological or practical experience of a work of art. Accessible and simple music, for example, might include chants and choruses, with melodic or lyrical lines that are repeated. The Taizé song "Jesus, Remember Me" and the Scripture song "I Love You, Lord" are examples of this. Accessible and complex music might include a hymn like Charles Wesley's "And Can It Be." Difficult and simple music might, for some, include black gospel "call and response" songs, such as "Oh Happy Day." Difficult and complex music might include polyphonic compositions or syncopated songs. Palestrina's music and City Harmonic's song "Manifesto" are instances of such music.

Whatever the music, all such art will usually be experienced as simple or complex, accessible or difficult *for a particular people, in a particular context.* What is felt to be simple by some may be felt to be complex by others. What is accessible to one congregation could be difficult to another. Because I believe that all art in worship should be seen as a vehicle for the formation of God's people into the image of Christ, I argue that both simple and complex art, both accessible and difficult, have a place within the life of the worshiping church.[14] And while notions of simplicity and complexity, accessibility and difficulty involve contextual dynamics, I nonetheless suggest that a broad range of art practices contribute to a holistic formation in the triune life.

Art: Particularity, Concentration, Representation

Eighth, works of art are characterized by particularity, concentration, and representation.[15] By particularity I mean that a specific work of art, such as the narrative of the Christ child, as told by the Virgin Mary to Saint Luke, is *this* thing, not any other thing. Once that story becomes written on the page, as Saint Luke does in his gospel, it becomes even more *this particular* thing. In its inscribed, pictureless form, it invites readers to imagine Luke's story with their own imaginations. And while there may be a range of plausible imagined scenes, circumscribed by the world that Luke describes, once pictures are added to the book, as the novelist Anne Rice does in her reimagining of the story in her 2005 novel *Christ the Lord: Out of Egypt,*

14. "Christian theologians were once well acquainted with the idea that the best art often delights only with difficulty, and through difficulty." Brown, *Good Taste, Bad Taste, and Christian Taste,* 253.

15. Here I am borrowing explicitly from Jeremy Begbie's essay "Faithful Feelings: Music and Emotion in Worship," in *Resonant Witness: Conversations between Music and Theology,* ed. Jeremy S. Begbie and Steven R. Guthrie (Grand Rapids: Eerdmans, 2011), 323–54.

the imagined world becomes *even more particular* in the mind of the reader. It is even more so the case with cinematic renditions, such as the 2016 film *The Young Messiah*, based on Rice's novel.

The property of concentration describes the way in which a work of art captures a *specific dimension* of human experience. The desire, for instance, to escape into a magical world is a common desire. We see it exhibited in Lewis Carroll's *Alice's Adventures in Wonderland* and Madeleine L'Engle's *A Wrinkle in Time*. Each story captures that peculiar desire but does so in a unique fashion. The property of representation, however, describes the way in which a work of art represents us—the viewer, the reader, the audience—rather than the author's perspective. In reading the *Chronicles of Narnia*, for instance, we find our own desires re-presented—for the Christlike figure of Aslan, for a magical adventure beyond the dullness of our own life, for evil that is named and conquered, or for an end that feels both sweet and sad, both necessary and unexpected.

The Near-Infinite Interests of Art

Ninth, the purposes of works of art are as varied as human and liturgical interests. Art has been marshaled on behalf of every human interest and in service of nearly every human activity. This is the case, for instance, for lullabies intended to soothe babies and for martial music that seeks to inspire bravery in those who fight the wars. For occasions of lament or times of penitence in the life of the church, there is a vast range of musical renderings of the *Kyrie* ("Lord, have mercy"). For days of celebration and situations that require an emboldened faith, there are triumphant songs like "A Mighty Fortress" or "All Hail the Power of Jesus' Name." There is no activity of corporate worship or purpose for the people of God at praise that the arts cannot serve in some befitting fashion.

Learning a New Art

Tenth, all media of art can be learned through sustained discipline within a community of thoughtful practitioners. One of the presumptions of this book is that it is never impossible, but only perhaps difficult, for a congregation to learn a new medium or use of art in worship. To learn such a practice of art in a way that promotes faithful, fruitful worship would require wise leadership, right training, patience, and a humble willingness to learn.[16] Whether it is desirable or needful for a congregation to learn a new practice of liturgical art is another matter. A congregation may refrain from introducing a new practice for any number of pastoral or practical reasons. In principle, however, any new practice of art can be learned and become intelligible to a congregation over time and in this way serve to form the congregation in the triune life.

Art and the Aesthetic Dimension of Human Life

Central to the argument of this book is that the arts foreground our experience of the sensory, the imaginative, and the emotional dimensions of human life, and they do so in metaphorically characteristic ways. The arts bring us, in this way, into concentrated experiences of the aesthetic dimension of our humanity. Because of the central role that this argument plays, I wish to develop it at length here in order to show how exactly the arts form our humanity within the context of corporate worship.

Art and the Senses

"All art," writes Joseph Conrad, "appeals primarily to the senses."[17] Rooted in the sensory domain, the arts make their appeal to the sense of taste and touch, of sight and sound and scent. A beautifully illustrated Bible appeals directly to my eyes. A Yamaha LL16 acoustic guitar appeals to the feel of my hand. Bach's *Goldberg Variations* appeals to my ear's love of repetition—and to its love of surprise, too. The freshly baked bread that I take in my hands, then bless, break, and offer to the congregation, appeals to my nose and what it knows about a eucharistically shaped life. When I taste the bread on my tongue, it reminds me to taste and see that the Lord is good.

16. For models of good leadership in corporate worship, see Constance M. Cherry, *The Worship Architect: A Blueprint for Designing Culturally Relevant and Biblically Faithful Services* (Grand Rapids: Baker Academic, 2010); Ruth C. Duck, *Worship for the Whole People of God: Vital Worship for the 21st Century* (Louisville: Westminster John Knox, 2013); Zac Hicks, *The Worship Pastor: A Call to Ministry for Worship Leaders and Teams* (Grand Rapids: Zondervan, 2016); Greg Scheer, *Essential Worship: A Handbook for Leaders* (Grand Rapids: Baker Books, 2016).

17. Cited in Simona Klimková, "A Man in Crisis: Selected Short Fiction of Joseph Conrad," *Ars Aeterna* 7, no. 2 (2015): 26.

The arts not only appeal to our physical senses, they also invite us to *inhabit* our senses and to discover the beloved world of God through our senses. For orthodox Christian faith, this is to be a welcomed thing. For regular human beings, this is a normal, even if not always a conscious, thing. Over against common assumptions in Western society, then, the body is not an accessory to perception; it is instead constitutive of it. "We think through our bodies," as Matthew Crawford writes in his book *The World beyond Your Head*.[18] And it is through our various embodied activities that we come to have "a grasp of the world." The arts simply intensify this grasp of things.

Describing the work of the Holy Spirit in relation to communal singing, Steve Guthrie says this about Ephesians 5: "the children of light are singing people, not *despite*, but *because* music engages body and sense."[19] Whereas sin desensitizes the human creature, robbing it of both its sense *in* the world and *of* the world, the Spirit of God resensitizes it, making it capable of holy sensory life *by way of* the physical act of singing.[20] In becoming resensitized, the Christian becomes more acutely sensitive to God and to neighbor. To sing to one another through psalms, hymns, and spiritual songs, then, is a gift of the Spirit, who instructs our "unstable" hearts and "weak" minds by way of the physical act of singing.

Rather than being a detriment to our humanity or an impediment to sanctification, then, the physical body is the condition of "creaturehood to which God condescends to meet us and mold us," as James K. A. Smith puts it.[21] This is something that the people of God experience in concentrated ways through the arts in worship. The stakes, as always, are high. "To starve the eye, the ear, the skin, the nose," writes Lewis Mumford, "is just as much to court death as to withhold food from the stomach."[22] At their best, liturgical artists nourish the eye, the ear, the skin, the nose, and the tongue, and thereby nourish a congregation with life that is basic to our humanity.

---

18. Matthew B. Crawford, *The World beyond Your Head: On Becoming an Individual in an Age of Distraction* (New York: Farrar, Straus and Giroux, 2015), 51. First John 1:1: "We declare to you what was from the beginning, what we have heard, what we have seen with our eyes, what we have looked at and touched with our hands, concerning the word of life" (NRSV).

19. Steven R. Guthrie, "Singing, in the Body and in the Spirit," *Journal of the Evangelical Theological Society* 46 (2003): 639, emphasis original.

20. This is a point that Tony Clark, following Guthrie, helpfully develops in *Divine Revelation and Human Practice: Responsive and Imaginative Participation* (Eugene, OR: Wipf and Stock, 2008), 186–89.

21. James K. A. Smith, *Imagining the Kingdom: How Worship Works* (Grand Rapids: Baker Academic, 2013), 111.

22. Lewis Mumford, *The City in History* (New York: Penguin, 1961), 344.

Art and the Emotions

The developmental psychologist Howard Gardner identifies six forms of human intelligence in his book *Frames of Mind: The Theory of Multiple Intelligences*.[23] One of them is musical-rhythmic. Mark Bangert summarizes a significant feature of Gardner's findings this way: "musical intelligence, though appearing in a variety of strengths, singularly provides an individual with the ability to perceive and apprehend aspects of feeling, as well as knowledge about feeling, that are unavailable through other intelligences."[24] Disaffected teenagers and Alzheimer's patients listening to particular kinds of music "get a feel" for their place in the world. Feelings are "identified," knowledge is "uncovered," identity is established.[25]

As with the senses again, the emotions become a way for human beings to name reality and to grasp the truth. They "are a primary means for our being in touch with our world."[26] Emotions are not only rooted in and generative of bodily behaviors, they are also "intrinsically social" and thereby a means by which we become relationally at home in the world.[27] The philosopher Robert Solomon argues that far from being irrational or an "illness of the mind," as Immanuel Kant saw them, the emotions are a fundamental aid to human wellbeing: "Emotions are intelligent, cultivated, conceptually rich engagements with the world, not mere reactions or instincts."[28]

In more theological terms, the arts can both reflect and shape an emotional life that is attuned to the heart of Jesus. As Jeremy Begbie offers, "Music can help us discover something that we *could* feel, that we have not felt before. And, we might add, we can also be educated emotionally: we might discover what we *should* feel in particular situations."[29] This is especially true, for ex-

23. Howard Gardner, *Frames of Mind: The Theory of Multiple Intelligences* (New York: Basic Books, 2011).

24. Mark P. Bangert, "The Last Word? Dynamics of World Musics Twenty Years Later," in *Worship and Culture: Foreign Country or Homeland?*, ed. Gláucia Vasconcelos Wilkey (Grand Rapids: Eerdmans, 2014), 126.

25. Iain McGilchrist, *The Master and His Emissary: The Divided Brain and the Making of the Western World* (New Haven: Yale University Press, 2009), 74, 88.

26. Mark Johnson, *The Meaning of the Body: Aesthetics of Human Understanding* (Chicago: University of Chicago Press, 2007), 65.

27. John A. Sloboda and Patrik N. Juslin, "Psychological Perspectives on Music and Emotion," in *Music and Emotion: Theory and Research*, ed. Patrik N. Juslin and John A. Sloboda (Oxford: Oxford University Press, 2001), 86. Cf. Begbie, "Faithful Feelings," 342–44.

28. Robert Solomon, *The Passions: The Myth and Nature of Human and Animal Emotions* (Notre Dame, IN: University of Notre Dame Press, 1983), ix.

29. Solomon, *The Passions*, 351, emphasis original.

ample, of the psalms. As prayers, the psalms offer us edited poetic language to give expression to our unedited emotions. Within the context of the liturgy, the psalms invite us, on certain days, to pray what we feel at the moment. On other days, they invite us to pray despite our feelings of the moment.

To pray in these two ways over the course of time is to cultivate the virtues of sympathy and empathy: of love for and with our neighbors. In this way our emotions are trained in the kind of neighborly care that Jesus proclaims and instantiates in his earthly ministry. To be emotionally "off," as Iain McGilchrist sees it, is to be "out of sorts," both personally and socially.[30] Because of the particular ways, then, in which the arts bring us into intentional and intensive experience of our emotions, they become an especially suited vehicle for becoming emotionally in tune with others. Within a liturgical context, the arts can form in us "faithful feelings."[31]

Art and the Imagination

As with the senses and the emotions, so with the imagination: it, too, is a fundamental way to discover our place in the world. With the imagination, humans are able to see things that are not immediately present or as yet actual.[32] Humans imagine what may yet be: flying cars, zero pollution, nanobots, a time when the wolf shall dwell with the lamb. Artists imagine what could be in another realm or how this realm might be rightly perceived. Such is the case with the playful architecture of Antoni Gaudí's *Sagrada Familia*, with its winged bulls, its "sequoia" columns, its whimsical colors, and its joyful vision of a world renewed by the resurrected Christ.[33] Such also is the case with Jesus's parables of the kingdom.

To see Michelangelo's *Last Judgment* is to imagine what God's justice might look like. The thirteenth-century Byzantine mosaic in the basilica of Santa

---

30. McGilchrist, *The Master and His Emissary*, 88.

31. Begbie, "Faithful Feelings," 323–54. Jeannette Winterson offers this insight: "Art shows us how to end the war, the war between heart and head, the war between reason and emotion." "What Is Art For?," in *The World Split Open: Great Authors on How and Why We Write* (Portland, OR: Tin House Books, 2014), 186–87.

32. Cf. Trevor Hart, *Between the Image and the Word: Theological Engagements with Imagination, Language and Literature* (Surrey: Ashgate, 2013), ch. 10; Leland Ryken, ed., *The Christian Imagination: The Practice of Faith in Literature and Writing* (Colorado Springs: Shaw Books, 2002); Peter Kivy, ed., *The Blackwell Guide to Aesthetics* (Oxford: Blackwell, 2004), ch. 1.

33. Cf. Luke Timothy Johnson, "Imagining the World Scripture Imagines," in *Theology and Scriptural Imagination*, ed. L. Gregory Jones and James J. Buckley (Oxford: Blackwell, 1998), 9.

Maria Assunta on the island Torcello (near Venice) invites us to imagine a different picture of God's judgment. An icon of Daniel in the lions' den invites Orthodox worshipers to imagine the moral shape of their lives in light of Daniel's life. "Look at Daniel, be like Daniel." When a congregation sings hymns from medieval, Celtic, and African liturgical traditions on All Saints Day, it becomes a way for them to imagine the day on which song from every tongue and tribe shall be lifted up to the Lamb, the everlasting desire of nations.

"Imagination, working at full strength, can shake us out of our fatal, adoring self-absorption, and make us look up and see—with terror or with relief—that the world does not in fact belong to us at all."[34] It belongs to God. What the writer Ursula K. Le Guin believes good novels can accomplish at their best might also be said about any art worth its salt. It describes, for instance, Maltbie Babcock's hymn "This Is My Father's World."[35] "This is my Father's world / O let me ne'er forget / That though the wrong seems oft so strong / God is the Ruler yet." It describes Solomon Raj's batik *Thirst for Justice*.[36] It likewise describes Jerusha Matsen Neal's dramatic monologues in *Blessed: Monologues for Mary*.[37]

As it relates to a liturgical anthropology in general and to corporate worship in particular, James Smith writes that "It is because I 'picture' [or imagine] the world as *this* kind of place, this kind of 'environment,' that I then picture 'the good life' in a certain way that draws me toward it and thus construe my obligations and responsibilities accordingly."[38] This is precisely what Jesus does in his preaching: he invites his listeners to imagine a world that resembles the "kingdom of heaven." This, too, is what Jesus invites the church to do through the arts: to imagine the world as God sees it, in faith, in hope, in love.

Art and Metaphor

In their joint book *Metaphors We Live By*, George Lakoff and Mark Johnson argue that our ordinary conceptual system is fundamentally metaphorical in nature.[39] General examples of this include "time is money," "the mind is a

34. Quoted in Julie Phillips, "The Fantastic Ursula K. Le Guin," *New Yorker*, October 17, 2016, https://www.newyorker.com/magazine/2016/10/17/the-fantastic-ursula-k-le-guin.

35. See https://hymnary.org/text/this_is_my_fathers_world_and_to_my.

36. See http://www.artway.eu/content.php?id=1315&lang=en&action=show.

37. Jerusha Matsen Neal, *Blessed: Monologues for Mary* (Eugene, OR: Cascade, 2013).

38. Smith, *Imagining the Kingdom*, 124–25, emphasis original.

39. George Lakoff and Mark Johnson, *Metaphors We Live By* (Chicago: University of Chicago Press, 1980), 3.

machine," and "argument is war." Those who think of an argument as war, for example, could imagine an argument-as-dance with no winners or losers *only with great difficulty*. Something similar is at work perhaps with metaphors that coordinate physical conditions with psychological ones. We say things like "I'm feeling up today" because physically erect postures typically go along with a positive emotional state—hence, happy is up. Physically drooping postures, conversely, typically go along with sadness, depression, and death.

Humans use metaphors in order to make sense of their entire experience in the world. This is certainly true for the New Testament community. Terms like "family," "people," "nation," and "foundation" are used to make sense of this new reality as a community constituted by the life, death, resurrection, and ascension of Christ and by the descent of the Spirit of God. Like a physical body, this community is now a "body" of Christ. Like Israel's temple, they are now a "temple" of the Spirit. For God's people, the meaning of the church was to be discovered not *beyond* but *through* these metaphors. While humans use metaphor in general ways, artists use metaphor in singular ways. And as I argue throughout the book, we cannot fully understand the formative power of art apart from its metaphorical character.[40]

The writer Ray Bradbury once remarked that, for artists, metaphors are the "breakfast of champions." For the American composer Leonard Bernstein, music was a "totally metaphorical language."[41] The literary critic T. R. Wright speaks perhaps for all artists when he says that the whole point of reading literature "is that it says something about life which cannot be said in any other way."[42] The arts marshal metaphors in a way that orients our sense of self in the world with a potency that cannot be easily matched by other media of communication. To be the family of God, for example, functions as a governing idea for the first generation of Christians.[43]

But family identity is also, and more crucially, an embodied reality. We can think all we wish about being a family of God. We can write books

40. As a point of clarity, while a piece of music—say, Adele's rendition of Bob Dylan's song "To Make You Feel My Love" or Edward Elgar's Cello Concerto in E minor, Op. 85—may express longing, the music itself does not express longing. It is rather that the music generated by the musician suggests *metaphorically* the experience of longing. Whether Dylan or Elgar were melancholy when they wrote the music, and whether Adele feels melancholy when she performs the song, is a separate question. What is common to these pieces of music is that they are expressive of feelings of longing in a *metaphoric* sense.

41. Cited in Begbie, *Voicing Creation's Praise*, 243.

42. Cited in Begbie, *Voicing Creation's Praise*, 249.

43. Family identity is theologically reconfigured by the advent of the Messiah; this much is clear from Jesus's words (Matt. 10:24–39; Heb. 2:11–12; cf. 1 Pet. 2:17; 1 John 3:10).

and preach sermons on the topic. But if our songs and our prayers, along with the seating configurations and the architectural arrangements of the spaces in which we regularly gather—if none of these artistic dimensions of our ecclesial life support a richly biblical idea of family, then we will never experience *familiness* in any formative sense. Without an appropriate artistic infrastructure—which enables us to say things like "This is what family *looks* like" or "This is how a family *feels*"—the idea of a church as family is, practically speaking, meaningless.

Conclusion

In worship we could preach about baptized imaginations, but we could also give our eyes something to look at, such as Matthias Grünewald's *The Crucifixion* or He Qi's *The Risen Lord*—which, as visual metaphors, show us Christ's life and death *vividly, acutely, concretely*—and trust that this experience of seeing will enable the worshiper to imagine the depths of Christ's agony on the cross or to perceive the glorious power of his resurrection.[44] A standard sermon, of course, performs a necessary service. Preachers at their best exposit texts, illustrate ideas, and show us how to apply them to our lives. Yet when the imagination is directly exercised through an immediate experience of a work of art, it acquires a potent capacity to "see" the world rightly, as Christ sees it.

When bodies are allowed to do the work of knowing in liturgical contexts, through postures of kneeling or prostration, they acquire instinctual capacities to serve as the humble Christ serves. When people are given a chance to feel rightly, for example, by praying Psalm 22 in lament on days when they might feel the exact opposite, they acquire muscles for feeling rightly beyond the liturgy, feeling for their neighbor with the sympathy of Christ. In all these ways our practices of art enable us to be tuned in to the Triune God and to be attuned to one another and to the world.[45] For all these reasons and more, it is no small thing how we think about art theologically and how art participates in *God's* work in corporate worship.

44. See http://www.artbible.info/art/large/9.html and https://www.heqiart.com/store/p94/48_The-Risen-Lord_Artist_Proof_.html. Roger Brown's painting *The Entry of Christ into Chicago* (1976) might also be a good thing for Christians to look at.

45. Smith, *Imagining the Kingdom*, 137.

After Sunday Mass at Pluscarden Abbey, Elgin, Scotland (Photograph by author)

CHAPTER 3

The Theological Meanings of Art in Worship

When [God's] hand was opened by the key of love, the creatures came forth.

Thomas Aquinas, *In sententiarum*, prologue

The artist himself always has to remember that what he is rearranging is nature, and that he has to know it and be able to describe it accurately in order to have the authority to rearrange it at all.

Flannery O'Connor, *Mystery and Manners*

The eschatological Creator God is not the enemy but the perfecter of the first creation.

Walther Eichrodt, *Theology of the Old Testament*

What roles do the arts in worship play in the economy of the Triune God? To answer this question we need first to ask a more fundamental question: What roles do *creation* and *culture making* play in God's economy? Whatever it is that we believe that the arts, as physical, aesthetic, cultural artifacts of human making, might accomplish in a liturgical context will be grounded in the purposes of God for creation and for human labor. How is the Father already at work in the physical world, blessing and gracing it to accomplish its God-given ends? How are the aesthetic aspects of our humanity already caught up in the redeemed humanity of Christ? How is the Spirit already enabling the work of humanity to resound with the glory of God? And how might the answer to these questions inform our practices of art in worship?

To ask how the Trinity is at work in creation is to begin to discover the manifold purposes of the arts within a liturgical context. To ask how the Trinity is at work in culture making, whereby humans make something of the world that God so loves, is likewise to begin to discover the purposes of art making in the context of corporate worship. The following affirmations seek to elaborate upon this twin conviction. Framed by a Trinitarian vision for creation and culture making, they suggest trajectories for the liturgical arts that are grounded in the distinctive work of the Father, the Son, and the Spirit. These affirmations are of course far from exhaustive—more could be added. But they enable us, I hope, to establish a kind of theological grammar for the faithful employment of the arts in corporate worship.

Twelve Affirmations

Creation is an expression of the pleasure of God.

Karl Barth once remarked that it is the Christian's duty "to love and praise the created order, because, as is made manifest in Jesus Christ, it is so mysteriously well-pleasing to God."[1] This is the first lesson in a distinctly Trinitarian theology of creation. To love creation is a way for human beings to participate in *God's* own pleasure in creation. How pleasing is the cosmos to God? We need only look at Jesus. He is the one who "opens up to us the mind and heart of the Creator."[2] To take pleasure in hue and texture, in the possibilities of fabric and metal, in the logic of wood and wind, in the patterns of sound and sinew and scent, is to take pleasure in the Word made flesh, the one through whom creation has its being, its glory, its perfect delight.

In his commentary on Genesis, John Calvin describes creation as a garden of the senses: "We see, indeed, the world with our eyes, we tread the earth with our feet, we touch innumerable kinds of God's works with our hands, we inhale a sweet and pleasant fragrance from herbs and flowers, we enjoy boundless benefits; but in those very things of which we attain some knowledge, there dwells such an immensity of divine power, goodness, and wisdom, as absorbs all our senses."[3] Because Christ stands at the center of the cosmic order, then, the created realm can be properly regarded as the beloved world of God and a source of Spirit-shaped delight and exploration for human beings.

In corporate worship the church takes the stuff of creation and makes an art of it: song from wind, dance from motion, architecture from stone, poetry from language, paint from pigments. The church does so not only

---

1. Karl Barth, *Church Dogmatics*, III.1, trans. J. W. Edwards, O. Bussey, and Harold Knight (Edinburgh: T&T Clark, 1958), 346.

2. Jeremy Begbie, *Resounding Truth: Christian Wisdom in the World of Music* (Grand Rapids: Baker Academic, 2007), 189.

3. John Calvin, *Commentary on* Genesis, "The Argument," vol. 1, in *Commentaries of John Calvin*, 46 vols. (Edinburgh: Calvin Translation Society, 1844–55; reprint, Grand Rapids: Baker Book House, 1979), emphasis added.

to make sense of its life before God in praise, nor only because of its desire to remain obedient to the will and Word of God, but also because liturgical art is a way for the people of God to take pleasure in God's beloved creation. To paraphrase the language of Genesis 2:9, the liturgical arts accomplish not only useful, necessary functions—serving prayer, praise, preaching, and so on. They also originate in our pleasure in creation's bounty and they generate pleasure in the Creator's good world.

Because our pleasure in creation is grounded in God's own pleasure, then, making art within the context of corporate worship is a delight, not just a requirement; it is an invitation rather than only a command.[4] And because it is the Holy Spirit who conforms the lives of the faithful to the perfect humanity of Christ, the faithful are freed both *from* undue anxiety over creation's "excesses" and *for* righteous pleasure in this theater of God's glory. The church delights in creation, in the end, on the conviction that we belong to God's economy of grace.[5]

Creation is an overflow of the grace of God.

Because creation is neither an accident nor a divine necessity but instead the absolute gift of a gracious God, human beings *get to* make something of it all, they do not only *have to*. For those with eyes to see, as Barth writes, the universe is revealed to them as the "theater of the history of the covenant of grace."[6] In such a grace-saturated universe, there is an *invitation*, not just an *obligation*. Humans *have to* make clothes for protection against the elements, but they *get to* make cassocks and bonnets and paisley ties. They *have to* build shelters, but they *get to* build chapels and cathedrals.

Human beings *have to* give glory to God, because their life depends on it, but they *get to* do so with a wealth of artistic goods: pipe organs and balalaikas, syncopated jazz and resplendent cantatas, whimsical sonnets and somber chants. In God's creation, and through the wonder of an eighty-eight-key piano, for instance, there is the possibility of 309,485,009,821, 345,068,724,781,056 chord voicings—an excess of possibilities. In God's

---

4. Creation as the result of a Trinitarian "bash" is an idea that Robert Capon imaginatively explores in his book *The Romance of the Word: One Man's Love Affair with Theology* (Grand Rapids: Eerdmans, 1995), 176–77.

5. Cf. my *The Theater of God's Glory: Calvin, Creation, and the Liturgical Arts* (Grand Rapids: Eerdmans, 2017), ch. 2, "The Work of the Material Creation," ch. 3, "The Work of the Material Symbols," and ch. 5, "The Double Movement of Creation in Worship."

6. Barth, *Church Dogmatics*, III.1, 44.

creation there is more than human beings need or deserve or could ever make good use of in one lifetime or several.

All of this is simply another way of saying that the "get to" of creation is a sign of God's grace. Because of the abundance that marks God's world, as an expression of the abundant life that characterizes the Triune Communion, the church at worship gets to revel in the sheer gratuity of it all. The church gets to wonder at things: why red is *red*, why appoggiaturas affect us so acutely, why Gothic cathedrals transport the affections upward, why just the right turn of phrase is everything, why a good story finds a way to send the imagination in the direction of hope.

The church at worship gets to explore bodily gestures for humility. It gets to tell parabolic stories and countercultural testimonies. It gets to ornament its spaces and to express its faith in a thousand tongues. The body of Christ gets to enjoy the things that God has made and to make something of these manifold things within a liturgical context. Inasmuch as the experience of creation's riches leads us by faith to honor God's grace, I argue that all our experiences of the liturgical arts, as expressions of creation's riches, also contribute to a grace-filled life.

Creation is a gift of God and the context for culture making.

The Father makes a world that, while wholly dependent on him, is also endowed with its own integrity, its own way of being. He places humanity in it to steward it and to draw out its riches and potentialities. The human creature does so in Christ's name, in whom creation discovers its fundamental logic. Human beings do so by the Spirit's power, by which creation accomplishes its divinely ordained purposes. According to Barth, it gives God a "sporting joy" to give the creature this space, "to be itself," to "its very depths," to freely make something of the world.[7]

In God's creation, then, there is a "place" for all the particular things of creation. This place is a gift; and it is a grace. This place is real, not apparent, and it is a place for the creature to "go of itself," in the freedom that both the Word and the Spirit make possible. This is what the poet Gerard Manley Hopkins might call the "inscape" of things: their unique quality.[8] "Once we realize the world has its *own* character," writes Jeremy Begbie, "its *own* ways of functioning, we will begin to attend to it more carefully *as it is*

---

7. Barth, *Church Dogmatics*, III.3, §49.

8. Hopkins describes this feature of creation in his poem "As Kingfishers Catch Fire," in Gerard Manley Hopkins, *Poetry and Prose* (London: Penguin Classics, 1953).

and *as it could be* and will be very wary of projecting onto it a theory of order unthinkingly imported from the philosopher's or the theologian's desk."[9]

The calling of the artist, on this understanding, to borrow the language of the writer Cynthia Ozick, is "to distinguish one life from another; to illuminate diversity; to light up the least grain of being, to show how it is concretely individual, particularized from any other; to tell, in all the marvel of its singularity, the separate holiness of the least grain."[10] Said otherwise, the calling of artists is to give loving attention to creation's "endlessly remarkable quiddity," as Richard Bauckham describes it.[11] This includes understanding the logics and powers of all the stuffs of creation.

What do the peculiar dynamics of the physical world—its constants and spontaneities, its sounds and its silences, its orders and non-orders, its spare and ornate qualities, its simplicities and complexities—say about the Creator?[12] How do color, stone, wood, metal, fabric, glass, and wind "work"? What do the different types of rock or wood make possible in works of art? How do human bodies shape social relations and psychological dispositions? How do spaces "learn" their inhabitants over time and form a way of being in the world?[13] To these questions, Calvin Seerveld offers this sensible piece of advice:

> If you must decide, so you can give leadership, on whether Chagall's stained glass window honouring the late Mayor Daley in the Art Institute of Chicago is more or less significant than the striking piece by Abraham Rattner that takes a whole wall of the downtown loop

9. Begbie, *Resounding Truth*, 194–95, emphasis original. He adds, "the created world is not good *despite* being different from God; it is good in its *very difference and distinctiveness*. It is created, and it will most fully honor God when it fulfills its role as created."

10. Cynthia Ozick, *Art and Ardor* (New York: Alfred A. Knopf, 1983), 248. Flannery O'Connor puts the point similarly when she says, "you cannot show the operation of grace when grace is cut off from nature . . . because no one will have the least idea of what you are about." *Mystery and Manners: Occasional Prose*, ed. Sally and Robert Fitzgerald (New York: Farrar, Straus and Giroux, 1961), 166.

11. Richard Bauckham, "Joining Creation's Praise of God," *Ecotheology* 7 (2002): 52. On this question, see also Colin Gunton, *The Triune Creator: A Historical and Systematic Study* (Grand Rapids: Eerdmans, 1998), 197–98.

12. Harold M. Best has a helpful way of relating these pairings to the practice of corporate worship. See *Unceasing Worship: Biblical Perspectives on Worship and the Arts* (Downers Grove, IL: IVP, 2003), 182–86.

13. "A sanctuary has a kind of creative capacity of its own." Ellen F. Davis, "The Tabernacle Is Not a Storehouse: Building Sacred Spaces," *Sewanee Theological Review* 49 (2006): 306.

synagogue, you don't go read Paul's letters, the Psalms or even Isaiah 40 to look for information on "beauty": instead, you go study the art for hours, learn the composer or artist's whole oeuvre to get context, examine the history of music, memorial and cult artistry, take a considered stand on the nature of art and slowly begin to discern what counts. All of this scrutiny is exceedingly difficult.[14]

Since the creation of God is, as it were, unfinished, he continues, "its variegated meanings are waiting there to be unleashed in a new chorus of praise for the Lord. This is our human calling."[15] Made in the image of a culture maker, of a Creator who makes both abstract and representational things, both gardens and cities, both clothes and families, human beings likewise make culture. They make Shaker furniture, illuminated Bibles, mystery plays, stone gargoyles, processional dances, ciboriums, and digital projections.[16] This difficult but blessed work is the work that human beings are called by God to do: to "till the ground" and thus to make culture.

The Father invites the human creature to discover, to attend, to name, to cultivate, and thereby to care for things in creation. In Christ human beings discover how to do this manifold work well. In the Spirit they are empowered to create and to keep culture in the love of God. Under this light, how might liturgical artists give voice to creation's varied praise? How might such artists give voice to the praise of every tribe, tongue, and nation? How might they convey the true knowledge of God and inspire affection for God? How might they bear witness to all that is right and wrong in the world, to the lighthearted and to the serious, to what is and to what might be?

14. Calvin Seerveld, *Rainbows for the Fallen World: Aesthetic Life and Artistic Task* (Toronto: Toronto Tuppence Press, 1980), 13–14. Flannery O'Connor argues against theologically impoverished approaches to the arts. The sorry artist, she writes, "will think that the eyes of the Church or of the Bible or of his particular theology have already done the seeing for him, and that his business is to rearrange the essential vision into satisfying patterns, getting himself as little dirty in the process as possible." *Mystery and Manners*, 163.

15. Seerveld, *Rainbows*, 24–25. Roger Hazelton says, "Creation does not happen all at once, nor is it entirely one complete and single act; God calls, forms, distinguishes, and names the multifarious world. Indeed, the more carefully we read and ponder the story told in Genesis, the more creation seems to take on the characteristics of a work of art." *A Theological Approach to Art* (Nashville: Abingdon, 1967), 53.

16. Cf. Andy Crouch, *Culture Making: Recovering Our Creative Calling* (Downers Grove, IL: InterVarsity, 2013), 101–17.

These, among others, are the kinds of questions that artists and worship leaders get to ask themselves in their role as makers and stewards of art in context of corporate worship.

Creation is marred by sin but not robbed of its grace.

In Genesis 3 we see that God's creation goes terribly wrong. But it is only in Christ that we see how terribly wrong it has gone. In Christ we see that creation is not simply caught up in forces of entropy; it is caught up in forces of sin and death. Through human disobedience, sin enters into the world and disfigures the world. Whatever else it is, sin is pathetic, idiotic, and irrational, just because it is good gone wrong.[17] Because of sin, creation is marred and the human creature seeks to play God and to fight God. Humanity becomes alienated from God, curved in on itself, and at odds with the rest of creation. Work becomes sweat and toil, death becomes "the last enemy," evil deforms the human creature, and an economy of scarcity, rather than an economy of abundance, marks the human experience.

What is required is the initiative of the Triune God to heal the world. In Christ's own initiative, to become "flesh from our flesh," we discover not only the extent of creation's brokenness but also its belovedness. In Christ we discover creation's original benediction as well as its eschatological destiny.[18] In Christ we discern not only the comprehensive corruption of the human creature but also its destiny to be hale and holy, capable yet again of intimate fellowship with the Father through the Spirit. As Gordon Lathrop describes it, in Christ we discover that "this life is the theater of sin and grace, death and life; that history matters and moves in a direction; that the structures of things, including the stars, had a beginning and may have an end; and that all creatures—animate and inanimate—stand before God."[19]

"The resurrection of the crucified humanity of Christ," writes Begbie, "is itself the embryonic promise for the entire physical cosmos.... In him

---

17. This is how the British theologian J. I. Packer would describe sin to his students at Regent College.

18. The end of creation is discovered in the end of Christ: creation is rightly seen not in its protological form ("in the beginning") but its eschatological form ("in the end"). We are looking, I argue, at a re-creation, not a return to Eden.

19. Gordon Lathrop, *Holy Ground: A Liturgical Cosmology* (Minneapolis: Augsburg Fortress, 2003), 45.

the destiny of creation has been set forth."[20] While it is in Christ that we discern the shape of redeemed culture making, then, it is by the empowering presence of the Spirit that the inordinate desires of "the flesh" are corrected and that human work is reoriented to its proper end. And so it is that with the help of the Godhead the faithful are enabled to become agents, here and now, of the new creation within a liturgical context.

The church's praise is correlative to creation's praise.

To draw the above comments in the direction of the church's corporate worship, I argue that the church's praise subsists in creation's praise. The manifold role, for example, that John Calvin perceives creation to perform—as a mirror, chock-full of the insignia of God, capable of refreshing the faithful, inviting them to revel in the abundance of God's work, an occasion for cataphatic feasting, and a stimulus to human praise in concord with the ongoing praise of irrational creatures—is the work that creation continues to perform in the life of the church inasmuch as creation is the proper context for any creaturely praise.

Worship occurs in and through creation because it is God's continual pleasure to call forth praise in all his works, at all liturgical times, and in all liturgical places. It is God's pleasure to be found in "the very beautiful fabric of the world," not "in his secret essence."[21] God does so, not as an unfortunate requirement, but as a way to honor human creatureliness. No other creaturely praise is in fact possible for human beings made from the fabric of God's good earth. "Given this utterly corporeal character of the human life lived by the Word of God for the redemption of the world, it is entirely congruous that he should choose to keep coming to his church by material means for the sake of our salvation."[22]

If it is true, as Augustine once argued, that human beings learn of God from the "book" of creation, then this will also be true of the faithful who gather together in liturgical contexts.[23] Job 12:7–8 says, "But now

20. Jeremy Begbie, *Voicing Creation's Praise: Towards a Theology of the Arts* (Edinburgh: T&T Clark, 1991), 176.

21. Calvin, *Comm.* Ps. 104:1, in vol. 6 of *Commentaries of John Calvin.* See also Gerald Hiestand and Todd Wilson, eds., *Creation and Doxology: The Beginning and End of God's Good World* (Downers Grove, IL: IVP Academic, 2018).

22. Geoffrey Wainwright, *For Our Salvation: Two Approaches to the Work of Christ* (Grand Rapids: Eerdmans, 1997), 11.

23. Augustine says this: "Some people read books in order to find God. But the very appearance of God's creation is a great book. Look above you! Look below you! Take note!

ask the beasts, and let them teach you; / and the birds of the heavens, and let them tell you. / Or speak to the earth, and let it teach you; / And let the fish of the sea declare to you" (NASB). The early church father Tertullian (AD 155–240) echoes this passage in his treatise on prayer, where he reflects on the capacity of creatures to serve as an example to humanity of right prayer: "Domestic and wild animals pray and bend their knees, and emerging from their stalls or dens look up to heaven not with closed jaws, but shaking the air with cries in their animal way. Birds too, when they awake, rise toward heaven and in place of hands lift their wings, which they open in the shape of the cross, chirping something that might seem to be a prayer."[24]

If it is possible for "irrational creatures," of both heaven and earth, to act as eloquent heralds of the glory of God, then it is theologically unreasonable to argue that these works of God—sound, stone, metal, glass, wood, light, flesh, fiber—will not also evoke God's glory in our spaces of worship. The purpose of the arts in worship, then, will not be to "get out of the way," but rather to serve the purposes of worship in their own creaturely ways. The purpose of artists, accordingly, will be to offer "articulate" voice to creation's praise, while never seeking to replace creation's own praise. And the purpose of creation will be, as always, to train the faithful to *taste* and *see* that the Lord is indeed good.

In corporate worship we join the praise of the firstborn of all creation.

Because Christ is the mediator of the whole world and the one who cares and keeps all of creation in its proper state, creation discovers its proper *end*: graced by the Father as the source of creation, grounded and oriented in the life of the Son, and animated and perfected by the Holy Spirit. Because Christ is the True Worshiper, the Chief *Leitourgos*, moreover, as Hebrews 12 describes him, the faithful join the praise of the Firstborn of all creation, who, by virtue of his Spirit-enabled resurrection and ascent to the right hand of the Father, is able to announce and enact the praise of the new creation.

Commenting on Hebrews 2:12, Calvin writes, "This teaching is the very strongest encouragement to us to bring yet more fervent zeal to the

Read!" Cited in Karlfried Froehlich, "'Take up and Read': Basics of Augustine's Biblical Interpretation," *Interpretation* 58 (2004): 5–16.

24. Cited in Timothy Verdon, *Art and Prayer: The Beauty of Turning to God* (Brewster, MA: Paraclete, 2013), 6.

praise of God, when we hear that Christ heeds our praise, and is the chief Conductor of our hymns."[25] As the incarnate temple of God, Christ gathers up all of creation's praise in a gift of love to the Father. Christ's praise, transposed in the church's praise, becomes an actual and symbolic prelude to the restoration of creation's perfect praise. In the name of Christ, then, the church gives voice to creation's own praise. As Calvin Seerveld describes the doxological calling of humanity, when we sing our praises to God, "[we] join in with the ecstatic praise continually being offered up to the Lord by trees and flowers, sunshine and rain, angels, dragons, and snakes, as well as monarchs and generals of the world. . . . To join the lightning and thunder and earthquake tremors in their praise of God, we should indeed pull out all the stops with flutes and drums, tubas, strings, woodwinds, trumpets, trombones, human voice, and dance to make a merry, raucous noise for the Lord."[26]

The Holy Spirit sustains creation's life and order.

In the Nicene Creed the church confesses its faith in the Third Person of the Trinity, "the Lord and Giver of life." By this confession the church affirms that it is the Spirit who animates creation, upholds it, and brings it to perfection. In faith the church affirms that it is the Spirit who mends the human creature, conforming it by grace, through faith, to the life of God in Christ. In faith the church likewise affirms that it is the Spirit who orders the cosmos. And while such a confession may be universally agreed upon, there is less concord about the order that the Spirit makes possible in worship.

The reason this matters is that our ideas about order will directly inform our practices of art in worship. If the Spirit is the divine person responsible for the order that characterizes the worship of the one, holy, catholic, and apostolic church, then we must look to the work of the Spirit of God in Christ to discern a proper answer. We can undoubtedly affirm that God is a God of order, not of chaos. But we can also affirm that a Spirit-constituted order will be an irrepressibly dynamic order, yielding new configurations of liturgical life and prompting praise to a God whose goodness is revealed through culturally varied expressions of order that mark the global body of Christ.

---

25. Calvin, *Comm.* Heb. 2:12, in vol. 12 of *Calvin's New Testament Commentaries*, ed. David W. Torrance and Thomas F. Torrance, 12 vols. (Grand Rapids: Eerdmans, 1959–72).

26. Calvin Seerveld, *Voicing God's Psalms* (Grand Rapids: Eerdmans, 2005), 141.

If the Spirit secures the order of the church's worship, then, it is important not to think of this order like that of a military or factory assembly line, where precision and sameness figure largely. It is instead a creative order—neither homogenous nor topsy-turvy. It is the kind of order that is capable of surprising and enthralling. The liturgical arts, on this view, contribute to a rich experience of order: the order that is experienced, for example, in syncopated music or that characterizes the Shakespearean sonnet in the hands of the liturgical poet Malcolm Guite;[27] the order that describes the "singing in the Spirit" of Latino Pentecostals or that typifies the Renaissance polyphonic choral works of *Stile Antico*.[28]

The Spirit enables humanity to praise God faithfully in and through creation.

Because the Spirit is poured upon the faithful *in Christ*, human beings can take "holy pleasure" in the works of creation. To say this is to argue against the presumption that disordered desires will have the last and most forceful word in our experience of art in corporate worship. It is to argue against the idea that extreme caution and constant worry should mark our practices of liturgical art.[29] Not only do such sentiments contradict a New Testament vision for the physical creation, they also underestimate the power of the Spirit to sanctify human desires, to purify human hearts and minds, and to rightly order physical bodies.

While Christians have no business taking sin any less seriously than Christ himself takes it, Christians also have no business taking the power of the Spirit less seriously than Christ himself does. If the arts can function as a vehicle of God's glory within a liturgical context, it is only because the Spirit enables the arts to be *fit for* such a task. It is only because the Spirit enables human beings to make good use of God's creation in the works of art that enter into the context of worship. The liturgical arts in this sense are enabled *by* the Spirit to serve the praise of God in Christ.[30] With con-

27. Malcolm Guite, *Sounding the Seasons: Seventy Sonnets for the Christian Year* (Norwich: Canterbury Press, 2012).

28. See https://www.stileantico.co.uk/about.

29. The second stanza of the 1911 Sacred Harp hymn "Where All Is Peace and Love" is representative of this view: "We're fettered and chained up in this clay / While in this body here we stay / By faith we know a world above / Where all is peace and love." Cited in *American Folklore: An Encyclopedia*, ed. Jan Harold Brunvand (Abingdon, Oxon: Routledge, 1996), 954.

30. Cf. Daniel W. Hardy, "Calvinism and the Visual Arts: A Theological Introduc-

fidence, then, in the effective work of the Spirit, the faithful are freed to explore a host of forms and medias and styles that might aptly serve the corporate worship of the church.

The Spirit enables the liturgical arts to serve the good purposes of God.
It is the Spirit who makes it possible for the arts, each in their own peculiar way, to reveal the invisible God through sensory media, to become a "school" for the church, to awaken joy through creation's powers and riches, to rebuke humanity of its ingratitude and pride, to summon the faithful to the praise of God and to take pleasure, as Richard Bauckham puts it, in that "strangeness, intricacy and difference" that God has entrusted to his creatures.[31] It is the Spirit who makes use of the arts to counter the idols of the mind, to repair forgetful memories, to rectify a will that is warped, to heal the disorder of broken bodies and dysfunctional affections, and to illumine the imagination to see the world as God sees it.

It is likewise the Spirit who enables the liturgical arts to become occasions for the care and celebration of each congregation's particular practice of worship. One of art's purposes is to accent the goodness of *this* particular place, *this* particular geography, along with the privileges and responsibilities and heart language that God has entrusted to *this* particular people at worship. It is the Spirit who makes wise a particular congregation to discern how it might bear witness to a culturally contextual artistic excellence, where this people take advantage of an opportunity to bring forward their particular artistic gifts in service of their worship to God.

While the physical creation enables a particular congregation to bear particular witness to God in worship, the physical creation will take on a second, especially crucial task within a liturgical context: to bear witness to the salvific work of God. In this way, creation makes salvation

---

tion," in *Seeing Beyond the Word: Visual Arts and the Calvinist Tradition*, ed. Paul Corby Finney (Grand Rapids: Eerdmans, 1999), 5. To argue this is to argue, with Trevor Hart, against a "free-for-all in which any and every material form may be appealed to as a likely site of encounter with" God, and instead to emphasize what God chooses to do—and indeed *wishes* to do. See Hart, "Unseemly Representations," in *Between the Image and the Word: Theological Engagements with Imagination, Language and Literature* (Surrey: Ashgate, 2013), 178.

31. Bauckham, "Joining Creation's Praise of God," 52. On this question, see also Gunton, *The Triune Creator*, 197–98.

dynamically sensible. Our places of public worship will be seen, on this view, not as static places, neutral placeholders for the operation of the ostensibly more important verbal and intellectual activities of worship, but rather as symbolically charged places that make visible the shape of God's salvation.

This is another way of saying perhaps that our places of worship will not simply "be" (as if it were possible for any space to be theologically neutral). They will be *for* something: for the Spirit's work of sanctification, shaping the way in which the faithful perceive their identity and vocation, their comings and goings, their acts of thanksgiving and reconciliation, their status as both settlers and strangers in the world, and enabling them to "read" the meaning of the world in light of the re-creative activity of the Triune God, played out in the drama of corporate worship.

Lastly, as Christ in his earthly ministry makes the invisible in some fashion *visible*, the ineffable somehow *effable*, the intangible partially *tangible*, the unknowable to some extent *knowable*, so Spirit-empowered artists make known, in some fashion, the goodness and glory of God within the context of corporate worship. As in Christ the mystery of God becomes heard, seen, touched, tasted, and sensed as an attestation of the grace of God incarnate, so too Spirit-empowered artists make the mystery of God known—but always, hopefully, in humility, in a way that resists our proclivities to master and manipulate it.

The physical body plays a determinative role in corporate worship.

The fundamental thrust of the New Testament is to understand the "spiritual" work of God as the work of the Holy Spirit to conform the whole human person to the life of Christ. This is a comprehensive reality. No sphere of life is left untouched by the Spirit-ual work of God. This includes the physical body, the "sphere" of the senses and a primary locus for artistic experience. One of the central places where the senses are sanctified and the faithful learn how to live a bodily "righteous" life is in public worship. It is here that the faithful learn what it means to disciple the human body. This too is a work of the Trinity.

Just as distinctively Christian worship ought to make space for spontaneous expressions of prayer and praise, as a way for our bodies both to be led by the movements of the heart and mind and to lead the movements of the heart and mind, it ought also to encourage ritualized and symbolic expression. A ritualized form of physical expression, on this understanding, will involve repeated activities that are performed for the good of our physical bodies, regardless of temperament or the feelings of the moment. A symbolic form of expression will take seriously the christomorphic shape of all of worship: worship that invites our physical bodies to "put on Christ" in every way imaginable.

To put the point in practical terms, the church does not do everything that could be done with the physical body in the context of public worship. While people may use bodies in playful ways, perhaps by dancing during a song, they will not play sports with them. They will only do certain things with the body, some of these repeatedly, some occasionally. But these things will remind them that they do not perceive their bodies rightly simply by moving them about throughout the week. They perceive them rightly by being gathered *in* their own bodies, *as* a body, *around* Christ's body.[32]

Triune worship is embodied, aesthetically mediated worship.

The worship that the Father seeks, that the Son exemplifies, and that the Spirit makes possible is worship that is embodied and aesthetically mediated rather than disembodied, otherworldly, and ethereal.[33] Key here is a right understanding of the language of John 4:23–24. When Jesus tells the woman at the well that a time "has now come when the true worshipers will worship the Father in the Spirit and in truth" (NIV), his point is a Trinitarian one. His point is not to give an account of the interior life—of her sincerity or capacity to be truthful. For the primary accent in John's Gospel rests *not* on the work of the human creature but rather on the work of the *Trinity* to enable disciples to worship God rightly.[34]

Worship that the Spirit makes possible, according to the Fourth Gospel, is made tangible in the new community that has been constituted by the work of God in Christ: in their speech, their actions, their bodies, and

32. Cf. Taylor, *The Theater of God's Glory*, ch. 7, "A Trinitarian Theology of the Physical Body."

33. Two traditions characterize the interpretation of this text: one that argues that John 4 points to the inner life of the individual worshiper and another that believes the text is best understood as a description of the activity of the Triune God to make faithful worship possible in this new "time," inaugurated by the coming of Christ and the descent of the Spirit. Cf. Taylor, *The Theater of God's Glory*, ch. 8, "The 'Simple' Worship of God," and ch. 9, "The Trinitarian Space of Worship."

34. Cf. R. G. Gruenler, *The Trinity in the Gospel of John: A Thematic Commentary on the Fourth Gospel* (Grand Rapids: Baker, 1986).

the physical media that liturgically symbolize the new life in Christ.[35] Richard Hays rightly argues that "this gospel's aesthetic vision is deeply grounded in the *particular*, the *palpable*, and the *embodied*."[36] John's Gospel points us therefore to a new covenantal worship where the physical creation plays an indispensable role: narratively through the story it tells (for example, in foot washing) and dramatically through the story it enacts (by way of, for instance, eucharistic gatherings).[37]

Put otherwise, in John we discover no disparagement of physical space; we discover no "sacred space," no secularizing of space.[38] We discover instead the possibility of an opening out of space significantly imbued with "Spirit and Truth." We discover a vision of the physical creation that has been hereby reconfigured by the work of the "Two Hands" of God. We discover, further, a way in which the shape of worship might become aesthetically and symbolically rich. To worship in the sphere of Christ and the Spirit, then, points to a reality in which the glory of God is expressed in artistically fashioned works of human hands, whether ornately or simply, whether extravagantly or economically.

A sound ecclesiology is essential to the flourishing of the worship arts.

To be a Christian is to be constituted by the body of Christ. Among other things, this means that Christians are knitted and tethered to one another by God's Spirit. It means that members of the universal church are *mutually implicated* in each other's lives. It means, also, that we are not the first to arrive on the liturgical art scene. Others have come before us, and we are much the poorer for refusing their wisdom. It means that others will follow us, and we get to hand over what has been entrusted to us: our insights into language, our musical discoveries, our investments in architecture and

---

35. It is noteworthy that the Scriptures include numerous examples of material objects that, both accompanied by and apart from faith, mediate the power and presence of God. These include the tabernacle altar, Moses's rod, Elijah's mantle, Elisha's bones, Paul's handkerchief, and Jesus's own robe.

36. Richard B. Hays, "The Materiality of John's Symbolic World," in *Preaching John's Gospel: The World It Imagines*, ed. David Fleer and Dave Bland (St. Louis: Chalice Press, 2008), 6, emphasis original.

37. Cf. N. T. Wright, "Worship and the Spirit in the New Testament," in *The Spirit in Worship—Worship in the Spirit*, ed. Teresa Berger and Bryan D. Spinks (Collegeville, MN: Liturgical Press, 2009), 23.

38. Cf. H. Wayne Johnson, "John 4:19–24: Exegetical Implications for Worship and Place," unpublished paper presented at the annual meeting of the Evangelical Theological Society, Baltimore, MD, November 2013.

institutions of patronage, our leaps of faith, our stories, and our faithful acts of worship on the stage of history.

To be *one* church means that we actively seek opportunities for collaboration and cooperation with the people of God, not just across town or across the planet, but also across cultural and linguistic and ethnic lines. It means that we read outside our own tradition. It means that we owe a debt of loyalty to the tradition of the church and that we owe a debt of responsibility to the future members of Christ's body. It means that we humbly incorporate the art practices of other members of Christ's body as a way to enrich our own worship and to implicate us in the common worship of the family of God. In doing such things, we become better at resisting the temptation to confuse the gospel with our home culture or to reduce the gospel to our own tradition.

To be a *holy* church means that we welcome the sanctifying work of the Spirit to make us whole and holy through our practices of art in worship. It means that we see ourselves as a temple of the Spirit, not a voluntary association of like-minded individuals, freely doing "whatever we please, whenever we please." We see ourselves instead as a Spirit-constituted, *holy ethnos*. At Pentecost a community "was created by the Spirit in which the embodiment of Christ's mission continued corporately after his ascension, as a household, a family, a koinonia."[39] At Pentecost, in other words, the disciples became something altogether new so that a community might be formed in Jesus's name from every tribe, tongue, and nation in order to be "a sign, instrument and foretaste of the kingdom of God," as the missionary bishop Lesslie Newbigin describes it.[40]

To be a *catholic*, or universal, church means that we actively seek to become familiar with what God is doing in the global church through the arts in worship. It means that we in the Global North identify with the blessings and sorrows of the church in the Global South, and vice versa. It means that we keep ourselves from ethnocentricity and monoculturalism, from the pride that arises in the thought that we have no need of other members of Christ's body. To be an *apostolic* church, finally, means that we seek always to remain faithful to the canonical witness of God's people. It means that we become careful students of how Holy Scripture talks *about* the arts and

---

39. Thomas Oden, *Classic Christianity: A Systematic Theology* (New York: HarperOne, 2009), 703.

40. Lesslie Newbigin, *Foolishness to the Greeks: The Gospel and Western Culture* (Grand Rapids: Eerdmans, 1986), 124.

how it also *does* art—how, for instance, the Bible employs the poetic arts but also how it conveys the true knowledge of God *through* poetry.

Conclusion

If the liturgical arts are viewed in a Trinitarian light, then the church at worship is looking not at an escape from the physical creation but rather at the preservation, healing, and liberation of creation so that the arts can become what the Father has eternally purposed for them. Rather than being seen as accommodations to human weakness, the arts in worship can be seen as media that fittingly symbolize the church's worship in light of the resurrection. Instead of being regarded as concessions to corporeal life this side of the eschaton, they can be regarded as physical media that remain commensurate with the creaturely condition and that function as glimpses of the new creation.

On this reckoning the liturgical arts do not diminish the worship of God's people. Nor do they endanger the faithful worship of God. Instead they ably serve the work of God, in the public praise of God, as a portrait of God's glory in and through the physical creation. In this way they become normative, rather than incidental, to the church's vision of the good world that the Father has remade by Christ and the Spirit. And by God's grace, the church at worship makes good on God's good world through its practices of art in worship.[41] How exactly the church does so, whether in music or painting, poetry or dance, architecture or drama, is the subject of the chapters that follow.

41. Jeremy S. Begbie, "Looking to the Future: A Hopeful Subversion," in *For the Beauty of the Church: Casting a Vision for the Arts*, ed. W. David O. Taylor (Grand Rapids: Baker Books, 2010), 198n6.

Hymns Ancient and Modern (ca. 1880) (Photograph by author)

CHAPTER 4

Worship and the Musical Arts

From harmony, from Heav'nly harmony
This universal frame began.

John Dryden, "A Song for St. Cecilia's Day"

Singing is not a neutral exercise. It should carry a governmental
health warning that it can affect minds.

John L. Bell, *The Singing Thing*

Tell me what you sing, and I'll tell you who you are!

Albert van den Heuvel, *Risk: New Hymns for a New Day*

The New Testament scholar Ralph Martin in his book *Worship in the Early Church* writes that the church was born in song.[1] Proof of this is not hard to come by. Like characters in a musical theater production, the protagonists of Luke's Gospel find mere speech insufficient to the task of expressing the astonishing events that occur to them. The Virgin Mary breaks out in song in response to Elizabeth's benediction. Zechariah sings his way out of silence at the pronouncement of his son's name. The angel choir sings of God's fantastic glory, while Simeon erupts in verse at the sight of the Christ child. And the early church sings the Psalter, the songs of David, which become the songs of Christ himself, even as the church at the end of the age joins the everlasting chorus of heaven: "holy, holy, holy."

Yet while singing has always been a welcomed practice in the life of the

---

1. Ralph P. Martin, *Worship in the Early Church* (Grand Rapids: Eerdmans, 1975), 39. On the contested question of song and hymnody in early Christianity, see Matthew E. Gordley, *New Testament Christological Hymns: Exploring Texts, Contexts, and Significance* (Downers Grove, IL: IVP Academic, 2018). Especially helpful for our purposes are his two sections "Hymns in the Lukan Infancy Narrative" and "Hymns in Revelation 4–5," 200–216.

church, not any kind of song has been seen to satisfy the requirement of faithful music making. *What* is sung, *how* it is sung, and *the character* that the practice of song produces has always been crucial.[2] Singing that generates unity, for instance, has been a perennial concern of the church. "Almost from the beginning," Calvin Stapert writes, "music was an expression of, a metaphor for, and a means toward unity."[3] For Saint Ambrose, the singing of a psalm represented a "pledge of peace and harmony, which produces one song from various and sundry voices."[4] Ignatius of Antioch argued that when Jesus Christ was sung rightly, it became a sign of the church's "harmonious love."

During the early centuries of the church, the singing of the psalms represented the superlative vehicle for unified praise. Yet psalm singing in worship may be the *only* practice that achieves near-universal consensus—and even then, Christians have rarely agreed on the sort of music that best fits the text of the Psalter, the context of corporate worship, and the requirement of concord. How exactly does singing forge unity? What practices are best suited to keep the faithful integrated? The unison chant of Benedictine monks? The concerted performance of a vocal ensemble in a Bach cantata? The improvisational syncopated song of African Pentecostals? And in what way do different practices of music making generate different kinds of *togetherness*?

In an essay on "The Wisdom of Song," Steven Guthrie contends that singing "is a sounding image of the unified church"[5] and "an enactment of the differentiated unity of the body of Christ."[6] Singing on this understanding performs not just good theological work; it also performs good physiological and psychological work. Guthrie explains: "Music, it would seem, is equipped to make sensible—as few other activities can—a self that is 'inhabited' or 'indwelled by others.' When I sing among others, I hear a voice that is both mine and not mine, a voice that is both in and outside

---

2. The editors of the official hymnal of the Presbyterian Church in America, the *Trinity Hymnal* (Suwanee, GA: Great Commission Publications, 1990), for instance, say this in their introduction: "It is well known that the character of its song, almost equal with the character of its preaching, controls the theology of a church."

3. Calvin Stapert, *A New Song for an Old World: Musical Thought in the Early Church* (Grand Rapids: Eerdmans, 2007), 26.

4. Cited in Stapert, *A New Song*, 26.

5. Steven R. Guthrie, "The Wisdom of Song," in *Resonant Witness: Conversations between Music and Theology*, ed. Jeremy S. Begbie and Steven R. Guthrie (Grand Rapids: Eerdmans, 2011), 385.

6. Guthrie, "The Wisdom of Song," 397.

of me. I hear my voice and your voice—and this third thing—our voices together: a sound which has properties which belong neither to your voice nor to my voice alone, but one that is nevertheless shaped and takes its substance from the individual voices comprising it."[7]

In more strictly scientific terms, as cognitive scientist William Benzon describes it, "Music is a medium through which individual brains are coupled together in shared activity."[8] He adds, "What makes this sonic communion possible is that all these physically distinct nervous systems are cut from the same mold, and all are attuned to the same patterns of sound."[9] When communal music making occurs, writes Steven Mithen in *The Singing Neanderthals*, it "leads to endorphin surges within the brains of the participants" and results in a "heightening of fellow feeling."[10] Put more colloquially, a community that sings together stays together.

But all of this good news about the powers of music to unite people in song still does not answer the double question: (1) What practices of music making do the job well, and (2) How do different practices of music, which may include a host of instruments and contexts of all sorts, unite people in different ways that remain faithful to the richly complex vision of ecclesial life that Holy Scripture presents to us? Singing together may well generate cognitive and emotional affinity between persons, bonding them in a way that nonmusical speech cannot quite achieve, but that fact by itself does not tell us how particular practices of song *form* distinctive identities and kinships.[11]

Beyond this specific instance of music's capacity to forge unity, how might monophony or polyphony form the church at worship? How might call-and-response practices shape the social identity of a congregation? How might the choral works of Thomas Tallis or Hildegard von Bingen en-

---

7. Guthrie, "The Wisdom of Song," 399. This is similar to what David Ford says: "In singing there can be a filling of space with sound in ways that draw more and more voices to take part, yet with no sense of crowding. It is a performance of abundance, as new voices join in with their own distinctive tones." *Self and Salvation: Being Transformed* (Cambridge: Cambridge University Press, 1999), 121.

8. William Benzon, *Beethoven's Anvil: Music in Mind and Culture* (New York: Basic Books, 2001), 23.

9. Benzon, *Beethoven's Anvil*, 43.

10. Steven Mithen, *The Singing Neanderthals: The Origins of Music, Language, Mind, and Body* (Cambridge, MA: Harvard University Press, 2006), 208–9.

11. "Acting together in rhythm to the music, people turn an individual psychological response into a social resource that brings communities, affinity groups, and entire societies into sync with one another." Timothy Rice, *Ethnomusicology: A Very Short Introduction* (Oxford: Oxford University Press, 2013), 50.

able a congregation to "say" things to God that it could not say otherwise? How might the voice of the global church be heard in ways that enable the often all-too-familiar gospel to become strange again? And how might the peculiar sounds of Irish ballads, rock and roll, or African-American work songs enable a congregation to testify to the Triune God in unique ways?

It is these kinds of questions that occupy the attention of the present chapter. Beginning with a brief exploration of the role that the musical arts play in the economy of the Triune God, we then examine the singular powers of music, specifically Western tonal music. We consider the question of context and the diverse role that music might play within corporate worship, and we examine two case studies that enable us to glimpse how specific practices of music open up and close down possibilities for the formation of our humanity in corporate worship.[12]

Music Theologically Considered

In his 1872 novel *Under the Greenwood Tree*, Thomas Hardy writes, "To dwellers in a wood, almost every species of tree has its voice as well as its feature. At the passing of the breeze, the fir-trees sob and moan no less distinctly than they rock; the holly whistles as it battles with itself; the ash hisses amid its quiverings; the beech rustles while its flat boughs rise and fall. And winter, which modifies the note of such trees as shed their leaves, does not destroy its individuality."[13] This is a novelist's way of saying what a theologian might say otherwise—namely, that God has vested the physical creation with particular sounds that glorify God in their own way: bird song as such and the particular trill of a dark-eyed junco; wind as such and the distinctive whisper of wind passing through an aspen forest; thunder

12. The presumption of this book stands over against a common presumption among Protestants, articulated here by Rick Warren, in *The Purpose-Driven Life* (Grand Rapids: Zondervan, 2002), 65: "Worship has nothing to do with the style or volume or speed of a song. God loves all kinds of music because he invented it all—fast and slow, loud and soft, old and new." The problem with Warren's comment is not the second half, with its encouragement of a broad range of musical sounds. The problem is with the first half. Perhaps it is only said in a generic sense, or perhaps Warren simply wishes to distinguish the personal act of worship from the musical accessories to worship. But to argue that worship has "nothing to do" with its musical shape is to underestimate the formative power of music.

13. Thomas Hardy, *Under the Greenwood Tree* (London: Penguin Classics, 1998), 7. Curiously, Hardy takes his title from a song in Shakespeare's play *As You Like It* (act 2, scene 5).

as such and the peculiar metallic roar of a lightning storm in West Texas. It is not only that it pleases the Spirit of Christ to secure particular capacities for sound in creation, and enabled these to be pleasing to the Father, it is that the morphology of creation becomes fodder for the musical creations of human beings—for instance, "woodwind 'birdsong' to evoke a pastoral scene, or glissandi violins to suggest the howling wind of a storm."[14]

Physical things have their own integrity by God's command, writes Jeremy Begbie. In human hands, musical sounds are "arranged in particular ways, and as such interact with me in particular ways so as to make sense—*musical* sense."[15] If all of creation's sounds worship God, precisely by fulfilling their created purpose, then humanity's calling is to give particular voice to creation's sonic praise and to do so in all sorts of ways, for all sorts of reasons, and in all sorts of contexts.[16] In the context of corporate worship, the musical arts can be enlisted to serve specific activities and purposes in a wide range of ways, and the Triune God would not have it otherwise.[17]

God delights in creation's song (Pss. 96:11–12; 150:6), the song of the morning stars when all the children of God shouted for joy (Job 38:4–7). God also delights in the song of his creatures: the song of the saints on earth (Neh. 12:46–47a), the song of the saints in heaven (Rev. 14:3), and the song of the heavenly host (Rev. 5:8–10; 14:2–3; 15:3). And as the seventeenth-century poet John Dryden imagines it, God creates the world and brings to completion the purposes of the world in song:

From harmony, from Heav'nly harmony
This universal frame began. . . .

So when the last and dreadful hour
This crumbling pageant shall devour,

14. Mithen, *The Singing Neanderthals*, 22. He adds this: "More than six thousand languages are spoken in the world today, this being a small fraction of the total number of languages ever spoken. The number of musics in the world is likely to be even greater and to display considerably more diversity" (13).

15. Jeremy Begbie, *Resounding Truth: Christian Wisdom in the World of Music* (Grand Rapids: Baker Academic, 2007), 50.

16. "[Music] refers to fundamentally distinct types of activities that fulfill different needs and ways of being human." Thomas Turino, as cited in Rice, *Ethnomusicology*, 63.

17. "When all Scripture references to music making are combined, we learn that we are to make music in every conceivable condition: joy, triumph, imprisonment, solitude, grief, peace, war, sickness, merriment, abundance, and deprivation." Harold M. Best, *Music through the Eyes of Faith* (New York: HarperOne, 1993), 186.

The trumpet shall be heard on high,
The dead shall live, the living die,
And music shall untune the sky.[18]

"We sing to God," it must be stressed, "because he first sang to us (Zeph 3.17)."[19] What exactly does God in Christ sing? Drawing on the text of Psalm 22, Reggie Kidd persuasively argues that Christ, whom Hebrews 2:12 presents to us as the Chief Worshiper, sings with many voices.[20] "One Voice sings above them all," Kidd writes, "and this Voice sings in all their voices, excluding none."[21] What are the songs that Christ sings "in the midst of the congregation"? He sings the song of all families (Ps. 22:23, 27), the song of the rich (22:29a), the song of the poor (22:26), the song of generations past (22:29b), and the song of generations yet to come (22:30–31).[22]

Put otherwise, Jesus sings both victory chants (Mark 14:26) and the laments of a broken world (Matt. 27:46). He sings folk songs and "high art" songs. Jesus sings earthy, simple songs, and he sings aesthetically complex songs.[23] He sings the ancient songs, the songs of our fathers and mothers in ages past, while also a new song and the songs of the new creation (2 Pet. 3:13; Rev. 5:9). "What David foretold in song, the Son of David fulfills by singing."[24] If Christ is the chief composer of the church's song, as Calvin and Wesley rightly believed, then we do well to sing this pluriform music so that our song on earth might become a faithful "antiphon" to Christ's song in heaven.[25]

If Christ is the one who shows us how to sing, then it is the Spirit who enables that song to be faithful to the Father, from whom all good things

18. John Dryden, "A Song for St. Cecilia's Day" (1687), https://www.poetryfoundation.org/poems/44185/a-song-for-st-cecilias-day-1687. Accessed June 22, 2018.

19. William Edgar, *Taking Note of Music* (London: SPCK, 1986), 133.

20. Reggie Kidd, *With One Voice: Discovering Christ's Song in Our Worship* (Grand Rapids: Baker Books, 2005). Psalm 22:22 (KJV): "I will declare thy name unto my brethren: in the midst of the congregation will I praise thee."

21. Kidd, *With One Voice*, 126.

22. On the question of what carries over from Old Testament practices of song and music into a New Testament vision for corporate worship, see W. David O. Taylor, *The Theater of God's Glory: Calvin, Creation, and the Liturgical Arts* (Grand Rapids: Eerdmans, 2017), ch. 1, "Musical Instruments in Calvin," and ch. 5, "The Double Movement of Creation in Worship."

23. On the question of "simple versus complex" music, see Greg Scheer, *Essential Worship: A Handbook for Leaders* (Grand Rapids: Baker Books, 2016), 149–53.

24. Michael O'Connor, "The Singing of Jesus," in Begbie and Guthrie, *Resonant Witness*, 438.

25. Kidd, *With One Voice*, 115.

flow. It is also the Spirit who keeps our music making fresh and transformative. It is the Spirit who enables all music making to give voice to our unique identities as worshiping congregations of every tongue, tribe, and nation. It is the Spirit who empowers the people of God to discover and to develop music, to judge it where sinfully employed and to let it heal where humanity may be broken, and to make new music in anticipation of the renewal of the cosmos that Christ announces and makes tangible in his own life.

By the Spirit music in worship becomes a way to deepen our love of God and our bonds as Christ's body. By the Spirit we are freed to delight in the sounds of creation and to make good use of them in our liturgies. By the Spirit we celebrate the forms of music as well as the freedoms that music offers the people of God at praise.[26] And it is by the Spirit that congregational song can become "an ecstatic act, in which the singer reaches out to others, becomes vulnerable before them, becomes a gift to them. And as such," concludes Michael O'Connor, "it is a fitting testimony to the eternal life of the Son before the Father, a self-emptying life of prayer, love, trust and obedience."[27]

What Is Music?

To affirm the theological goodness of music is a relatively uncontroversial thing. More controversial perhaps is what counts as music, what counts as *good* music, and how does music *mean*.[28] However we perceive music's formative powers, it will hinge on our understanding of music and what we think its purposes are for the church at praise. While a proper answer to this question cannot be accomplished in this book, we can perhaps draw from Jeremy Begbie's work in *Resounding Truth* in order to suggest a working definition for our purposes here. Begbie defines music this way: "We

---

26. To argue this is to argue that any musical instrument, in principle, can be enlisted to serve the faithful worship of God, over against the assumptions, for instance, of T. David Gordon: "There is no good musical reason to insist on accompanying congregational song with a guitar; it is poorly suited to the task, and it profoundly limits the other choices that can be made once it is chosen." *Why Johnny Can't Sing Hymns: How Pop Culture Rewrote the Hymnal* (Phillipsburg, NJ: P&R, 2010), 99. Cf. *The Folksinger's Hymnal*, ed. Wayne Hooper, Gary Hullouist, and Steve Guptill (Glendale, CA: Key Music Company, 1969), 4–5.

27. O'Connor, "The Singing of Jesus," 453.

28. Edgar, *Taking Note of Music*, in chapter 3, is particular helpful on this question of how music *means*.

are going to propose that to be true to the Western tonal tradition, it is best to think of music primarily as an art of *actions*—the most basic actions being music making and music hearing. These actions nevertheless involve things that have their own particular integrity—*sound producing materials and sound waves*, the *human body*, the dimension of *time*, and *distinctively musical sound patterns*. We shall also stress that the actions of music are closely intertwined with a rich and complex *context*."[29]

Five characteristics of Begbie's definition deserve careful attention. First, music involves a set of actions. Music is not to be confused with naturally or randomly occurring sounds, such as the sound of a hiccup or the hum of a computer. Music is what human beings make when they purposefully arrange sounds in particular ways for specific reasons.[30] In Nicholas Cook's terms, music "is what we make it, and what we make *of* it."[31] Humans make sad songs, like dirges and blues, in order to make sense of the sad nature of human life. Christians make love songs to say how much they love God: Isaac Watts (1674–1748) sings of his "Infinite Lover!," while Anne Steele (1717–1778) sings of "the rich depths of love divine!"

Second, the "sonic order" has its own particular integrity. By this Begbie means that sound-producing materials, the human body, sound waves, and time involve "patterns of constraints" that are rooted in the physical creation. Music is not simply sociocultural "nurture": what humans say it is. Music is also "nature": what God's world makes it to be, such as catgut, sugar pine, breaths, or ear drums.[32] The clash of bronze cymbals, for instance, might more "logically" befit the sudden appearance of angelic hosts to shepherds in Luke 2, while Ennio Morricone's oboe composition, from the 1986 film *The Mission*, might more "logically" befit the exchange between the angel Gabriel and the young Virgin Mary—a sweet, haunting sound to characterize the mystery of the annunciation.

---

29. Begbie, *Resounding Truth*, 38, emphasis original. Begbie also offers this perspective: "The paradox of music is that it is 'organised time,' an artificially created order which is nevertheless recognisably related to the dynamics of the created world." *Voicing Creation's Praise: Towards a Theology of the Arts* (Edinburgh: T&T Clark, 1991), 246.

30. "Ordinary folksingers make music to enhance work with animals and crops, to raise children and keep family ties, to give voice to their beliefs, hopes, and identities, or to signal that they understand their place in society." Mark Slobin, *Folk Music: A Very Short Introduction* (Oxford: Oxford University Press, 2001), 3–4.

31. Nicholas Cook, *Music: A Very Short Introduction* (Oxford: Oxford University Press, 1988), vi, emphasis original.

32. Cf. Begbie, *Resounding Truth*, 49.

Third, the experience of making music has a direct relation to the human body. However else we may describe the power of music, we must always remember that music's effects upon us are rooted in our bodily experience. Music moves us not just because of what it evokes in us—the thought of God or the joy of life. Music also moves us because of how it moves us physically. Morehouse College's drumline moves the body one way, while Brahms's "Lullaby" moves the body otherwise. The Bach Guild's forceful rendition of "A Mighty Fortress Is Our God" arouses our physical bodies; Enya's atmospheric interpretation of "O Come, O Come Emmanuel" quiets our physical bodies.[33]

Fourth, the making and reception of music are inextricably related to specific contexts.[34] Context includes my state of mind and body when I listen to a work of music, the associations that I bring to a piece of music, and the sociocultural conventions that frame my experience of music.[35] The spiritual "Swing Low, Sweet Chariot" means one thing for the Fisk Jubilee Singers, an African-American ensemble first organized in 1871. It means quite a different thing for fans of the English national rugby team, for whom the song functions as an official anthem.[36] The Brooklyn Tabernacle Choir in New York City, we might imagine, heard one thing when it sang the gospel song "God Is Able" on Sunday, September 9, 2001.[37] It heard a different thing the Sunday after, in the wake of 9/11. The words remained the same:

33. "The 'music' of the body includes pulse (heart rate), tempo (speeded or slowed heart rate), fluctuation (a sudden quickening of the pulse). It includes the sounds we make, involuntarily and voluntarily, in the course of simply being: the crying infant and the cooing mother; the rattling of a chest infection; the sounds of conversation—its pitches, rhythms, volumes, and tempos." Tia DeNora, *After Adorno: Rethinking Music Sociology* (Cambridge: Cambridge University Press, 2003), 101. Our most fundamental experience of music occurs in our mother's womb, which some have called a "sonorous envelope of the self" or a "sonorous space." Cf. DeNora, *Music in Everyday Life* (Cambridge: Cambridge University Press, 2000), 102; Peter Althouse and Michael Wilkinson, "Musical Bodies in the Charismatic Renewal: The Case of Catch the Fire and Soaking Prayer," in *The Spirit of Praise: Music and Worship in Global Pentecostal-Charismatic Christianity*, ed. Monique M. Ingalls and Amos Yong (University Park: Pennsylvania State University Press, 2015), 31.

34. "Music, like any art form, is a social discourse, structured by a set of social relations between artist and perceiver." Kathryn Kalinak, *Film Music: A Very Short Introduction* (Oxford: Oxford University Press, 2010), 25.

35. Cf. Begbie, *Resounding Truth*, 54–56.

36. Andrew Keh, "How a Slave Spiritual Became English Rugby's Anthem," *New York Times*, March 7, 2017, https://www.nytimes.com/2017/03/07/sports/rugby-swing-low-sweet-chariot.html.

37. See http://www.songlyrics.com/brooklyn-tabernacle-choir/god-is-able-lyrics/.

God is able
God is able
To deliver from the fire
He will rescue those who serve him
When the flames are burning higher.

The context, however, changed altogether, and the words took on a radically different meaning. And so, fifth, time is a definitive power of music.

The Singular Powers of Western Tonal Music

With this idea of music in mind, how might we understand its singular powers? To describe music's powers is to discover the distinctive ways in which music forms our humanity. While we cannot do full justice to all of music's powers, the following registry might help us get a good sense of how music works and therefore how it shapes us. A fundamental power of music is *time*.[38] Unlike sculpture, music does not attempt to escape time or to be "timeless." It seeks its meaning *through* time. For example, with a jack-in-the-box toy, which uses the melody to "Pop! Goes the Weasel," it is impossible to "get" the song apart from the anticipation that builds to the point at which the weasel "pops" out.

What most of us might call a *note*, such as G or C-sharp, scientists call a *tone*. Both are related to the power of a *pitch*. And the pitch that works in the recording studio with a professional musician may prove difficult, if not off-putting, for a congregation full of nonprofessional singers. *Rhythm* describes the duration of a series of notes and how they group together into units. A particular rhythm, for instance, helps to regulate work on the railroad.[39] Rhythm also helps to distinguish a unique feature of African music with its inherently physical quality.[40] "In these settings, to make

38. Cf. Paul Westermeyer, *Let Justice Sing: Hymnody and Justice* (Collegeville, MN: Liturgical Press, 1998), 89.

39. This is what William H. McNeill calls "muscular bonding" as a way to describe the effect of moving muscles and singing rhythmically. See *Keeping Together in Time: Dance and Drill in Human History* (Cambridge, MA: Harvard University Press, 1995), 2. Daniel J. Levitin says, "Notes and words unfold in a precise sequence and at a precise time, and motor actions are learned to synchronize with them." *The World in Six Songs: How the Musical Brain Created Human Nature* (New York: Dutton, 2008), 208.

40. "Blacks love singing at all times. At work, when lifting anything heavy, it is done

music is to dance, to move."[41] Here music is meant to be *felt*, not just heard; and as often as not it occurs in synchronization to other physical bodies.[42]

Another power of music, *tempo*, describes the overall speed of a piece of music. A lively pace will seem perfectly normal for one congregation (like the charismatic church Holy Trinity Brompton in London) but wholly destabilizing for another (like the "high church" Great St. Mary's Church in Cambridge). This will also be true for the *volume* of music. With Jesus Culture's "Unstoppable Love," a loud volume becomes the way *through which* the idea is established that God's love cannot be "stopped" by sin, fear, or death. A similar thing might be at play in certain organ works of George Frideric Handel or Johann Pachelbel, used frequently in liturgical postludes: fullness of sound "says it all."

Reverberation describes the persistence of a sound after its source has stopped. What a singing congregation might accomplish in the context of a cozy living room, full of rugs and plush furniture, is accomplished with difficulty in the cavernous room of Gothic cathedrals, full of stones and hard surfaces, where individual voices seem to ricochet in an incoherent manner. *Repetition* is a source of frequent controversy for church musicians.[43] When is music excessive? And on what grounds, for example, might we argue that too much repetition marks William Cowper's "There Is a Fountain" or Taizé's "Wait for the Lord"?[44] However we answer the

---

with song. When digging trenches, rhythm regulates the raising and falling of the pick. Singing permeates the life of a black person." Makhubu, cited in Thomas Oduro, "Church Music in the Life of African Christian Communities," in Roberta King, with Jean Ngoya Kidula et al., *Music in the Life of the African Church* (Waco, TX: Baylor University Press, 2008), 92.

41. Mary E. McGann, *Exploring Music as Worship and Theology: Research in Liturgical Practice* (Collegeville, MN: Liturgical Press, 2002), 22, 68.

42. Begbie remarks, "given rhythm's connections with emotion, it is one of the quickest ways in which emotion is spread and shared. As we join in the movements of others, through 'feedback,' a mood is easily generated." "Faithful Feelings: Music and Emotion in Worship," in Begbie and Guthrie, *Resonant Witness*, 344.

43. "The same principles and patterns of repetition of sounds that occur in the rhetoric of speech are possible in the rhetoric of music—such as alliteration, anaphora, epizeuxis, mesarchia, mesodiplosis, epistrophe, epanadiplosis, anadiplosis, epiploce, and climax." Scotty Gray, *Hermeneutics of Hymnody: A Comprehensive and Integrated Approach to Understanding Hymns* (Macon, GA: Smyth & Helwys, 2015), 227.

44. Debates about repetition in worship music often appeal to the common refrain of Psalms 118 and 136, "for his mercy endures forever," to establish a biblical precedent for the right use of repetition. On this issue, see Jeremy S. Begbie, *Theology, Music and Time* (Cambridge: Cambridge University Press, 2000), 175: "The way in which musical repetition will function and be received in any particular setting depends on a vast network of con-

question, repetition in music becomes a powerful means to underscore an idea, to deepen an emotion, or to generate a contemplative mood.[45]

Much more could be said, of course, about the powers of music, whether about meter, melody, harmony, timbre, or even silence. And no doubt music's capacity to be "omnipresent" is a considerable power that neither the sculptural nor the visual arts possess, the latter of which are bound or fixed to particular places. But perhaps the above list of powers gives us a sufficient sense of what we might find if we "opened up the hood" on the engine of music and asked what made music *music* and how it worked. Yet as anthropologists and ethnologists would remind us, no music forms us out of context.

The Power of Context

Context powerfully shapes how we experience music, and it describes several things, not just one.[46] Context involves cultural dynamics. William Benzon writes, "While music certainly travels across cultures more easily than language does, it remains culture-specific. Sounds that are music in one culture may be noise in another."[47] What is music to the ears for members of Worship Central in the United Kingdom, with their love of Fender guitars, pedal boards, and condenser mics, may be experienced as utter noise for the Guild of Church Musicians, also in the United Kingdom, with their preference for pipe organs and cathedral choirs.

---

straints—acoustics, expectations, the music people are used to hearing, biological makeup, the way the music is introduced, and so forth." See also Jacob Sensenig, "In Defense of Repetition: A Philosophy for Planning Music for Corporate Worship," *Artistic Theologian* 5 (2017): 82–93, http://artistictheologian.com/journal/artistic-theologian-volume-5-2017/in-defense-of-repetition-a-philosophy-for-planning-music-for-corporate-worship/.

45. "Every neuroimaging study that my laboratory has done has shown amygdala activation to music, but not to random collections of sounds or musical tones. Repetition, when done skillfully by a master composer, is emotionally satisfying to our brains, and makes the listening experience as pleasurable as it is." Daniel J. Levitin, *This Is Your Brain on Music: The Science of a Human Obsession* (New York: Penguin, 2006), 167.

46. Cf. Kalinak, *Film Music*, 12; Rice says, "Arguably ethnomusicology's most important theoretical move has been a sustained attack over more than a half-century on the notion, purveyed until recently by its sister musicological disciplines, that music is primarily an art form made for its own sake, mystically transcendent in its effects, and with little or no social or practical significance." *Ethnomusicology*, 44.

47. Benzon, *Beethoven's Anvil*, 44.

Context also involves the arrangement of physical bodies. What difference does it make, for instance, if a congregation turns its bodies towards one other when it sings, rather than looking only at each other's backs? Might it shift not only how they sang but also how they perceived themselves as a body? Might such a physical posture enact Saint Paul's injunction in Ephesians 5:18–19 to "speak" to one another in psalms, hymns, and spiritual songs? Context also involves the set of expectations that a community brings to liturgical music. What a rural Caribbean Methodist congregation assumes is both possible and desirable, musically speaking, may contrast sharply with what an urban Singaporean Presbyterian congregation assumes is possible and desirable.

Context includes the way in which similar sounds are heard differently—by different communities. "In Hollywood," to use an example from popular culture, "the brass instruments have conventionally connoted heroism, but in Hindi film, brasses often signify villainy."[48] When blues music entered into the liturgical sphere, on the tails of black gospel, some felt that it introduced "the devil's music."[49] Others felt that it introduced the psalmist's voice of lament into a practice of worship that had largely been allergic to the "minor key" of Christian faith. For communities that are discomfited by expressions of sadness in worship, blues music feels out of place.[50] For communities that have suffered greatly, blues music *says what needs saying* to God in the presence of the people of God.[51]

Context likewise includes specific liturgical activities. If Richard Gillard's hymn "Servant Song" is sung prior to the confession of sin, it might be heard one way: as a way to underscore the relational effects of sin. If it is sung during the Lord's Supper or at the benediction, it will perhaps be heard a different way: as a way to stress the nature of the Suffering Servant who feeds and sends us into the world in his name, to serve as he serves. Liturgical activities include calls to worship, the reading of Scripture, testimonies, confessions of faith, offertory, prayer, and opportunities for ministry to one another. The musical arts can serve all the activities that comprise our corporate worship, and they can do so in all sorts of ways.

---

48. Kalinak, *Film Music*, 14.

49. Cf. Giles Oakley, *The Devil's Music: A History of the Blues* (London: Da Capo, 1997).

50. Cf. Tim Dowley, *Christian Music: A Global History* (Minneapolis: Fortress, 2011), 86, 173.

51. Cf. Michael Fox, "Don't Nobody Know My Troubles but God: Discursive, Social, and Aesthetic Connections and Distinctives in 'Sacred' and 'Secular' Black Music," in *Readings in African American Church Music and Worship*, ed. James Abbington, vol. 2 (Chicago: GIA Publications, 2014), 377–98.

Context, lastly, might describe the role that participants play in making music. A pastor who sings alone the words of the ninth-century hymn "Come, Creator Spirit" might be experienced one way: as a priestly prayer of invocation of the Spirit's presence on behalf of the people. For a choir to sing this hymn might become a way for "one member" to give eloquent, harmonious voice to the petition of "all the members" for the Spirit's power. For certain African churches, in predominantly oral communities, individuals might participate in the song through hand clapping and "talking back" as a way corporeally to welcome the Spirit's work in their midst.[52]

On the Formative Possibilities of Music in Worship

With this contextual perspective in mind, we turn now to two case studies: "Oceans (Where Feet May Fail)" by Hillsong United and the Keith Getty and Stuart Townend hymn "In Christ Alone." A close look at the music of each song becomes a way, I suggest, to discover how they might open up and close down possibilities for the formation of a congregation. They become also a way to explore how *any* work or practice of music might form a congregation. A similar exercise could be done with Romance Watsons's 1949 rendition of the spiritual "'Tis the Old Ship of Zion" or the eighteenth-century carol "Jesus Christ the Apple Tree" performed by the Choir of King's College, Cambridge.

Among other reasons, I focus on "Oceans" and "In Christ Alone" because of the way in which they have crossed denominational, cultural, and geographic lines in their appeal to Christians at worship in recent years.

The Formative Power of "Oceans"

Unlike the musical template that characterized folk songs of the 1970s, like "Seek Ye First" or "Father, I Adore You," with their simple texts and their "minimal sophistication in instrumental or vocal amplification,"[53] a

---

52. Jean Ngoya Kidula, "Music Culture: African Life," in King with Kidula et al., *Music in the Life of the African Church*, 43.

53. Swee Hong Lim and Lester Ruth, *Lovin' on Jesus: A Concise History of Contemporary Worship* (Nashville: Abingdon, 2017), 61.

song like "Oceans," released in 2013, occupies a different musical world. A more rhythmically dynamic, professionally produced, and instrumentally propulsive "arena rock" generally characterizes Hillsong United's musical practice.[54] And whereas the music that came out of Calvary Chapel in Southern California during the Jesus Movement was made for local congregational use, the music of Hillsong, based in Australia, is made for listeners on the go and on portable devices everywhere.[55]

Not just a band, it is a "brand" that includes churches in London, Kiev, and Buenos Aires. No longer a product of an Assembly of God church in the suburbs of Sydney, it occupies a "media-dense culture."[56] Hillsong tends to eschew the "unplugged" approach of early Maranatha! Music for a "wall of sound": multiple keyboards and electric guitars, drum kit, brass instruments, backing vocalists, full choirs, and multimedia presentations. And much like the music that came out of Youth for Christ in the mid-twentieth century, Hillsong United draws directly from the sound and sense of youth culture. On YouTube, the nine-minute-long lyric video for "Oceans" has, to date, 97 million views.[57]

To ask how the pop-rock music of "Oceans" forms a congregation, however, cannot be done in the abstract. For our purposes here, I imagine a performance of "Oceans," led by lead singer Taya Smith, that follows the sermon and that takes place within a stadium/arena context, common enough for most Hillsong United concerts.

The first thing to note about the song is its length. The official album version of the song is nine minutes long.[58] The song begins with a quiet instrumental opening, with vocals entering at 0:39. At 2:40 there is a surge of sound matched by an escalation of vocals. At 3:09 the sound subsides

---

54. Cf. Mark Evans, *Open Up the Doors: Music in the Modern Church* (London: Equinox, 2006), ch. 5; Mark Evans, "Hillsong Abroad: Tracing the Songlines of Contemporary Pentecostal Music," in Ingalls and Yong, *The Spirit of Praise*, 179–96. The beats per minute (BPM) on the average pop-rock song, coincidentally, is 120, which aligns roughly with average human walking speed or with the tempo of crowd applause at a music concert.

55. Cf. Gesa Hartje-Döll, "(Hillsong) United through Music: Praise and Worship Music and the Evangelical 'Imagined Community,'" in *Christian Congregational Music: Performance, Identity and Experience*, ed. Monique Ingalls, Carolyn Landau, and Tom Wagner (New York: Routledge, 2016), 137–52. See also the "fact sheet" on the official Hillsong website: https://hillsong.com/media/.

56. Evans, "Hillsong Abroad," 182.

57. See https://www.youtube.com/watch?v=dy9nwe9_xzw.

58. When performed in concert or in a proper Hillsong worship service, the song lasts between seven and nine minutes.

and cedes to thirty seconds of an ambient sound, leading eventually to the bridge. The bridge is repeated no less than six times, each time with an upsurge in sound and vocal emphasis, after which the sound "goes huge" (as one band member puts it) and the vocals take on an improvisational mode. At 7:40 the vocals come to an end and yield again to an atmospheric sound.

The considerable length of the song, combined with a pattern of swelling musical sounds mimicking the swell of ocean waters, allows, I suggest, for an immersive contemplation of Christ in the rise and fall, push and pull of desire for God that typically charismatic theology emphasizes in its worship music.[59] With the text of the song, a theme of risky faith, characterized by an implicit motif of Saint Peter, matches a musical composition that gives representative expression to the heart that yearns, both insistently and persistently, for a God who calls the Christian into a trust that dares to believe the impossible. This again is a central attribute of charismatic faith.

What the surplus of time makes possible is a space for a personal appropriation of the song's meaning. Because the music is unrushed and the text is recursive, the singer is able to enter affectively into an act of adoration of God. On this account, Ellie Holcomb, a CCM singer, remarks, "We typically fill up every moment musically . . . but 'Oceans' gives us space to sit in the truth. . . . There is space to be still and rest . . . space to absorb the prayers being sung."[60] Similar to certain devotional practices in Christian mysticism, whether Carmelite or Franciscan, the musical practice of Hillsong opens up the possibility for a leisurely contemplation of Christ's character.

What the amplification of Taya Smith's whispery voice makes possible is the communication of a kind of tender intimacy. This in turn invites the congregation to seek a similarly intimate encounter with God.[61] It is also important to underscore the fact that a woman functions here as lead singer. For other female worship leaders this makes it plausible to imagine

---

59. David Douglas Daniels III helpfully draws attention to the characteristic of "ambient sound" in early Pentecostal sound in his essay "'Gotta Moan Sometime': A Sonic Exploration of Earwitnesses to Early Pentecostal Sound in North America," in Abbington, *Readings in African American Church Music and Worship*, vol. 2, 353–76.

60. Ellie Holcomb, "'Oceans' Keeps Rising," *Christianity Today*, June 10, 2015, https://www.christianitytoday.com/ct/2015/june-web-only/oceans-keeps-rising-hillsong-united.html.

61. Erik Routley worries, rightly perhaps, about the "the fictitious intimacy of the microphone." *Twentieth Century Church Music* (New York: Oxford University Press, 1964), 156.

their place in the world of contemporary pop-rock worship, largely dominated by male singers.[62] What does Smith's vocal practice close down? What it closes down is its extreme range points. As Greg Scheer remarks, "Music that flatters a performer's voice is often at odds with the technical limitations of the group voice."[63]

The use of a complex light system, projected images, and stadium seating, I offer, enables a massive group of people to have a "massive" experience of worship that could not be experienced in smaller, technologically minimalist settings. The use of screens instead of books, moreover, frees physical bodies to express themselves during the song.[64] While the "arena rock concert" context may generate "arena rock concert" instincts—that might preference the actions of "performers" on stage over the actions of "audience" off the stage—it may also be true that participants at a Hillsong worship event are psychologically disposed to sing in fulsome fashion.[65]

An effective performance of this song can only be pulled off, of course, by musicians who possess the requisite skill and a "stage presence," which for Pentecostal Christians is the way that one makes space for the presence of the Holy Spirit. For those for whom this liturgical culture is normal, *this* particular song, sung in *this* particular fashion, is how Christians demonstrate their unity in musical manner. To shorten the song or to sing it at a clip robs "Oceans" of its inherent formative power. It "makes sense" only in its proper context: *how* it is sung and *who* sings it, not just *what* is sung. But it also closes down a transformative experience of the song by congregations whose culture is radically different.

---

62. As a principal female worship leader, Taya Smith "makes sense" because Darlene Zschech, Hillsong Church's official music director from 1995–2007, shaped the culture of Hillsong Worship in its early years. Cf. Lim and Ruth's explanation in *Lovin' on Jesus*, 78. See also Tanya Riches's comments in "'Oceans' Keeps Rising," *Christianity Today*, June 10, 2015, https://www.christianitytoday.com/ct/2015/june-web-only/oceans-keeps-rising-hillsong-united.html.

63. Greg Scheer, "Shout to the Lord: Praise and Worship from Jesus People to Gen X," in *New Songs of Celebration Render: Congregational Song in the Twenty-First Century*, ed. C. Michael Hawn (Chicago: GIA Publications, 2013), 188.

64. On what may be lost for a congregation's life together with the loss of hymnbooks in contemporary practice, see Ashley Hales, "What We Lose When Hymnbooks Disappear," *Christianity Today*, August 6, 2018, https://www.christianitytoday.com/ct/2018/august-web-only/hymnal-christopher-phillips.html. The essay involves a review of Christopher N. Phillips, *The Hymnal: A Reading History* (Baltimore: Johns Hopkins University Press, 2018).

65. Cf. Scheer, *Essential Worship*, 135–36.

The Formative Power of "In Christ Alone"

As with "Oceans," I have imagined a similar liturgical purpose for a performance of "In Christ Alone"—namely, as a response to the preaching of a sermon. Unlike Hillsong United, however, I imagine a Reformed evangelical congregation of roughly 250 members, worshiping in a distinctively Colonial architectural space, led by a small band, with Keith Getty at the piano and Kristyn Getty on lead vocal, and supported by a twenty-five-member choir along with a four-person string orchestra.

A first thing to note is that "In Christ Alone" is written as a traditional hymn. To call it "traditional," however, requires qualification. The Getty-Townend hymn belongs to a specific cultural tradition—namely, an evangelical British one that can be linked to the work of Isaac Watts (1674–1748), Anne Steele (1717–1778), and Charles Wesley (1707–1788).[66] Such a tradition is distinct in shape and sound from the tradition of sixteenth-century Lutheran hymns or post–Vatican II Catholic hymns. So while there is no such thing as *the* traditional hymn, "In Christ Alone," with its strophic structure, makes possible a sound that will be familiar to many Protestants.[67]

For Getty and Townend, the Irish ballad melodic form is determinative. As Getty explains, "My melodies tend to be heavily influenced by Irish music, and the Irish melodic style is essentially congregational." By this he means that it has the ability "to be experienced and sung by large groups of people—whether in our homes, schools, or even at a sports match." Beyond its accessibility to nonprofessional singers, the Irish ballad is narrative in nature. "All Irish music," Getty writes, "centers on stories, whether of love or war or of people and places."[68] What this makes possible is a musical vehicle that lends itself easily to a narration of the Christian faith.

Under this light, Getty and Townend aimed to give voice to the "whole" gospel story. "I knew I wanted to tell the gospel story in one song." This again means something particular rather than self-evident. It means

---

66. On this question of definition, see Emily R. Brink, "When in Our Music God Is Glorified: Classic Contemporary Protestant Hymnody," in Hawn, *New Songs of Celebration Render*, 39–68, esp. 54. See also Donald P. Hustad, *Jubilate! Church Music in the Evangelical Tradition* (Carol Stream, IL: Hope Publishing, 1981), ch. 14, "Evangelicals and Congregational Singing."

67. Here I argue against a presumed definition of a hymn, as Austin C. Lovelace might do, for example, in *The Anatomy of Hymnody* (Nashville: Abingdon, 1965), 6–7.

68. Keith Getty and Stuart Townend, "In Christ Alone," *Worship Leader*, August 18, 2015, https://worshipleader.com/articles/in-christ-alone/.

narrating the "theological truths about the life, death, and saving power of Christ through his sacrificial death on the cross."[69] A hymn that tells such a story, as Getty and Townend would have it, arouses praise for the majesty of God and gratitude for the work of Christ, while also inviting a hearty experience of singing, underscored in the third line of each stanza, with its melodic surge.

Inasmuch as it draws musical inspiration from the Irish ballad, "In Christ Alone" easily crosses cultural lines. This is due in part, Getty argues, to the use of the pentatonic scale by folk melodies, whether Celtic or Chinese. Getty writes, "when we write modern hymns, we are aiming to write melodies that people of different ages and backgrounds can (and will) sing."[70] Scotty Gray adds this observation, in *Hermeneutics of Hymnody*: "The AABA unison musical setting [of "In Christ Alone"] has intergenerational and interdenominational appeal, bearing the text in its own unpretentious way."[71]

As with the hymns of Watts and Wesley, Getty and Townend's aim was to write a hymn that would be simple and catchy, in a familiar meter (88 88 D), while also fresh and interesting.[72] A hymn that appealed only to a high level of musical skill or to a specific demographic was to be rejected. The ultimate goal was for people to easily recall the song throughout the rest of the week and, in this way, to sustain Christians with the good news of Christ in all the circumstances of their lives. As Getty and Townend envisioned it, *this* particular melody, sung in *this* particular fashion, moving with *this* particular regularity, is how Christians might demonstrate their unity of faith.

The culture of our imagined congregation will seek to sing the hymn lustily, engaged in heart and mind, but also with a "decent and orderly" use of the physical body. The architecture of the space, evoking a classroom

69. Getty and Townend, "In Christ Alone."

70. Keith Getty, "Hymns and Innovation," in *It Was Good: Music to the Glory of God*, ed. Ned Bustard (Baltimore: Square Halo Books, 2013), 280. John Wilson makes a similar point in "Looking at Hymn-Tunes: The Objective Factors," in *Duty and Delight: Routley Remembered*, ed. Robin A. Leaver and James H. Litton (Norwich: Canterbury Press, 1985), 123–52.

71. Gray, *Hermeneutics of Hymnody*, 273, 251.

72. On this point, see Gray, *Hermeneutics of Hymnody*, 242–44. Nicholas Cook says, "It is a common enough experience among musicians and non-musicians alike to get a familiar tune 'on the brain.'" *Music, Imagination and Culture* (Oxford: Oxford University Press, 1990), 86.

learning environment, will reinforce a "dignified" practice of singing, as the people confess their faith in musical form. Like "Oceans," the performance of "In Christ Alone" will feature the use of a band on a stage. Unlike Hillsong United, the Getty-led band will involve a more kinesthetically reserved practice.

While we might readily concede that the melody of "In Christ Alone" is broadly accessible, it remains a culturally particular form of music. How it sounds and how it moves a people through time is a reflection of Getty and Townend's Reformed, evangelical, folk-musical, British context. Similarly, while "In Christ Alone" represents a classic evangelical hymn, such hymnody emerges from an Anglo-American context and cannot be therefore regarded as "timeless" or "universal," as some might describe it.[73] Such hymnody is culturally contextual. So while we may say that this song is widely accessible, for some it is still a matter of "your music, your sounds, not ours."

While people of all sorts of backgrounds, using any number of musical instruments, might sing the hymn, it does not mean that it will articulate their understanding of the Christian faith—of the "whole" gospel story. In fact, it may be felt to leave out significant parts of that story or to stress the wrong ones. Lastly, while the hymn's musical structure supports a dense amount of text, the tempo of the music has a sense of "marching" the singer swiftly to the end. While the hymn opens up the possibility of a sung story, then, it closes down the possibility of focused attention or leisurely contemplation of any one part of the song.

Conclusion

It is impossible to escape the question of "heart" language in a chapter on music. Whatever the merits or demerits of a practice of music, inevitably a congregation returns to the music that enables them to express most deeply their knowledge and love of God. A congregation may readily concede the relational benefit of singing a hymn in a cappella fashion. It may

---

73. Getty concedes this point in "Hymns and Innovation," 277: "I think every culture has its own indigenous musical language and is poorer for not making more use of it. But that said, the fact of the matter is that Western music is wanted all over the world. So, Western music does translate in terms of popular culture, but I think it's a sad thing when it completely replaces the indigenous music."

reshape its seating arrangements in order to emphasize the communal nature of worship. It may introduce a new instrument as a way to give fresh voice to creation's praise or it may sing a song in a foreign language to forge unity with the global church. But always there is its musical "mother tongue."[74]

For members of Indelible Grace, for example, with its largely Presbyterian, Tennessean roots, folk Americana music is the music that enables the community to sing to God from the heart.[75] For Israel Houghton, as a Pentecostal African-American worship leader, black gospel represents the musical language that enables the people to sing "with soul."[76] It may be "fine" or "folk," chant or chorus, classical or jazz—whatever the musical practice, a congregation always has its "heart song" to God. Yet while this "heart song" should be preserved, a congregation might also need to experiment with its music in order to be formed more deeply in the triune life.

A last thought is this: before we rush to tout music's "sacred" or "transcendent" qualities, or its capacity to pave the road "for the Spirit's coming," we must always keep clear that music's formative powers are first and foremost *musical.*[77] Whatever "holy" benefits it may yield the church at worship, music does its good work *through* the sounds of God's creation, not despite them, nor beyond them. In configuring these sounds in particular ways, the faithful make musical sense of their life before God. And however a congregation resounds its faith, it inevitably forms a peculiar Christ-shaped identity and a Spirit-constituted tie to other members of the church.

74. This is the argument of chapter 11.

75. See http://www.igracemusic.com.

76. See http://newbreedmusic.com.

77. Chris Tomlin and Darren Whitehead, *Holy Roar: 7 Words That Will Change the Way You Worship* (Brentwood, TN: Bowyer & Bow, 2017), 46. On the different ways in which the language of "transcendence" is used in relation to the arts, see Jeremy S. Begbie, *Redeeming Transcendence in the Arts: Bearing Witness to the Triune God* (Grand Rapids: Eerdmans, 2018).

Duke University Chapel, Duke University, Durham, North Carolina (Photograph by author)

CHAPTER 5

Worship and the Visual and Architectural Arts

My own eyes are not enough for me, I will see through those of others.

C. S. Lewis, *Experiment in Criticism*

Churches orient us. The word "orientation" means literally "turned towards the east" (*oriens* in Latin means "rising," and so where the sun rises). It is a word derived from church building.

Margaret Visser, *The Geometry of Love*

Of this I am certain, that God desires to have his works heard and read, especially the passion of our Lord. But it is impossible for me to hear and bear it in mind without forming mental images of it in my heart. For whether I will or not, when I hear of Christ, an image of a man hanging on a cross takes form in my heart, just as the reflection of my face naturally appears in the water when I look into it. If it is not a sin but good to have the image of Christ in my heart, why should it be a sin to have it in my eyes?

Martin Luther, *Against the Heavenly Prophets*
in the Matter of Images and Sacraments

David Freedberg, the Pierre Matisse Professor of the History of Art at Columbia University, summarizes the power of images this way: "People are sexually aroused by pictures and sculptures; they break pictures and sculptures; they mutilate them, kiss them, cry before them, and go on journeys to them; they are calmed by them, stirred by them, and incited to revolt. They give thanks by means of them, expect to be elevated by them, and are moved to the highest levels of empathy and fear. They have always responded in these ways; they still do. They do so in societies we call primitive and in modern societies."[1]

---

1. David Freedberg, *The Power of Images: Studies in the History and Theory of Response* (Chicago: University of Chicago Press, 1989), 1.

For all these reasons, and plenty more, images are powerful. They represent us in family portraits. They reflect us in the movies. They *want* things from us: our money, our loyalty, our worship. They inundate and "swallow us up."[2] "Images not only express conviction," writes Thomas Matthews, "they alter feelings, and end up justifying convictions."[3] Images ornament our world and define our differences. In any given week we are confronted with Photoshop manipulations, graphic deceptions, virtual realities, smoke and mirrors, and all sorts of what the Oxford intellectual George Hakewill in 1608 called "vanities of the eye," distorting our sense of reality.[4]

This is imagery at its worst. At its worst, a work of art like Warner Sallman's *Head of Christ*, painted in 1940, leads the average American to believe "It's what Jesus looks like," with its decidedly non–Middle Eastern features.[5] At its worst, a work of visual art can distort our perceptual capacities and occlude the true knowledge of God. At its best, however, a work of visual art has the power to "teach us to refuse evil and choose the good," as George MacDonald once wrote.[6] At its best, as Thomas Aquinas believed, echoing Gregory the Great before him, images have the power to instruct the "unlettered," to secure a remembrance of the Trinity, and to arouse the emotions with desire for a holy life.[7]

At its best, visual art, in both its two- and three-dimensional forms, becomes a sensible vehicle for the contemplation of invisible things— God's love, Christ's kingdom, the unity that the Spirit makes possible. At its best, art helps us to see signs of God's presence in the world.[8] At its best, visual art inculcates the capacity to see other persons as Jesus sees them, in

2. W. J. T. Mitchell, *What Do Pictures Want? The Lives and Loves of Images* (Chicago: University of Chicago Press, 2005), 80.

3. Thomas Matthews, *The Clash of the Gods: A Reinterpretation of Early Christian Art* (Princeton: Princeton University Press, 1993), 11.

4. Cf. Stuart Clark, *Vanities of the Eye: Vision in Early Modern European Culture* (Oxford: Oxford University Press, 2007), 5.

5. David Morgan, *Icons of American Protestantism: The Art of Warner Sallman* (New Haven: Yale University Press, 1996), 3.

6. George MacDonald, "The Imagination: Its Function and Its Culture," in *A Dish of Orts, Chiefly Papers on the Imagination, and on Shakspere* (New South Wales: Wentworth Press, 2016).

7. Cf. Freedberg, *The Power of Images*, 162.

8. T. J. Gorringe, *Earthly Visions: Theology and the Challenges of Art* (New Haven: Yale University Press, 2011), 14–16.

charity.[9] At its best, visual art enables us "joyfully to imagine that things need not and will not go on just as they are but as God will have them," to paraphrase Stanley Hauerwas.[10] At its best, finally, visual art and architecture can enable us to perceive the world as the theater of God's glory and to love it as God loves it.

Controversy around the visual and architectural shape of corporate worship has, of course, marked every era of church history.[11] On one side stand the cautionary voices, suspicious of the powers of images, ambivalent about the importance of architecture, and convinced that the dominant message of the New Testament involves a categorical preference for the aural over the visual, and for the invisible over against the visible. A line from William Cowper's 1769 hymn "Jesus, Where'er Thy People Meet" is representative of this view: "For Thou, within no walls confined / Inhabitest the humble mind."[12] More colloquially: the church is a people, not a building.

Works of architecture may be necessary and useful but, as some might argue, they are fundamentally incapable of signifying the presence of God. "God spoke so that he might be heard," the Old Testament scholar Bruce Waltke would tell his students, "He did not appear so that he could be seen." Those who hold this position would seem to be right if certain biblical texts—such as Romans 10:17 ("Faith comes by hearing") or 1 Corinthians 5:7 ("We walk by faith, not by sight")—are privileged in the discussion, and if such texts are seen to support a theological antipathy to visual media as vehicles for faithful Christian worship.

But this represents only one reading of Scripture and one position, among many, in church history. On the other side stand those who have felt that the organ of sight and the media of art and architecture are gifts of God to teach the church and to become perceptible signs of the goodness and grace of God.[13] The views of the twelfth-century French Abbot Suger

9. Margaret R. Miles, *Image as Insight: Visual Understanding in Western Christianity and Secular Culture* (Eugene, OR: Wipf & Stock, 2006), 29.

10. Stanley Hauerwas, "On Keeping Theological Ethics Imaginative," in *Against the Nations: War and Survival in a Liberal Society* (San Francisco: Harper & Row, 1985), 58.

11. Robin M. Jensen, *The Substance of Things Seen: Art, Faith, and the Christian Community* (Grand Rapids: Eerdmans, 2004).

12. For the full text of the hymn, see: https://hymnary.org/text/jesus_whereer_thy _people_meet.

13. Sight, within both Catholic and Orthodox traditions, is a privileged organ in worship. The Greek term *oida*, "I know," in classical Greek is the perfect form of the classical

may be representative: "The detractors also object that a saintly mind, a pure heart, a faithful intention ought to suffice for this sacred function; and we, too, explicitly and especially affirm that it is these that principally matter. [But] we profess that we must do homage also through the outward ornaments of sacred vessels ... with all inner purity and with all outward splendor."[14]

To hear about Jesus's resurrection was one thing; even better was to have been "eyewitnesses of his majesty" (2 Pet. 1:16 NASB).[15] To write a letter was a gift for Saint Paul; but what he longed for was *to see* the saints in the flesh (1 Thess. 3:6; Rom. 1:11). As Scripture reminds us repeatedly, God is in the business of revealing himself: in the burning bush, in the pillar of cloud and fire, in the sign of the stars, in the Passover meal, and, supremely, in Jesus.[16] The Orthodox theologian Paul Evdokimov remarks, "in an architectural and structured form, the Word opens the door of the church building.... Drawn in lines of mystery, the Word offers himself for contemplation in the 'visual theology' of the icon."[17]

When it came to the relative adornment of church buildings, the Puritans of sixteenth-century England registered a double charge against their Anglican counterparts: that the practices of the Elizabethan church revealed a prideful heart and that God took no pleasure in "chargeable pomp." God instead was most acceptably worshiped in humble structures—that is, in "the houses of poor men." The grounds for this claim, they believed, were as manifestly sure as the "nakedness of Jesus" and the "simplicity of his Gospel."[18]

Against this, Richard Hooker, a spokesman for the Anglican party, argued that sumptuous architecture and visual fecundity gave an expression of humanity's "cheerful affection" for God and bore witness to creation's

---

Greek verb *eido*, "I see," and thus means "I have seen and therefore I know." To see something, on this view, is to know that it exists and to enter into a kind of visually oriented relationship to it.

14. *Abbot Suger on the Abbey Church of St. Denis and Its Art Treasures*, 2nd ed., ed. and trans. Erwin Panofsky and Gerda Panofsky-Soergel (Princeton: Princeton University Press, 1979), 67.

15. Cf. 1 John 1:1–3; Luke 1:2; 24:48; Rom. 15:17–19; 1 Cor. 9:1; 2 Cor. 12:12.

16. Cf. Calvin, *Institutes of the Christian Religion*, IV.10.15.

17. Paul Evdokimov, *The Art of the Icon: A Theology of Beauty*, trans. Steven Bigham (Pasadena, CA: Oakwood Publications, 1989), 174.

18. Richard Hooker, *Of the Laws of Ecclesiastical Polity*, in *The Folger Library Edition of The Works of Richard Hooker*, vol. 2, ed. W. Speed Hill (Cambridge, MA: Harvard University Press, 1977), 51.

riches. Just as Bezalel was commended for building a sanctuary for God that was as "beautiful, gorgeous and rich as art could make them," so the church, he maintained, should build its own sanctuaries that gave sensible witness to the majesty of God.[19] As Hooker saw it: the external bore witness to the internal; the earthly corresponded to the heavenly; the visible resembled the invisible.

While internality, invisibility, and aurality factor largely in the thinking of one side of the debate, externality, visibility, and visuality govern the thinking of the other. This is of course to speak exceedingly simplistically of what is in reality far more complex and variegated. For most Christians, however, no matter their place on the ecclesial spectrum, there is little doubt about the power of visual and architectural art. The capacity of the plastic and spatial arts to serve or to distort the corporate worship of the church is clear to all—to iconodules as much as to iconoclasts.

Less clear, perhaps, is how visual and architectural art uniquely "work." What does visual art *do* that other media of art cannot do in quite the same way? What role do the visual and architectural arts play in the economy of the Triune God? How do they "work" and "speak" and "shape" a sense of self in the world? What are their singular powers? And how do the media of visual and architectural art open up and close down possibilities for the formation of our humanity in corporate worship? This chapter explores each of these questions in turn.

Visual Art and Architecture Theologically Considered

In order to discover the good that the visual and architectural arts might bring to the church at worship, we need to get some sense of the good that the visual and architectural arts in particular, and that images and the eye in general, perform within the economy of the Triune God. I offer two arguments here.

First, as God is an image maker, so human beings are image makers. In making creation, God makes a physical "painting" of the divine glory.[20] God makes the human creature "in his own image" (Gen. 1:27 NIV), and in the visible signs of smoke and fire, God's presence is somehow perceived.

---

19. Hooker, *Of the Laws of Ecclesiastical Polity*, vol. 2, 59.

20. This is language John Calvin uses to describe creation in the *Institutes of the Christian Religion*, I.5.10.

God appears to people in theophanies, dreams, visions, and angelic visitations. God appears in the *Logos* made flesh—by the Spirit the faithful behold his glory (John 1). The miracles of Jesus, when seen by the disciples in faith, lead to belief in God (John 2:11). And in the Lord's Supper we see an image of the body and blood of Christ.

Our ethical actions also make visible the kingdom of God (Matt. 25), while Holy Scripture images the Word in scripted form. Just as Scripture opens with a scene in which God takes pleasure in that which he beholds (Gen. 1:31), so too Scripture ends with an epic spectacle of beholding as the climax of history (Rev. 1:7). To be a creature made in the image of an image-making God, then, is to be an image maker too. Every act of human creativity, in fact, from garden making to city building, involves a capacity to image that activity.[21]

How do the Scriptures speak about eyesight? A proper answer lies beyond the scope of this chapter, but we might say this for starters. When the Bible speaks about the activities of the eye, it speaks of them as an experience characterized by certitude. Deuteronomy 4:3 says, "You have seen for yourselves what the LORD did with regard to the Baal of Peor" (NRSV). In Luke 24:39 Jesus says, "Look at my hands and my feet.... A ghost does not have flesh and bones, as you see I have" (NIV). Acts 5:32 declares, "we are witnesses of these things; and so is the Holy Spirit" (NASB). It is the apostles' sight of the Messiah that underscores the veracity of their testimony.[22]

Sight may deceive, but it retains a privileged place in God's self-revelation.[23] It is also important to note that the Scriptures present the

21. This would include graphic images (pictures, statues, designs); optical images (mirrors, projections); perceptual images (sense data, "species," appearances); mental images (dreams, memories, ideas, phantasmata); verbal images (metaphors, descriptions, writing); and symbolical images (national flags, religious insignia).

22. John 1:1–4 is the paradigmatic text; cf. Rom. 15:17–19; 1 Cor. 9:1; 2 Cor. 12:12. In the transfiguration (Matt. 17; Mark 9; Luke 9) the disciples are shown the true nature of Jesus as a form of encouragement to remain faithful in the face of the imminent experience of suffering and loss.

23. More precisely: while the ear is relationally *in via*, the eye is relationally *terminal*. We hear in faith and obedience *in order to* behold the beloved. The knowledge of another person, as the New Testament sees it, is ultimately for the sake of intimate presence. This is what is at stake, I believe, in the biblical language of "face-to-face" and "in the sight of." While the Second Commandment (Exod. 20:3–4; Deut. 5:8) must be taken with utter seriousness, it must also be read in context. On the possibility of seeing a positive outcome for the visual arts on the terms of the Second Commandment, see John D. Witvliet, "The Worship," in *For the Beauty of the Church: Casting a Vision for the Arts*, ed.

relationship between eye and ear as interdependent rather than opposi-tional. Both ear and eye are a gift to humanity. Both are broken; both are made new in Christ; both are central to the mission of the church. The seminal text here is Isaiah 6:9–10, which Jesus reiterates in every Gospel account,[24] while Acts 4:20 functions as a primary text for future reflection on the visual and aural arts: "For we cannot but speak the things which we have seen and heard" (KJV).

Second, two kinds of physical places in Scripture play a determina-tive role in Christian reflection on church architecture: the literal and the figurative. The literal places include the tabernacle (Exod. 25–40; Deut. 23:15; 2 Sam. 7:6–7) and temple of Israel (1 Kings 5–8; 2 Chron. 2–7), both of which harken to the garden of Eden as sacred space; the synagogue as the place where prayer and preaching occur (Acts 9:20; 13:5, 14); the upper room (Acts 1:13; 20:8); and the New Jerusalem (Rev. 3:12; 21:2). The figurative places include: Jesus as temple (John 1:14; 2:19); the church as temple (1 Cor. 3:16–17; 2 Cor. 6:16; Eph. 2:21; 1 Pet. 2:5; Rev. 3:12); the human body as temple (1 Cor. 6:19–20); the earthly tabernacle as a kind of heavenly tabernacle (Heb. 8–9); and the vision of a new temple (Ezek. 33–48).

W. David O. Taylor (Grand Rapids: Baker Books, 2010), 63–64. Other helpful resources include Natalie Carnes, *Image and Presence: A Christological Reflection on Iconoclasm and Icono-philia* (Stanford, CA: Stanford University Press, 2018); Adrienne Chaplin, "Visual Spiritu-ality: Is Religious Art, Like Michelangelo's 'Creation of Adam,' a Violation of the Second Commandment When God Is Portrayed?," *Christianity Today* 50, no. 5 (2006): 58; J. C. Cooper, "The Theology of Image in Eastern Orthodoxy and John Calvin," *Scottish Jour-nal of Theology* 35, no. 3 (1982): 219–41; Joseph Gutmann, "The 'Second Commandment' and the Image in Judaism," *Hebrew Union College Annual* 32 (1961): 161–74; Mary Charles Murray, "The Image, the Ear, and the Eye in Early Christianity," *ARTS* 9, no. 1 (1997): 17–24; Jaroslav Pelikan, *Imago Dei: The Byzantine Apologia for Icons* (Princeton: Princeton University Press, 2011); David VanDrunen, "Iconoclasm, Incarnation and Eschatology: Toward a Catholic Understanding of the Reformed Doctrine of the 'Second' Command-ment," *International Journal of Systematic Theology* 6, no. 2 (2004): 130–47; Gerhard von Rad, "The Veto on Images in the Old Testament," in *Old Testament Theology*, vol. 1 (Louisville: Westminster John Knox, 2001), 214–16.

24. Matt. 13:11; Mark 4:12; Luke 8:10; Acts 28:26. See also Luke 10:21–24. The philoso-pher Abraham Kuyper puts the point this way: "Because God himself hears, he also planted in man the ear, so that also hearing would be in him; and because God himself can behold things, he also formed in man the eye, so that also man could see." Cited in H. David Schur-inga, *Hearing the Word in a Visual Age: A Practical Theological Consideration of Preaching with the Contemporary Urge to Visualization* (PhD diss., Theologische Universiteit te Kampen, 1995), 139.

The Old Testament is admittedly full of theological engagement with place in general and with architecture in particular. But in the New Testament, this engagement often takes on more of a figurative character. For many Christians, especially of the Protestant sort, this results in a positive *disinterest* in the theological and artistic importance of buildings. Does the New Testament offer any vision for church architecture? Murray Rae, in *Architecture and Theology: The Art of Place*, answers yes: "Good architecture is a vital ingredient of living well in God's world—and a signpost pointing to the New Jerusalem he's fashioning."[25]

Historically, Christians have taken this positive instinct and run with it in three specific architectural directions.[26] For many Catholics, Orthodox, and Anglicans, church architecture tends to take its cue from the idea of "building as house of God." Here church buildings draw inspiration from the architectural plan of Israel's temple. This might include basilicas, cathedrals, monastic abbeys, and centralized plans. A second sense, church architecture as "schoolhouse," draws inspiration from the synagogue. In this context, a "teacher-preacher" presides over a "classroom" full of "student-learners" who gather in order to pray and to read and to learn. Classical works of church architecture, along with colonial and meetinghouse plans, tend to represent this view of church buildings.

A third sense, church architecture as "domestic house," draws inspiration from the upper room of Mark 14:15 and Acts 1:13. Here a senior "family member" presides over a "family-like gathering" in celebration of "table-fellowship" activities. For some, this will be a house as "hearth" or a sanctuary as "living room," such as we might find in the meetinghouses of Anabaptists, the "house church" and charismatic movement, or congregations in contexts marked by extreme poverty or persecution. For others, it will be a house as "theater," as is the case with Willow Creek Community Church, in Barrington, Illinois.[27]

---

25. W. David O. Taylor, "Buildings That Bear Witness to God," *Christianity Today*, November 27, 2017, http://www.christianitytoday.com/ct/2017/december/buildings-that-bear-witness-to-god.html.

26. Allan Doig, *Liturgy and Architecture: From the Early Church to the Middle Ages* (London: Routledge, 2008); Nigel Yates, *Liturgical Space: Christian Worship and Church Buildings in Western Europe 1500–2000* (London: Routledge, 2008).

27. Cf. Jeanne H. Kilde, *When the Church Became Theatre: The Transformation of Evangelical Architecture and Worship in Nineteenth-Century America* (Oxford: Oxford University Press, 2005).

The Singular Powers of Visual Art and Architecture

With these all-too-brief ideas on visual and architectural art in mind, how might we describe their singular powers? Partly their powers reside in the basic elements and materials that characterize the two media; partly they reside in the particular styles that are employed with the two media. A defining power, I argue, is their "material fixity." Let me take the first of these two powers (elements and materials) briefly and develop the third (material fixity) at greater length.

The basic elements of visual art and therefore the means by which visual art exercises its power include the following. *Lines* in art, which are one-dimensional, can communicate information through their character and direction as well as feelings or ideas.[28] *Shapes* can be rectangular, oval, circular, or otherwise. *Space* in a work of art refers to a feeling of depth and can be "positive" or "negative" space. *Texture* describes the surface quality of an object that we sense through touch. In a two-dimensional work of art, texture gives a visual sense of how an object depicted would feel in real life if touched. In three-dimensional works, artists use actual texture to add a tactile quality to the work.

Color has three main characteristics: hue (red, green, blue, etc.), value (how light or dark it is), and intensity (how bright or dull it is). Colors can be described as warm or cool and are used to convey feeling or mood in a work of art. Artists use color value to create different moods. For example, Rembrandt primarily used dark colors, while van Gogh tended to use bright colors. Intensity identifies the purity or strength of a color. Bright colors are often associated with positive energy and heightened emotions. Dull colors create a sedate or serious mood.

Perspective is where a flat surface is used to convey multiple dimensions. *Emphasis* is what catches the viewer's eye. *Balance* is where an image or space is symmetrical or asymmetrical. *Contrast* describes elements within a work of art that are intentionally contrasted with one another. *Movement* describes the direction that a viewer's eye takes through a work of visual art. *Pattern* is the repetition of an object, line, symbol, and so on. *Proportion* is the feeling of unity created by all the parts of a work of art. And *rhythm* is when one or more element is repeated in order to give the work of art a certain dynamism.

28. This is a point that the illustrator Molly Bang persuasively makes in her delightful book, *Picture This: How Pictures Work* (San Francisco: Chronicle Books, 2016).

The basic materials of visual art and architecture include such things as leather, fabric, metal, iron, plastic, ceramic, concrete, brick, hair, water, fiber, wood, glass, stone, and light. Each material opens up and closes down possibilities for what can be made of works of visual art and architecture. The styles of visual art and architecture include, among other things, classical, Byzantine, medieval, Romanesque, Renaissance, Gothic, Celtic, Baroque, Romantic, realist, impressionist, surrealist, abstract, conceptual, modern, postmodern, contemporary, and global. These are like emotionally and imaginatively rich languages that speak with a characteristic grammar and vocabulary, fully intelligible only within context.

The most characteristic singular power of visual and architectural art is the power of what I am calling "material fixity."

In contrast to the dramatic arts, which occur "through time," works of visual and architectural art occur fixed "in time." While music occupies a diffuse "space," visual and architectural art occupy a fixed space. And whereas the potency of dance lies in its immediate experience, the potency of visual and architectural art lies in its durative permanence over time. A painting does not unfold over time like a song does. A Romanesque work of architecture does not expire in the way that a musical note does. A cast-iron sculpture does not bend to the subjectivity of a particular audience as might be the case with an anthem, which is sung one way by a professional choir and in a rather different manner by untrained folk.

In language borrowed from Katie Kresser, I suggest that the quality of material fixity in visual or architectural art is characterized by "simultaneity," "permanence," and "monumentality." By *simultaneity* I mean that they do not unfold over time; by *permanence* that they do not expire like a song does; and by *monumentality* that they retain their own character without the need for human beings to keep them active.[29] The art historian W. J. T. Mitchell describes an image's peculiar characteristic this way: "The picture wants to hold, to arrest, to mummify an image in silence and slow time."[30] What the visual and architectural arts enable humans being to do, then, is to *fix* before our eyes a thing or an image solidified in time.

---

29. Katie Kresser, "Contemporary Art and Worship: *Imago Dei* in the Twenty-First Century," in *Contemporary Art and the Church: A Conversation between Two Worlds* (Downers Grove, IL: IVP Academic, 2017), 117–35.

30. Mitchell, *What Do Pictures Want?*, 72.

Take the color blue, for example. In music the color blue may represent the experience of "getting the blues." When listening to a melancholy song, like "Will the Circle Be Unbroken?," one's thoughts may wander in any number of directions while the song plays. With a painting, however, like Giovanni Bellini's *Madonna of the Meadow*, a fixed work of art confronts the viewer. Dressed in blue, symbolizing both truth and heavenly grace, the Virgin Mary invites the viewer to contemplate a life of faithful devotion to the Son, which, for those who love Jesus as Mary does, inevitably involves suffering.[31] Meaning is concretized in a fixed image; it neither wavers nor wanders. Such is the power of visual art.

In Emily Dickinson's poem "Ah, Teneriffe!," the terrific nature of mountains is thematically explored. All a person can do in the face of a mountain's massive presence, the poem seems to say, is bow. Whether distinct or vague memories of the poem remain, its power to suggest the experience of a mountain depends on the initiative of the reader. With a cathedral, like Chartres Cathedral in France, however, a mountain is symbolized in glass and stone. Its obdurate presence confronts the viewer regardless of the viewer's initiative. Its mountainous form engulfs the worshiper despite the expectations that a worshiper may bring to the space. Its massive character resists expiration, the forces of wind and water notwithstanding.[32] Such is the power of architectural art.

Like all media of art, the power of visual and architectural works of art is necessarily contextual. A pope's miter means one thing to Italian Catholics gathered at the Sistine Chapel; it means another thing altogether if that same miter is on display at the Metropolitan Museum of Art. An image of Sallman's *Head of Christ* imprinted on a coffee mug means one thing to the pastor of a rural, largely white United Methodist congregation, while it may mean a different thing when that image hangs in the foyer of an urban, largely black African Methodist Episcopal Church. A church building situated in the public square (the *marktplatz*) of a European town retains a particular relation to civic power that a church building embedded within a strip center in a suburban neighborhood will not possess.

---

31. "The main space of prayer illustrated here is again Mary, shown in profound meditation, her head bent, eyes almost closed and hands slowly coming together." Timothy Verdon, *Art and Prayer: The Beauty of Turning to God* (Brewster, MA: Paraclete, 2013), 59.

32. Cf. Peter Fingesten, "Topographical and Anatomical Aspects of the Gothic Cathedral," *Journal of Aesthetics and Criticism* 20, no. 1 (1963): 3–23.

Visual Art and Architecture in a Liturgical Context

Five types of art and architecture play a definitive role in the corporate worship of the church. One type is ornamental art. Such art makes a space aesthetically pleasing, and by enlisting the detailed ornamental qualities in creation it is able to give a personal and culturally contextual quality to a congregation's life. Examples of this include the use of limestone in the building of First Evangelical Free Church, in Austin, Texas, the adobe clay that marks the San Francisco de Asis mission church in Ranchos de Taos in New Mexico, and the use of wood and light in the Thorncrown Chapel in Eureka Springs, Arkansas.

A second type is representational art. This type of art re-presents things in creation, things in church history, and things from God's works in Scripture and in the world. The symbols of fish and cross are obvious examples of this. The image of almonds embroidered on a priestly vestment, as a less familiar example, represents divine favor (cf. Num. 17:1–8). Images of bears represent evil powers (cf. Dan. 7), while images of the dove may represent the energetic power or the gentle quality of the Holy Spirit.[33] The Jubilee Church in Rome includes the architectural representation of a ship that ploughs the seas of the third millennium as well as three shells that signify the Trinity.

A third type of art is abstract art. This type uses a visual language that operates largely independently from visual references in the world. Such art might also be regarded as nonobjective or nonfigurative art.[34] Examples of this include cathedral columns that symbolize the people of God. The color purple symbolizes imperial power, while the color red serves as symbolic of Pentecost and of the blood of the martyrs. The use of light in the design of Singapore Life Church, a Presbyterian church in Singapore, is intended to serve as a beacon of light to the immediate neighborhood of the congregation.

A fourth type of art, typographic art, makes use of letters or words to convey specific ideas. This includes, for example, the INRI that stands for *Iesus Nazarenus Rex Iudaeorum* ("Jesus of Nazareth, King of the Jews"), church signs, and the use of graphic art in announcements. A fifth type is

---

33. Judith Couchman's book *The Art of Faith: A Guide to Understanding Christian Images* (Brewster, MA: Paraclete, 2012), is a wonderful introduction to the meaning of images, figures, and symbols in the devotional and liturgical practices of Christians throughout history.

34. Cf. *The Yale Dictionary of Art and Artists*, ed. Erika Langmuir and Norbert Lynton (New Haven: Yale University Press, 2000), 2.

pragmatic art. This accomplishes utilitarian purposes. The color of carpet and of pews may serve to hide dirt, while the color of text on a video screen may serve to give cues for when the congregation and the worship leader speak, respectively. The architecture of an elevated pulpit, which makes use of a sounding board, such as is found in St. Pierre Cathedral in Geneva, serves to amplify sound.

The Purposes of Visual Art and Architecture in Corporate Worship

What are the purposes of visual and architectural art in corporate worship?[35] One purpose is aesthetic—that is, to decorate a place, as is the case with the use of light and color in many church buildings. A second purpose is didactic. Such art seeks to teach about the Christian faith. Gothic architecture seeks to bear witness to the transcendence of God, while modern church architecture seeks to emphasize the immanence of God.[36] A third purpose is devotional. Such art seeks to kindle affection for God and for a holy life. This includes such things as Catholic pilgrimage art, the use of Stations of the Cross imagery in an Anglican sanctuary space, or the presence of inspirational banners in many free-church congregations.

A fourth purpose is liturgical-functional, which aims to reinforce a particular activity of corporate worship. Vestments, for instance, reinforce the distinct authority of the worship leader. The colors that correspond to the church calendar function as visual reminders to the congregation of specific "seasons" of Christ's life. A last purpose, missional, aims to inspire a congregation with a vision of God's mission in the world. From basilicas to theater spaces, Christians have appropriated the architectural styles of the time as a way to assert that God speaks in the architectural tongue of every time.[37] At Hope Chapel in Austin, Texas, a banner of the resurrected Christ hangs on the back wall of the sanctuary to remind the congregation that God makes all things new in our private and public life.[38]

35. Lisa DeBoer's book *Visual Arts in the Worshiping Church* (Grand Rapids: Eerdmans, 2016) offers a fascinating sociological perspective on the visual art practices of Eastern Orthodox, Roman Catholic, and Protestant congregations.

36. On this point, see Mark Torgerson, *An Architecture of Immanence: Architecture for Worship and Ministry Today* (Grand Rapids: Eerdmans, 2007), 49, 62.

37. Against such a conviction, see Moorya Doorly, *No Place for God: The Denial of the Transcendent in Modern Church Architecture* (San Francisco: Ignatius Press, 2007), 1.

38. See http://www.bcartfarm.com/pp199.html.

The Formative Possibilities of Visual Art and Architecture

How might the visual and architectural arts form our humanity within the context of corporate worship?

The Formative Power of Permanent and Occasional Visual Art

One way is through the use of permanent and occasional art. Permanent works of art possess a particular power to shape how human beings see their place in the world. That power is a durative, definitive one. Permanent works of art can outlast the first generation of a church and often define a church's singular identity. This is what permanent art opens up formatively. The stained glass windows that belong to Duke Chapel, for example, illustrate this point.[39] Depicting various biblical characters and stories, the seventy-seven windows, installed sometime after the initial dedication of the space in 1935, took nearly three years to complete and used more than one million pieces of glass. When examined closely, the figures depicted in the windows have a European cast about them.

This by itself is not absolutely problematic. What becomes problematic is the idea, unconsciously inferred perhaps, that Duke Chapel belongs principally to white people and that white people most closely resemble the people of the Bible. It is this "story" that nonwhite Christians may hear most loudly. Such a story can be tempered or countered, however, by occasional works of art. Occasional art holds the power to give in-the-moment expression to how Christians view their life before God. When Duke Chapel installs an exhibit on the walls of the nave, then, such as an exhibit of the prints of Sadao Watanabe, which translate biblical narratives into Japanese settings using the traditional Japanese folk art of katazome stencil dyeing, it becomes an opportunity to tell other stories that mark the character of the congregation.[40] What occasional artwork closes down is the possibility that a congregation will forget or no longer be deeply formed by art that has disappeared from a common space.

To remain with Duke Chapel, the use of windows in a church building can form a sense of self in the world. Stained glass tells one story; clear

39. See John M. Bryan, *Duke University: An Architectural Tour* (New York: Princeton Architectural Press, 2000), 26–31; https://chapel.duke.edu/mission/building/windows.

40. See https://chapel.duke.edu/art and Sandra Bowden, *Beauty Given by Grace: The Biblical Prints of Sadao Watanabe* (Baltimore: Square Halo Books, 2012).

glass panes tell another story. At its most basic level, stained glass serves to decorate a space with color.[41] In this way it becomes an occasion for aesthetic joy as an instantiation of God's shalom. When stained glass windows give voice to color's praise, so to speak, a congregation can become inspired to join creation's radiant adoration of God. When representations of persons, animals, or landscapes are included in the windows, the story that the stained glass tells is enhanced with symbolic meaning. At Duke Chapel the stained glass windows tell a specific story, not just through their depiction of the "usual" Old Testament characters, but through their inclusion of Rebekah and Hagar and of archangels too. It is a way for their unique stories to intersect the stories of individual parishioners. What does stained glass close down? It cannot tell *any* other story but the one represented.

A very different story is told with the windows in Goodson Chapel, the primary worship space for Duke Divinity School. When the chapel was renovated in 2005, a deliberate choice was made to keep the window-panes clear rather than colored. The leadership wished to remind faculty, staff, and students when they gathered for worship that God's mission lay near at hand. Both creation (piney woods) and history (Duke University) are seen to represent a sphere for witness and service and for the display of God's glory.[42] Both, they believed, should be witnessed without the mediating character of color or figures. While clear-paned windows could merely be a medium to let sunlight into a space, for Duke Divinity they represent an opportunity to be deeply formed.[43] "To watch the leaves

41. On the complicated and fascinating process of making stained glass, see Virginia Chieffo Raguin, *Stained Glass: From Its Origins to the Present* (New York: Harry N. Abrams, 2003), 34–41.

42. In email correspondence, March 16, 2018, Susan Pendleton Jones, who served as chair of the committee that oversaw the construction of the chapel, wrote this: "The tree-line fits perfectly with the placement of the windows above the chancel area but actually doesn't extend much beyond them on either side. On the northern apse side (opposite the organ) there are no (or maybe few) trees, but when seated you mainly see the sky. When standing, you see the Duke LSRC [Levine Science Research Center] building off in the distance which gave us the sense of combining both the beauty of nature in worship (as you look outside toward the chancel) with the realities of the everyday world, symbolized by a generic classroom building out the baptismal apse side windows."

43. "As a transparent as well as a colored material, glass resonated profoundly with the concepts of clarity and opacity that functioned as primary dichotomies for both moral and ontological systems. Light was transparent as it left the Creator, acquiring color, and thus its ability to be visible, as it penetrated the material world. Colors can there be seen

change color throughout the seasons of the year behind the chancel area has endless theological possibilities for enhancing worship."[44] What does clear glass close down? Worshipers may see nothing but their own bored and broken imaginations.

The Formative Power of Church Buildings

Our choices in a church building represent a distinctive way that architecture shapes our humanity in worship. The New Testament uses a variety of images to describe the life of the church. One image describes the identity of the church as "rooted" in Christ (Col. 2:7). Another image portrays it as "raised with Christ" and therefore compelled to set its heart and mind "on things above" (Col. 3:1–3 NIV). Church architecture often reinforces one image over another and in this way shapes a congregation's imagination. Romanesque architecture, for example, tends to draw the eye downward. Standing in such a space, a person might feel weighted down by the heaviness of the stones. The gravitational pull of the space is "down" and in this way functions as an architectural metaphor for the idea of being "rooted" in Christ.

Gothic architecture, in contrast, tends to draw the eye upward, toward the lightness of the ceiling. The eye rises heavenward by way of the rising arches and out through the expansive but fragile windows. The gravitational pull of the space is "up" and in this way functions as an architectural metaphor for the idea of being "raised" in Christ. "A Gothic cathedral that soars and sings," writes the philosopher Nelson Goodman, "does not equally droop and grumble."[45] Goodman's observation underscores the fact that models of architecture, along with seating arrangements and the overall design of a building, acquire a distinguishable character about them. They also acquire a particular inertia: a way that "forces" human beings to occupy a space in a definitive manner.

Whatever church we choose to build, the model of architecture will inevitably orient a way in which people think about God, perceive themselves, and imagine their relation to the world at large. Every choice of

---

as representing the diversity and imperfection of creatures, although they still betray the radiance of their origins." Raguin, *Stained Glass*, 13.

44. Susan Pendleton Jones in email correspondence, March 16, 2018.

45. Nelson Goodman, "How Buildings Mean," *Critical Inquiry* 11, no. 4 (1985): 642–53.

church architecture inescapably opens up and closes down possibilities for the formation of Christ's body on earth.[46]

The Formative Power of an Art Exhibit in the Sanctuary

A last example involves an art exhibition that took place in the church I pastored in Austin, Texas. In 2007, Hope Chapel, a nondenominational, moderately charismatic congregation, invited Laura Jennings, one of our members, to exhibit a series of paintings that she had created while pursuing her master's degree at the University of North Texas. While the work was originally created for her MFA, we felt that it would serve our context too. When her art first appeared in the sanctuary, I explained to the congregation that, as with all the visual art that hung there, Laura's work was not here only to ornament our space. It was here to help us to see the gospel afresh and to inspire us to live out the gospel afresh. Just as Jesus repeatedly directed his disciples to notice things that society ignored, so Laura's work drew our attention to groups we frequently overlooked: in this case, the Dalits of India and victims of war violence.[47]

But it was more than the subject that challenged us; it was the style, which was more abstract than literal. The work did not yield its meaning easily, and while some folks saw only strange figural shapes in vibrant colors, others saw nothing but a token of decoration to the sanctuary. Some, though, took time to look, and to look again and again, as a way to persevere with the abstraction. The space in which the work had been hung was essential to its formative possibilities. The artwork hung in the sanctuary space on walls that ran parallel to the pews, from back to front. In part the paintings functioned as environmental art, peripheral to the focal activity of worship.

46. Helpful resources for congregations that face the option to build a new structure or to renovate existing buildings include Richard Giles, *Re-Pitching the Tent: Re-Ordering the Church Building for Worship and Mission* (Collegeville, MN: Liturgical Press, 2004), and Mark A. Torgerson, *Greening Spaces for Worship and Ministry: Congregations, Their Buildings, and Creation Care* (Herndon, VA: The Alban Institute, 2012). For historical perspectives on the practice of church architecture, see Richard Kieckhefer, *Theology in Stone: Church Architecture from Byzantium to Berkeley* (Oxford: Oxford University Press, 2008), and Jeanne Halgren Kilde, *Sacred Power, Sacred Space: An Introduction to Christian Architecture and Worship* (Oxford: Oxford University Press, 2008).

47. I wrote a blog post in 2012 that included some images of her artwork: "Appendix to My CT Article on Visual Art and Worship," Diary of an Arts Pastor, http://artspastor.blog spot.com/2012/03/appendix-to-my-ct-article-on-visual-art.html.

At the time when Jennings's work hung in the sanctuary, in the months of autumn, the congregation found itself during the season of Ordinary Time. Two banners, which hung on the front and back walls of the sanctuary, gave a colorful expression to this season of the church's life. Unlike the banners, however, which remained in the direct line of sight for the congregation, Jennings's artwork remained on the periphery. People might notice the artwork when they walked into the church, and they might glance at it on their way out of the sanctuary. As often as not, the work remained tangential to the activities of worship and functioned as visual ambience rather than direct aid to worship. At times a preacher might include in his sermon a comment on the art. How, then, did the congregation "participate" in the work of visual art? Inasmuch as they contemplated the work, they might find the work interfacing with the activities of worship or find the work speaking to their lives beyond the context of corporate worship.

Three contextual variables augmented the art's ability to form the congregation. First, the art functioned as an official activity. The senior leadership, with its authority to "let in" and "to keep out," basically said: "This art matters." The art was not an extracurricular activity; it belonged at the center of the church's life. Second, the art was placed within the sanctuary, not in the foyer or a Sunday school space. As the place that church authority usually deems the most "sacred," the sanctuary is a strictly protected space. To put art in the sanctuary, then, was to make a statement about the importance of art.[48] Third, the art was placed in direct relation to the narrative of the church calendar, in this case the season of Ordinary Time. To embed the art in the tradition of the liturgical calendar helped, I hoped, to resist tendencies to approach the art in consumeristic and or narrowly subjective ways.

What formative possibilities did it open up? By showing us pixelated bodies rather than solid ones, Laura's art reminded us that we do not see people rightly simply by looking at them; our sight is damaged and needs mending. In depicting fragmented bodies, the art also reminded us of our fragmented perceptions. The art depicted issues related to suffering, slavery, injustice, and death. To place the issues close at hand was a way to counter the benumbing effects of nightly news. Against the temptation to despair that suffering would have the last word, the art also invited us to imagine what often feels impossible: that God is in fact present to people's

48. Cf. Elaine L. Graham, *Transforming Practice: Pastoral Theology in an Age of Uncertainty* (New York: Mowbray, 1996), 103.

suffering. And finally, the art challenged us to love the "poor and needy," those far from home as well as those close by. In experiencing Laura's art over the course of seven weeks, our congregation was given the opportunity to perceive the poor and the needy in gospel ways. We "prayed with the eyes" and, by faith, were changed accordingly.

What formative possibilities did the artwork close down? The difficult style of art, abstract rather than representational, may have caused people easily to give up on the art, especially if they felt that contemporary artists sought to "make regular folk feel stupid." With no extensive verbal commentary accompanying each individual work, the art could be all-too-easily ignored. And the work's imagery might have been swallowed up by a consumerist approach to imagery in general. How might these drawbacks have been avoided? We might have integrated the art more thoroughly into the congregation's life. We could have preached a sermon series on the topic of the artwork. Our Scripture readings could have been intentionally connected to "the poor and the needy." Or the congregation might have been regularly encouraged to practice the disciplines of prayer, fasting from media communications, service to neighbors, and, as the Spirit led, feasting with the poor and needy.

If Laura's art formed us in anything particular, however, it formed us to resee the people who sat in the pew nearby, whose brokenness on certain days (if we were honest) we often had no interest in seeing. With the aid of this art, though, we were given an invaluable opportunity: to see them with a hopeful love. Did this formative experience for Hope Chapel come about automatically? No. Did a re-*formed* habit of sight occur immediately? No again. If it happened at all, it was a slow, uneven process, and if the art formed sanctified habits of sight, that was due in no small part to a long and purposeful "training" period. Our congregation recognized that the sanctification of our eyes would need to occur over a great deal of time. And we would need to cultivate an "ecclesial culture" to help us engage visual art in a transformative fashion.

Conclusion

A popular children's song, often taught in Sunday school classes and around campfires, includes a line thrice repeated in its first stanza: "Oh, be careful little eyes what you see." The presumption of the song is that our eyes can lead us astray and that we must therefore guard our eyes from the temptations that are peculiar to the faculty of sight. While the stanza is framed by this cautionary note, the stanza's center pivots on a specific action of the First Person of the Trinity: "There's a Father up above / And He's looking down in love." Whether this divine gaze is perceived as gracious or ominous might depend on the child and if the accent falls on the act of "looking down" or on the manner in which the Father regards us, "in love." Subsequent stanzas march through additional powers of the human body, reiterating the same exhortation to ears, hands, feet, and mouth.

Yet while the injunction to "be careful" might be freighted with the presumption that eyesight deceives and distorts, and that visual media are not just useless aids to the knowledge of God but dangerous too, I would like to suggest another reading of the song: as an invitation to a Spirit-led, *care*-filled use of the eye through the church's liturgical works of visual art and architecture. While eyesight may warp our sense of reality, it can also become a vehicle for Spirit-ual vision, as both biblical prophets and patristic theologians believed. While images can certainly be "dead and dumb," they can also become potent stimuli to prayer, offering "a feast for the eyes, just as the spectacle of the countryside spurs my heart to glorify God," as Saint John of Damascus felt.[49] And while Scripture affirms the ear as a medium of faith, works of architecture can both reinforce and testify to the faith in concrete terms.

The service that visual artists and architects offer the church is a vital one. They draw our attention to often-overlooked things, like the wonder of the color red and to delight in it as God delights in it. They fix before us an image of a world broken by our own doing but not abandoned by God. They make a plain room exceedingly lovely by the rich use of line and light. They combine absurd things to reveal the comical or fractured side of human life. They invite us to notice the depth of creation and the ways in which the physical world discloses the glory of God—lilies of the field, granite stones, the ant and the antelope, "the chains of the Pleiades," Ceylon cedarwood, a well-made coffee or chalice. Visual artists question our habits of sight and they invite us to "pray with the eyes" as a way to see the world as God sees it—our lives, our homes, our neighborhoods and cities—and to be changed accordingly.

49. Cited in Verdon, *Art and Prayer*, vi. In this vein, I cannot more highly recommend to church and worship leaders, along with teachers and scholars, the following online resource: The Visual Commentary on Scripture, https://thevcs.org.

Stanley Hauerwas writes, "That God is lord of history means we must be able joyfully to imagine that things need not and will not go on just as they are but as God will have them."[50] In the case of this chapter's subject, it means, finally, not just the avoidance of false images in our spaces of public worship or the absence of good architecture in our corporate lives; it also means the provision of visual and architectural works of art that offer the physical eyes something good and true and beautiful to look upon in order that the eyes of our minds might be clarified and that the eyes of our hearts might be aroused for the sake of a deeper love of God and a more faithful engagement with a world that God so loves. When such visual and architectural art is offered to the church, it is given a chance, as Bonaventure once believed, to perceive the splendor of Christ's own beauty.

50. Stanley Hauerwas, "On Keeping Theological Ethics Imaginative," in *Against the Nations: War and Survival in a Liberal Society* (San Francisco: Harper & Row, 1985), 58.

Image from Psalm 19 in *The Message* (Photograph by author)

CHAPTER 6

Worship and the Poetic Arts

Where language is weak, theology is weakened.

Madeleine L'Engle, *Walking on Water:*
Reflections on Faith and Art

I found that keeping company with poets, men and women who care
about words and are honest with them, who respect and honor their
sheer overwhelming power, kept me alert—biblically alert, Jesus
alert.

Eugene Peterson, *Holy Luck*

When Poetry thus keeps its place, as the handmaid of Piety, it shall
attain, not a poor perishable wreath, but a crown that fadeth not away.

John Wesley, *A Collection of Hymns*
for the Use of the People Called Methodists

Poetry is about the wonder and ways of words—of their sounds and their
sense and their capacity *as words* to make the world meaningful. A poet
delights in the musicality of words, or as the Nobel Prize–winning Irish
poet Seamus Heaney puts it, a poet revels in the "stability conferred by a
musically satisfying order of sounds."[1] In the hands of a poet, a prayer
after Communion is more than a perfunctory affair, transitioning the congregation from one thing to the next. It is a sonorous petition of God to
"grant us strength and courage, to love and serve you, with gladness and
singleness of heart."[2]

---

1. Seamus Heaney, *Opened Ground: Selected Poems 1966–1996* (New York: Farrar, Straus
and Giroux, 1998), 430.
2. This comes from the prayer after the Eucharist in *The Book of Common Prayer* (New
York: Seabury, 1979), Rite II, 365.

A poet retrieves words "from being ground to cliché and turned to pap or propaganda."[3] In the hands of a poet, the cross is more than just about the "power of the blood." It is of course about that, but it is *much more* than that. As Percy Dearmer (1867–1936) and John Mason Neale (1818–1866) translate the sixth-century hymn *Pange, lingua*, by Venantius Fortunatus (AD 530–609), addressing the cross, the blood of Christ is a marvelously rich reality:

Thou alone wast counted worthy
This world's ransom to uphold
For a shipwreck'd race preparing
Harbour, like the Ark of old,
With the sacred Blood anointed
From the smitten Lamb that rolled.[4]

In the hands of a "Negro bard," as John Work describes the supposed author of a popular spiritual in his book *American Negro Songs*, the cross is a cosmic dilemma to the angelic host:

The angels done bowed down
The angels done bowed down
The angels done bowed down
The angels done bowed down

While Jesus was hanging upon the cross,
The angels kept quiet till God went off.
The angels hung their harps on the willow tree,
To give satisfaction till God was pleased. . . .

Go down angels to the flood,
Blow out the sun turn the moon into blood!
Come back angels bolt the door,
Because the time that's been goin' to be no more.[5]

---

3. Marilyn McEntyre, "Why Read a Poem at a Time Like This?," accessed on November 8, 2016, https://medium.com/active-voice/why-read-a-poem-at-a-time-like-this-8b1f 884de94d#.jpxzwvwbc.

4. Cited in *An Annotated Anthology of Hymns*, ed. J. R. Watson (Oxford: Oxford University Press, 2002), 26.

5. John W. Work, *American Negro Songs: 230 Folk Songs and Spirituals, Religious and Secular* (Mineola, NY: Dover Publications, 1998; Crown Publishers, 1940), 24–25.

A poet, like all good artists, tells the truth but tells it slant, as Emily Dickinson famously said it.[6] With its densely woven speech, poetry is suggestive rather than scientific.[7] It works precisely by being ambiguous and allusive. And while poets are "always telling us that grass is green, or thunder loud, or lips red," as C. S. Lewis writes in his essay "The Language of Religion," they are also always telling us that green is more than merely green, thunder more than only loud, lips exceedingly red.[8] This is another way of saying that God's creation is more than "just stuff," empirically classifiable.

It is, as John Calvin would have it, a theater, a spectacle, a mirror of divinity, a painting, and a beautiful fabric that elicits both superlatives and expletives, as the case may be. In the hands of a poet, the morning sun becomes a perfectly particular sun: "a new husband / leaping from his honeymoon bed / The daybreaking sun an athlete / racing to the tape," as Eugene Peterson translates Psalm 19 in *The Message*. "That's how God's Word vaults across the skies," Peterson continues, capturing the psalmist's sense of creation's praise in the light of God's law: "from sunrise to sunset / Melting ice, scorching deserts / warming hearts to faith."

Poetry is not chiefly about the transfer of information. It is instead a kind of language that says more and says it more intensely than does ordinary language, to paraphrase Laurence Perrine's definition.[9] Poetry is also not about the sprucing up of language, as if it were a matter of adding decorative but ultimately unnecessary ornamentation to our words. It is rather a matter of delighting in the very nature of words, in their powers and possibilities.[10] Poetry, finally, is not a mere forerunner to propositional

6. This is the title of one of Emily Dickinson's poems; see https://www.poetryfounda tion.org/poems-and-poets/poems/detail/56824.

7. John Goldingay, *Psalms*, vol. 1, *Psalms 1–41* (Grand Rapids: Baker Academic, 2006), 42: "Prose language majors on clarity; poetic language majors on suggestiveness."

8. C. S. Lewis, *The Seeing Eye and Other Selected Essays from Christian Reflections* (New York: Ballantine Books, 1986), 174.

9. Laurence Perrine, *Literature: Structure, Sound, and Sense*, 5th ed. (New York: Harcourt Brace Jovanovich, 1988), 509, emphasis original.

10. It should be stressed here that I am working with a broad rather than narrow sense of poetry. A broad understanding would include not just Shakespeare, Coleridge, Dickinson, and Angelou, but also the slam poetry of Mayda del Valle, the hip-hop poetry of Lecrae, the haiku poetry of Matsuo Bashō, the free verse poetry of Christina Rossetti, and the narrative poetry of Robert Burns. Cf. John McWhorter, *Doing Our Own Thing: The Degradation of Language and Music and Why We Should, Like, Care* (New York: Gotham, 2003);

or practical speech. It is instead a native language of God and of the people of God.

In biblical perspective, poetry is a mother tongue of the Word Incarnate on whose lips the psalmist's words came naturally. And as the Psalter might have it, it is *through* poetry, not despite it nor beyond it, that faithful worship occurs. For all these reasons the church needs its poets. Poets are "shepherds of words."[11] They teach us to be careful with our words in an often-careless world. They remind us that words are agents of energy and grace. "They take us to the edge of 'what can't be said.'"[12] They help us to feel the truth. They assist us to define reality. And in the case of the church's worship, a good poet aims to make the praise of God faithful in its choice and use of words.

This chapter briefly explores the role that the poetic arts play in the economy of God, followed by an investigation of poetry's singular powers, both in general and in the biblical canon. I then consider the various roles that poetry might play within corporate worship and conclude with an investigation of the formative possibilities of three distinctive hymn texts.

Poetry Theologically Considered

It goes without saying that poetry has not always had an easy lot in the life of the church. While it struggles to survive in contemporary Western culture, poetry especially struggles to find a positive role in corporate worship.[13] "For all that concerns ornaments of speech, similitudes, treasure of eloquence, and such like emptinesses, let it be utterly dismissed." That is how the English philosopher Francis Bacon (1561–1626) felt about poetry. His sentiments are far from rare in Christian circles. In specific Protestant communities there is a resolute, at times obdurate, preference for so-called straightforward, undecorated, discursive speech.

Kevin Coval, Quraysh Ali Lansana, and Nate Marshall, eds., *The BreakBeat Poets: New American Poetry in the Age of Hip-Hop* (Chicago: Haymarket Books, 2015).

11. "Poets are caretakers of language, shepherds of words, protecting them from desecration, exploitation, misuse." Eugene Peterson, *Holy Luck* (Grand Rapids: Eerdmans, 2013), xiv.

12. McEntyre, "Why Read a Poem at a Time Like This?"

13. David Orr names a common apprehension about the term *poetry* itself: "That's because poetry is *poetry*—it supposedly comes to us wrapped in mystery, veiled in shadow, cloaked in doubt, swaddled in . . . well, you get the idea." *Beautiful and Pointless: A Guide to Modern Poetry* (New York: Harper Perennial, 2011), ix–x.

This preference inevitably reflects a predilection for certain texts of Holy Scripture over others—the epistolary over the poetic, for example. This preference also reflects a particularly modern Western relationship to language. Here scientific speech, the language of biologists and engineers, is seen to possess an exclusive capacity to tell us how "the world really is." Information transfer is favored over figurative language. Ideas matter, of course. Doctrine matters. Reasonable and analytic speech matter. But these specific communicative activities do not constitute the sole work of the faithful Christian.

While they are a crucially important to our capacity to speak in discrete, precise fashion about the God and Father of our Lord Jesus Christ, whom the Holy Spirit through the words of Holy Scripture makes real to us, they are not the whole of it. They aptly serve the work of confessional definition, yes. They enable us, yes, to discriminate (in the best sense of that term) between a faithful confession and an unfaithful confession. They belong in this sense to the church's dogmatic work.[14] Yet they also belong to a large constellation of communication media by which God reveals himself to us and by which we communicate to God in response.

That constellation includes not only historical and doctrinal but also devotional and lyrical language. In the context of corporate worship, poetry enables us *by way of poetic language, both spoken and written*, to express our knowledge and love of God faithfully, to perceive our lives and our neighbors' lives truthfully, and to live fruitfully in the world that God so loves. There are a host of ways in which poetry can be enlisted to serve specific liturgical activities and purposes. It is this particular service that our chapter here seeks to explore.

What Is Poetry?

Poetry is a medium of art that we more easily recognize than we are able to define. It is also the case that things are said about poetry that could just

---

14. "*Human language has been incorporated directly into the momentum of God's self-communication* in such a way that it is irreplaceably intrinsic to that momentum. . . . Our speech, no less than any other dimension of our humanity, has, in this speaking person, the Word-made-Word-user [the Incarnate Christ], been purged and renewed, re-forged and re-shaped." Jeremy Begbie, "The Future of Theology amid the Arts: Some Reformed Reflections," in *A Peculiar Orthodoxy: Reflections on Theology and the Arts* (Grand Rapids: Baker Academic, 2018), 205, emphasis original.

as easily be said about music or painting or films. So what are the distinctive characteristics of poetry? How might we describe its singular powers? How might poetry serve the church's worship? And how might poetry open up and close down possibilities for the formation of our humanity within various liturgical contexts?

In an essay for the *New Yorker*, Dan Chiasson writes that poetry gives us "the testimony of the senses, the power of words in new and arresting combinations, and an unwavering belief in what Keats called the 'holiness of the heart's affections.'"[15] In Chiasson's job description for poetry, only one thing can be regarded as unique to poetry: a concern with the power of words. While the senses and the affections are a concern of all the arts, what poetry offers us uniquely is intricately rich communication, "densely woven with complex internal connections, meanings, and implications."[16] More at length, Robert Alter writes "that poetry, working through a system of complex linkages of sound, image, word, rhythm, syntax, theme, idea, is an instrument for conveying densely patterned meanings, and sometimes contradictory meanings, that are not readily conveyable through other kinds of discourse.... Poetry is a way of using language strongly oriented toward the creation of minute, multiple, heterogeneous, and semantically fruitful interconnections in the text."[17]

When the American poet Jeanne Murray Walker argues that poetry can rescue us from "the tyrannical business of everyday language," she captures a peculiar quality of poetry.[18] This idea is similar to what Marilyn McEntyre contends when she says that poetry ought to "purify the dialect of the tribe."[19] Poetry not only enables us to see human language afresh, it also invites us to feel the weight of human language—to attend carefully both to its capacities and to its limits.[20] As Walker sees it, poetry rehabilitates "the big, practical English language."[21]

---

15. Dan Chiasson, "The Poetry I Was Grateful for in 2017," *New Yorker*, December 19, 2017, https://www.newyorker.com/culture/2017-in-review/the-poetry-i-was-grateful-for-in-2017.

16. Robert Alter, *The Art of Biblical Poetry* (New York: Basic Books, 2011), 141.

17. Alter, *The Art of Biblical Poetry*, 113.

18. Jeanne Murray Walker, "On Poets and Poetry," in *The Christian Imagination: The Practice of Faith in Literature and Writing* (Colorado Springs: Shaw Books, 2002), 371.

19. McEntyre, "Why Read a Poem at a Time Like This?"

20. "Preachers need poetry if for no other reason than to be reminded of the palpable weight of language." Kolby Kerry, "Ten Poets Every Pastor Should Read," http://www.leaderworks.org/ten-poets-every-pastor-should-read-part-one/. Accessed January 10, 2017.

21. Walker, "On Poets and Poetry," 375, 377.

One way to get at the essence of poetry is to observe the basic aims of a poet. According to Howard Gardner, the aims of a poet, among others, are to be superlatively sensitive to the shades of meanings of a word;[22] to be superlatively sensitive to the meanings of words in relation to each other; to be superlatively sensitive to the sounds of words and their musical interactions upon one another; and to know the rules of language well enough before she can bend or break them to a satisfying end.[23] For those who have the vocation of a poet, there is a manifest, persistent "love of language and the eagerness to explore its every vein."[24]

The Singular Powers of Poetry

How then might we describe the singular powers of poetry? Perhaps we might suggest the following five powers. Assumed throughout is the basic tool chest of poets: repeated lines, rhyme, meter, voice, assonance, alliteration, imagery, metaphor, and so on. Following this list of powers I offer a brief description of the powers of biblical poetry, so central to distinctively Christian worship.

Poetry Accents the Musical Textures of Human Language

Laurence Perrine writes, "Our love of rhythm and meter is rooted even deeper in us than our love for musical repetition. It is related to the beat of our hearts, the pulse of our blood, the intake and outflow of air from our lungs. Everything that we do naturally and gracefully we do rhythmically."[25] Poets savor, on their tongues and in their ears, the musicality of words.[26] Poets love "hanging around words, listening to what they say," as

---

22. T. S. Eliot felt that the search for just the right word requires "just as much fundamental brainwork as the arrangement of an argument." St. John Perse, *Anabasis* (New York: Harcourt Brace Jovanovich, 1970), preface.

23. Howard Gardner, *Frames of Mind: The Theory of Multiple Intelligences* (New York: Basic Books, 2011), 80.

24. Gardner, *Frames of Mind*, 81.

25. Laurence Perrine and Thomas R. Arp, *Sound and Sense: An Introduction to Poetry* (New York: Harcourt College Publishers, 1991), 148.

26. Malcolm Guite, *Faith, Hope and Poetry: Theology and the Poetic Imagination* (Surrey: Ashgate, 2010), 26.

W. H. Auden once remarked.[27] "Lord of all being, throned afar / thy glory flames from sun and star / centre and soul of every sphere / yet to each loving heart how near!" (Oliver Wendell Holmes, "God of All Being, Throned Afar").[28] "Ol' Satan's got a slippery ol' shoe / And if you don't mind he will slip it on you / Ol' Satan's like a snake in the grass / Waitin' to bit you as you pass" (nineteenth-century spiritual).[29]

Stephen Spender explains this aspect of his work as a poet this way: "when I am writing, the music of the words I am trying to shape takes me far beyond the words, I am aware of a rhythm, a dance, a fury, which is as yet empty of words."[30] For the Christian the invitation is to taste and to savor, like actual honey, the words of the Word. Psalm 119:103: "How sweet are Your words to my taste! / *Yes, sweeter* than honey to my mouth!" (NASB; cf. Ps. 19:10). The 1662 Book of Common Prayer, in its collect prayer for the second Sunday in Advent, enjoins the Christian to embrace the words of Holy Scripture this way: "Help us so to hear them, to read, mark, learn and inwardly digest them."[31] However else poetry exercises power over us it is a power that is exercised on our musical ear. Malcolm Guite: "We have to let words *be* music, and in that music to let them play counter-melodies to one another."[32]

Morning has broken
Like the first morning;
Blackbird has spoken
Like the first bird.
Praise for the singing!
Praise for the morning!
Praise for them, springing,
Fresh from the Word! (Eleanor Farjeon, 1931)

---

27. Cited in Gardner, *Frames of Mind*, 80.

28. For the full text of this hymn, see https://hymnary.org/text/lord_of_all_being _throned_afar.

29. Work, *American Negro Songs*, 23.

30. Stephen Spender, "The Making of a Poem," in *The Creative Process: Reflections on the Invention in the Arts and Sciences*, ed. Brewster Ghiselin (Berkeley: University of California Press, 1985), 125.

31. *The Book of Common Prayer: 1662 Version* (London: Everyman's Library, 1999), 110.

32. Guite, *Faith, Hope and Poetry*, 27.

Poetry Brings Us into Linguistically Metaphor-Rich,
Image-Rich Territory

Poets use words to say, "The world is like this image, juxtaposed to that past thing, as it intersects this present reality, in this particular metaphor."[33] Poetry in this way gives voice to the multilayered nature of reality. As Charles Wesley sees it in his hymn "Glory Be to God on High":

> See the eternal Son of God
> A mortal son of man,
> Now dwelling in an earthly clod
> Whom heaven cannot contain!
> Stand amazed, ye heavens, look at this!
> See the Lord of earth and skies
> Low humbled to the dust he is
> And in a manger lies!

A good poet is a student of how things are connected to each other. Amy Lowell describes the work of a poet this way: "No subject is alien to him, and the profounder his knowledge in any direction, the more depth will there be to his poetry."[34] A poet draws attention to the linkages that constitute human experience. In his poem "Prayer (1)," George Herbert captures the multifaceted nature of prayer.[35]

> Prayer the church's banquet, angel's age,
> > God's breath in man returning to his birth,
> > The soul in paraphrase, heart in pilgrimage,
> The Christian plummet sounding heav'n and earth
> Engine against th' Almighty, sinner's tow'r,
> > Reversed thunder, Christ-side-piercing spear,
> > The six-days world transposing in an hour,
> A kind of tune, which all things hear and fear;
> Softness, and peace, and joy, and love, and bliss,

---

33. Guite, *Faith, Hope and Poetry*, 28.

34. Amy Lowell, "The Process of Making Poetry," in Ghiselin, *The Creative Process*, 112.

35. *George Herbert: The Complete English Works*, ed. Ann Pasternak Slater (New York: Alfred A. Knopf, 1995), 49.

Exalted manna, gladness of the best,
Heaven in ordinary, man well drest,
The milky way, the bird of Paradise,
Church-bells beyond the stars heard, the soul's blood,
The land of spices; something understood.

Poetry Helps Us to Re-see the Particularity of Things

Good poets, like all good artists, are interested in the concrete over the abstract, the particular over the generic. This is not just out of a conviction that the universal is discovered by way of the particular. It is also out of a love for the details of life. A poet believes that it is the details that constitute unique identity. The poet Andrew Rumsey writes, "Poets are driven—albeit in many different ways—by the desire to *really* see what is before them, to *attend* to particulars in all their uniqueness and diversity."[36] The English poet Gerard Manley Hopkins captures this desire of poets in his 1877 poem "As Kingfishers Catch Fire."

Each mortal thing does one thing and the same:
Deals out that being indoors each one dwells;
Selves—goes its self; *myself* it speaks and spells,
Crying *What I do* is *me: for that I came.*[37]

For the Christian, the mystery of existence is not that everything is the same but "that everything is what it is and not another thing."[38] The calling of the believer poet, accordingly, to borrow the language of the essayist Cynthia Ozick, is "to distinguish one life from another; to illuminate diversity; to light up the least grain of being, to show how it is concretely individual, particularized from any other; to tell, in all the marvel of its singularity, the separate holiness of the least grain."[39] Malcolm Guite, in

36. Andrew Rumsey, "Through Poetry: Particularity and the Call to Attention," in *Beholding the Glory: Incarnation through the Arts*, ed. Jeremy S. Begbie (Grand Rapids: Baker Academic, 2001), 51, emphasis original.

37. "As Kingfishers Catch Fire," in Gerard Manley Hopkins, *Poetry and Prose* (London: Penguin Classics, 1953), 51.

38. Colin Gunton, *The One, the Three and the Many: God, Creation and the Culture of Modernity* (Cambridge: Cambridge University Press, 1993), 206.

39. Cynthia Ozick, *Art and Ardor* (New York: Alfred A. Knopf, 1983), 248.

his sonnet "O Rex Gentium," helps us to see—*really* see—something particular about Christ as King.

> O King of our desire whom we despise,
> King of the nations never on the throne,
> Unfound foundation, cast-off cornerstone,
> Rejected joiner, making many one,
> You have no form or beauty for our eyes,
> A King who comes to give away his crown,
> A King within our rags of flesh and bone.
> We pierce the flesh that pierces our disguise,
> For we ourselves are found in you alone.
> Come to us now and find in us your throne,
> O King within the child within the clay,
> O hidden King who shapes us in the play
> Of all creation. Shape us for the day
> Your coming Kingdom comes into its own.[40]

Poetry Invites Us to Slow Down as a Way to Pay Careful Attention

We cannot speed-read a poem. Poetry forces us to slow down. This characteristic of poetry is directly related to that thing that both frustrates and repels the would-be reader. Poetry refuses to behave like prose, which most of us prefer because we (think we) know what to do with it. As Eugene Peterson reminds us:

> A poem requires re-reading. Unlike prose which fills the page with print, poems leave a lot of white space. . . . We sit before the poem like we sit before a flower and attend to form, relationship, color. We let it begin to work on us. When we are reading prose we are often in control, but in a poem we feel like we are out of control. . . . In prose we are after something, getting information, acquiring knowledge. . . . But in poetry we take a different stance. We are prepared to be puzzled, to go back, to wait, to ponder, to listen.[41]

40. Malcolm Guite, *Sounding the Seasons: Seventy Sonnets for the Christian Year* (Norwich: Canterbury Press, 2012), 12.

41. Eugene H. Peterson, "Novelists, Pastors, and Poets," in *Subversive Spirituality* (Grand Rapids: Eerdmans, 1997), 180.

"This attending, this waiting, this reverential posture," Peterson continues, "is at the core of the life of faith, the life of prayer, the life of worship, the life of witness."[42] It is not tangential to worship, nor is it peripheral to our knowledge of God. When poets slow us down, when they ask us to read it again and again and again, they are reminding us of a fundamental virtue of faithful worship. Faithful worship is not like a grocery list—something to get through as efficiently as possible. Nor is faithful worship only a matter of reciting right ideas about God. Faithful worship is, in the end, an invitation to contemplate God: to adore, to attend, to linger, and to live our lives in light of this wonder-filled encounter. Poetry cultivates this liturgical virtue.

Poetry Brings to Our Awareness the
"More than Just" Quality of Things

The scientist and philosopher Michael Polanyi famously said that we know more than we can tell. In this he draws our attention to the obvious: namely, that our knowledge of God and of the world involves more than just conscious intellectual knowledge; it involves intuitive, emotional, subconscious, kinesthetic knowledge. "The world, though, is also so much more," as Derek Mahon's poem "Tractatus" says it.[43] Malcolm Guite, in his book *Faith, Hope and Poetry*, writes, "To hear snatches from the huge unknowable symphony of experience, to catch them and transpose them to a key that resonates with our understanding, so that at some point they harmonise with that unheard melody from heaven we are always trying to hear—that is the purpose of poetry."[44]

If we were to read about the "heavens" from a science magazine, we would discover important properties about cumulus clouds, air currents, solar patterns, moon phases, and so on. But we would not learn all that there is to learn, as human beings actually experience the God-shaped heavens. Poets tell us about the "more than just" nature of the atmosphere above our heads. Eugene Peterson translates Psalm 19:1–4, 6 in *The Message* this way:

God's glory is on tour in the skies,
    God-craft on exhibit across the horizon.

---

42. Peterson, "Novelists, Pastors, and Poets," 180–81.
43. Polanyi and Mahon are both cited in Guite, *Faith, Hope and Poetry*, 6.
44. Guite, *Faith, Hope and Poetry*, 23.

Madame Day holds classes every morning,
    Professor Night lectures each evening.
Their words aren't heard,
    their voices aren't recorded,
But their silence fills the earth:
    unspoken truth is spoken everywhere. . . .
    warming hearts to faith.

To say that poetry offers us a taste of the multilayered, "more than just" quality of things is to say that it invites us to embrace ambiguity as a good in the kingdom of God. Guite explains ambiguity this way: "we are entering a realm where only multiple meanings will do if we are at last to find 'something understood.'"[45] Ambiguity is not to be confused with vague, anything-goes speech. Ambiguity does not stand in contrast to our capacity to speak positively and precisely about the Triune God. It does stand against the reductionisms of rationalism and scientism and propositionalism. Properly understood, ambiguity belongs to the mystery of creaturely existence as it is lived under the sovereign care of God. It belongs to the kind of speech that marks faithful worship, where the Christian stands in wonder before the transcendence of the Holy Trinity.

O mystery of love Divine
That thought and thanks o'erpowers!
Lord Jesus, was our portion Thine,
And is Thy portion ours?[46]

On the Singular Powers of Biblical Poetry

Because of the central place that biblical poetry plays in Christian worship, it may be useful to offer a brief comment about its own singular powers. A first characteristic of biblical poetry is its terseness. Things are said in the most economic way possible; it is not a flowery or rhapsodic style of poetry. Additional characteristics include ellipsis (the omission of a word within a poetic or grammatical unit where it would otherwise be expected, such

45. Guite, *Faith, Hope and Poetry*, 29.
46. This is the first stanza to the hymn "O Mystery of Love Divine" by Thomas Gill, written in 1864, https://hymnary.org/text/o_mystery_of_love_divine.

as we find in Ps. 114:4); the use of strophe and stanza (Pss. 13; 19); the use of refrain (Pss. 67; 80); the use of acrostic (Ps. 119; Prov. 31:10–31; Lam. 1–4); an interest in the sound of words, such as rhyme or paronomasia (Judg. 3:8, 10), alliteration (Ps. 127:1), and assonance (Ps. 102:6); and a richer use of imagery and metaphor (John 10) than is employed in prose or legal passage.

The most recognizable mark of biblical poetry is parallelism. Parallelism describes the practice whereby words in the second unit or line correspond in some way to those in the first unit or line. For some scholars, this is *the* distinguishing mark of Hebrew poetry. Various types of parallelism include synonymous (Ps. 77:11), antithetic (Ps. 30:5), synthetic (a heightening or specifying of first line; Ps. 96:6), grammatical, or lexical (Pss. 33:8; 6:5). It is never *mere* repetition, of course. It is more of an echo or expansion of one line in relation to another line. What results is a dense sentiment. The eighteenth-century Hebrew scholar Johann Herder remarks, "The heart is never exhausted, it has forever something new to say."[47] This is the concrete effect of parallelism. Through the device of reiteration, the heart is given an opportunity to sink itself in the reality announced by poetry.

Typical examples of parallelism in the Psalter include (from the NRSV):

1. Ps. 24:7: "Lift up your heads, O gates! / and be lifted up, O ancient doors!"
2. Ps. 77:16: "When the waters saw you, O God / when the waters saw you, they were afraid; / the very deep trembled."
3. Ps. 33:2: "Praise the LORD with the lyre; / make melody to him with the harp of ten strings."

Specific Purposes of Poetry in Worship

With these singular powers of poetry in mind, in what ways might poetry serve the activities of corporate worship?

The first, and perhaps most pervasive, service of poetry is to the songs we sing. The way in which Eugene Peterson translates Psalm 19 in *The Message* calls to mind one of my favorite Christmas poems, written by

---

47. See E. C. Lucas, "Terminology of Poetry," in *Dictionary of the Old Testament: Wisdom, Poetry and Writings*, ed. Tremper Longman III and Peter Enns (Downers Grove, IL: IVP Academic, 2008), 520–25.

Phillips Brooks. Born in 1836 in Massachusetts, the Harvard-educated pastor of Trinity Church is perhaps best known for two things. He wrote and delivered the funeral oration for Abraham Lincoln in 1865, and in 1891 he published a poem that he titled "O Little Town of Bethlehem." But it is an unpublished poem that deserves, to my mind, special appreciation for its Tennysonian, psalmic language. The first two verses go like this:

> The silent skies are full of speech
> For who hath ears to hear;
> The winds are whispering each to each,
> The moon is calling to the beach,
> And stars their sacred wisdom teach
> Of faith and love and fear.

> But once the sky the silence broke,
> And song o'erflowed the earth;
> The midnight air with glory shook,
> And angels mortal language spoke,
> When God our human nature took,
> In Christ the Saviour's birth.[48]

A good poem, as Brooks's song might illustrate, does double duty. In addition to its fundamental task to facilitate the praise of God, a good poem both delights and instructs. It arouses the affections, and it teaches theology. Most Christians' primary exposure to theology will occur through the songs they sing. The Dutch theologian Albert van den Heuvel commented in 1966 at the World Council of Churches, "It is the hymns, repeated over and over again, which form the container of much of our faith. They are probably in our age the only confessional documents, which we learn by heart. As such, they have taken the place of our catechisms."[49]

In certain cases, as the Anglican pastor George Herbert knew firsthand, "a verse may finde him, who a sermon flies / And turn delight

---

48. Cf. Andrew Gant, *The Carols of Christmas: A Celebration of the Surprising Stories Behind Your Favorite Holiday Songs* (Nashville: Thomas Nelson, 2015), 38–40.

49. Cited in C. Michael Hawn, ed., *New Songs of Celebration Render: Congregational Song in the Twenty-First Century* (Chicago: GIA Publications, 2013), xxvi.

into a sacrifice." This is why thoughtful, well-crafted poetry matters to the songs we sing in public worship.[50] Phillips Brooks gets the birth narrative of Christ right, while plenty of our popular carols get them wrong as often as not because of what they ignore about the intertextual, theologically dense nature of the Matthean and Lukan accounts of Christ's birth.

As I explore more thoroughly in the final section of this chapter, the lyrical content of our songs exercises an inordinate power to form our ideas of God and of the Christian life. Hymns may be "the poor man's poetry," but they are also "the ordinary man's theology."[51] Or as the New Testament scholar Gordon Fee often told his own students, "Let me hear you pray, let me hear you sing, and I will write your theology." Just so.

A second service of poetry to public worship can occur in the "call to worship." One exemplary instance of this is found in the call to worship that *The Covenant Book of Worship* uses during the season of Advent. The language is sharp, vivid, and memorable. The "call" employs active verbs and metaphors drawn from the biblical story. In its use of a call-and-response pattern, it mirrors the call-and-response rhythm so typical of poetry in the prophetic literature of the Bible.

Call: The news is still fresh! The messenger is coming! He will bring with him the covenant in which we delight. The valley shall be filled, mountains and hills leveled; what is crooked shall be straightened up and rough places made smooth.

Response: Our mouths are filled with laughter; with our tongues we shout for you. You have done great things for us, O God. We come before you with gladness and rejoicing.

Call: Watch! Wait! The day of God is at hand!

Response: Like the bud on a tree, God's promises are about to blossom!

50. It bears mentioning that for certain nondenominational congregations, the use of carefully scripted poetry as song lyrics will represent the one exception that worship leaders and musicians will make to the normative preference for extemporaneous, and therefore "authentic," speech. I have Lester Ruth to thank for this observation.

51. Donald Hustad, *Jubilate! Church Music in the Evangelical Tradition* (Carol Stream, IL: Hope Publishing, 1981), 243.

Call: Stay awake! The reign of God is very near.

Response: We are here, watching and waiting with hope.

All: May God bring justice to all people on this day. May God's reign come on earth as in heaven.[52]

While this second example is not a proper call to worship, the "Invitation to the Table," which *The Covenant Book of Worship* employs as a call to the celebration of the Lord's Supper, recommends itself to us for its use of poetry characteristic of African-American worship contexts. Though the language will find a more natural home within these contexts, the poetry could become a way for other liturgical contexts to feel afresh the invitation to partake of Communion.

Call: We're gonna sit at the welcome table!

Response: We're gonna sit at the welcome table one of these days! Hallelujah!

Call: All kinds of people around that table one of these days! Hallelujah!

Response: All kinds of people round that table gonna sit at the welcome table one of these days.[53]

A third service to the liturgy is in prayers, whether offered ad hoc or in pre-scripted fashion. Two examples are offered here: one from Thomas Cranmer and one from a spiritual.

A COLLECT FOR THE 24TH SUNDAY AFTER TRINITY

Lord, we beseech thee, absolve thy people from their offenses, that through thy bountiful goodness we may be delivered from the bands of all those sins, which by our frailty we have committed. Grant this, we ask, through our Lord Jesus Christ.

---

52. *The Covenant Book of Worship* (Chicago: Covenant Publications, 2003), 60.
53. *The Covenant Book of Worship*, 59.

GOD IS YOUR COMFORTER
(Based on Isaiah 40:1–11 and the Negro Spiritual "Over My Head")

One: God says, "I am here for mothers bound in slavery and pain;
    I am here for fathers stripped of dignity and duty;
    I am here for children imprisoned and pressed down from birth."
    God is your comforter.

Many: Over my head, I see trouble in the air
    There must be a God somewhere.

One: We gather in need of an encouraging and witnessing word.
    God says, speaks, shouts:
    "I am eternal!"

Many: Over my head, I see music in the air
    There must be a God somewhere.

One: "Bruised and beaten worshippers, your slavery from sin and shame
       is gone."
    Today, right now, invite God among us.
    Tell God to come, come, come.
    Come among us, O Lord,
    come among the disgusted, downed, and discriminated people,
    so we may be encouraged and blessed.
    Come comforter, come!

Many: Over my head, I see glory in the air
    Over my head, I see glory in the air
    Over my head, I see glory in the air
    There must be a God somewhere.

A fourth way in which poetry might service corporate worship is in the reading of the Psalter. Many Christians may be surprised to hear that 30 percent of the Bible comes to us in poetic form. Through poetic speech God reveals something to the world, so it seems, that could not be revealed any other way. Poetic speech likewise enables the human creature to say things to God and about God that it could not otherwise say. It is not insignificant that very early on, the church regarded the Psalter as its official devotional book. It has done so for many reasons, not least of which is the prominent place that the psalms played in the life of Jesus and the apostles, appearing no less than 196 times in the New Testament. In the context of the Gospels, Jesus quotes the Psalter more than any other book of Israel's Bible. When Jesus faces trouble in the Gospels, he inevitably summons the language of the psalms.

When challenged by the teachers of law for his actions in the temple, in Matthew 21:12–17, Jesus responds by quoting Psalm 8:2. When the chief priests question his authority, Jesus appeals to Psalm 118. In conversation with the Pharisees in Matthew 22:41–45, Jesus cites Psalm 110 as evidence of his Davidic vocation. Predicting his betrayal at the hand of one of his disciples, in John 13:18 Jesus quotes Psalm 41:9. A little later he appeals to Psalm 35:19 and Psalm 64:4 to show how his ministry is the fulfillment of the law. On the cross, he gives voice to his terrible pain by uttering the words of Psalm 22:1. After walking the road to Emmaus with two disciples, Jesus opens their eyes by way of exposition of the things concerning himself "in the Law of Moses, in the prophets, and in the psalms" (Luke 24:44 KJV).[54]

For Jesus, then, the psalms frame both his life and his ministry, his relationship to God and to others, because he has internalized their words through a lifelong habit of prayer. It is a habit that the church would do well to emulate in its use of the psalms if it wishes to be formed in the life of Jesus. It can do so by the weekly reading of a psalm, the preaching of the psalms, the praying of the psalms, and the singing of the psalms.

A fifth way for poetry to serve worship is in sermons. This can take two forms: (1) the preaching of poetic texts, not just in the Wisdom literature but also in the Prophetic literature; and (2) enlisting poetry in sermons in general. For some, the sermons of preachers like Frederick Buechner, Barbara Brown Taylor, Walter Brueggemann, Aimee Semple McPherson, George Herbert, and the early church fathers may readily come to mind. But it is in the sermon practices of African-American preachers that poetry more readily finds a home. As Kenyatta R. Gilbert

---

54. Following Christ's ascension, when the church has gathered to wait for Pentecost, the disciples choose a replacement for Judas by appeal to Psalms 69 and 109. When the Spirit descends on these same disciples, the first Spirit-anointed sermon Peter preaches to the crowds is an exegesis of two psalms (Acts 2:25–35). And when the early church regularly gathered for worship, they were to speak to one another with psalms, as Saint Paul enjoined them in his letter to the saints of Ephesus (Eph. 5:19).

summarizes, "African American prophetic preaching is not only concrete and particular speech but is also daringly poetic. . . . These preachers are creative poets who possess the 'will to adorn.' . . . Instead of singular reliance on expository prose, the preacher-poet communicates in signs and symbols that 'extend the spatial and temporal boundaries of prose' to multiply the dimensions through which a listener may encounter God in the preached Word."[55]

A sixth service of poetry to the liturgy is through "special" performances of poetry. This might include what the pastor, poet, and theologian Malcolm Guite once did at his home church in Cambridge, St. Edwards, namely, to write a series of sonnets inspired by the church calendar and to read them in worship. The final result of that experience was a published book, *Sounding the Seasons: Seventy Sonnets for the Christian Year*. Or it could include instances of spoken word, as poets like Trip Lee or Amena Brown might show us.

A final way for poetry to enhance the worship of God's people is in the benediction. While many congregations do not end their corporate gathering with a benediction, plenty do. Some will give the benediction extemporaneously. Others will adopt benedictions taken from the Bible, such as this one: "The Peace of God, which passeth all understanding, keep your hearts and minds in the knowledge and love of God, and of his Son Jesus Christ our Lord: And the Blessing of God Almighty, the Father, the Son, and the Holy Ghost, be amongst you, and remain with you always. Amen."[56]

Still others will write original benedictions that then become part of the church's tradition. One of my favorite benedictions is taken from the Kenyan Book of Common Prayer. Imagine a straightforward blessing. Now imagine this blessing, where the people accompany the first three responses with a sweep of the arm toward the cross behind the Holy Table, and their final response with a sweep toward heaven.

Minister: All our problems

People: We send to the cross of Christ

55. Kenyatta R. Gilbert, "Making the Unseen Seen: Pedagogy and Aesthetics in African American Prophetic Preaching," in *Readings in African American Church Music and Worship*, vol. 2, ed. James Abbington (Chicago: GIA Publications, 2014), 297–98.

56. *The 1929 Book of Common Prayer*, "The Order for Holy Communion," http://www.episcopalnet.org/1928bcp/communion.html. Accessed December 18, 2018.

Minister: All our difficulties

People: We send to the cross of Christ

Minister: All the devil's works

People: We send to the cross of Christ

Minister: All our hopes

People: We set on the risen Christ

Minister: Christ the Sun of righteousness shine upon you and scatter the darkness from before your path: and the blessing of God Almighty, Father, Son and Holy Spirit, be among you, and remain with you always. Amen.[57]

If I experienced this benediction weekly, I can imagine myself thoroughgoingly blessed!

On the Formative Possibilities of Poetry in Worship

Because of the considerable amount of space that our practices of corporate worship devote to singing, it is reasonable to focus our investigation of the formative powers of poetry in the songs we sing. I focus here on three songs: (1) "Oceans (Where Feet May Fail)," by Hillsong United (2013); (2) "In Christ Alone," by Keith Getty and Stuart Townend (2002); and (3) "'Tis the Old Ship of Zion," a nineteenth-century spiritual. By no means are these songs comprehensive. They are only representative and suggestive. With each I ask what they open up and what they close down for the formation of our humanity in public worship.

A first observation about the poetry of "Oceans" relates to the interplay between a motif of Saint Peter on the water and the image of John the Beloved. The former suggests the power of God; the latter points to

---

57. "The Kenyan Rite: A Eucharistic Service from the Anglican Church of Kenya," *Reformed Worship* 127 (March 2018), https://www.reformedworship.org/article/march-2018/kenyan-rite. Accessed December 18, 2018.

the experience of intimacy. While the former captures a sense that God is able and willing to do the impossible in our lives, the latter, in the piling on of imagery in the text, seeks to stimulate desire for the Divine Lover, affectively familiar to us in Christ Jesus. The line "My soul will rest in Your embrace / For I am Yours and You are mine" is language that one might just as easily find in Catholic mystical writings that promote an intensely sensory encounter with God.[58] When matched to a pattern of swelling sounds, itself mimicking the swell of ocean waters, the poem invites the singer to a leisurely, immersive contemplation of Christ, in the rise and fall, push and pull of desire for God that often characterizes our spiritual lives.

Ultimately such an encounter is a "mystery." "Mystery" and "oceans deep" are metaphorically linked in the text, the latter image concretizing the former and investing the idea of mystery with a physical reality that enables a charismatic Christian to name an encounter with Jesus. This is what the poetry of "Oceans" opens up formatively. If the element of intimacy in poetry is used exclusively, however, problems may result. God may be perceived as an object of love that can be fully possessed. The idea of the church as the bride of Christ—that is, the whole community as the bride, rather than only the individual—may be missed.[59] And a narrow conception of love for God may occur. Jenell Williams Paris argues that romantic worship songs should be conserved but that the church should remember that love is more than this. "Love is also about commitment, hard work, change over time, and, at times, confusion and doubt."[60]

Whereas the poetry of "Oceans" invites the singer to a raptured affection for God, "In Christ Alone" takes the pilgrimage motif and invites the singer to immerse himself in the "whole" story of salvation. Here we have Saint Peter matched not to Saint John but to Saint Paul. Here we have the birth of Christ and the resurrection of Christ. Here

---

58. For lyrics to the whole song, see "Oceans (Where Feet May Fail)" (Words and Music by Matt Crocker, Joel Houston & Salomon Lightelm), https://hillsong.com/lyrics/oceans-where-feet-may-fail/.

59. This is a point Keith Drury points out in his essay "*I'm Desperate for You*: Male Perception of Romantic Lyrics in Contemporary Worship Music," in *The Message in the Music: Studying Contemporary Praise and Worship*, ed. Robert Woods and Brian Walrath (Nashville: Abingdon, 2007), 63.

60. Jenell Williams Paris, "'I Could Sing of Your Love Forever': American Romance in Contemporary Worship Music," in *The Message in the Music*, 52.

we have the gift of righteousness and a divine wrath that is satisfied by the cross at Golgotha. Here guilt is removed, death robbed of its sting, and life lived in confidence that no power of hell or scheme on earth can rob the Christian of the irresistible love of God. Because the poem is tied to a melodic form that resembles an Irish ballad, characteristically simple and accessible, it makes possible a broadly communal embrace of the hymn. In grateful response to the salvific work of Christ, the Christian finds herself, one imagines, humming the infectious melody all throughout the week.

In Getty and Townend's poem, a piling on of imagery occurs in verse 1 that is grounded in a narration of Christ's work. While the poem seeks to carry the Christian from beginning to end, from earth to heaven, inviting one to feel caught up in the glory of the "gospel story," it also risks a hurried march through a dense field of ideas. This is perhaps typical of a certain Reformed sensibility. Very little breathing room is created for the singer to linger on any one idea. Instead of making, for instance, the final refrain in each verse the same, as a way to make possible an experience of affective intensification, four different refrains are offered. Only one reference to God appears in the poem, and the Holy Spirit remains an absentee person to the "whole" story. These are things that "In Christ Alone" opens up and closes down.

With a spiritual like "'Tis the Old Ship of Zion," our notions of "proper" poetry get questioned. In this particular song the verses follow a call-and-response pattern. The leader sings: "Ain't no danger in de water / Ain't no danger in de water / Ain't no danger in de water." The people sing: "Git on board, git on board." Subsequent verses remind the singer that the "old ship" was good "for my dear mother" and "my dear father." If it was good for them, it will be good presumably for us today, too. For those of us who have taken swim lessons as a child, "the water" holds the promise of joy and recreation. But this is not true for all. As Luke Powery remarks in his book *Rise Up, Shepherd! Advent Reflections on the Spirituals*, slaves were thrown overboard from slave ships and left to drown in the seas during the Middle Passage. "Water became a natural grave."[61] To sing "git on board, git on board," then, is a way to identify with the plight of black Christians, with the powerless and the helpless.

But it is not "get"—it is "*git*." The editors of the hymnal *Songs of Zion*

---

61. Luke Powery, *Rise Up, Shepherd! Advent Reflections on the Spirituals* (Louisville: Westminster John Knox, 2017), 7.

instruct singers not to change the dialect "into correct English" because it "would *destroy* the intent of the composition."[62] Typical of the spiritual, simple stories are prioritized over abstract ideas. And like the exegetical practices of the patristic era, the stories of the Bible are read in typological manner. The singer imagines herself on that "old ship," *both* the slave ship *and* the ship of Zion; and in doing so, she *feels* equally the danger and the good news. And the call-and-response lyric promotes dialogical rather than monological speech. The strengths in a spiritual like this are perhaps mirrored by its weaknesses: for instance, a micro-story that may drift far afield from the larger story of Scripture or a *feel* for the "old ship" that remains theologically ungrounded and therefore idiosyncratic or emotionalistic only.

The poetry, in each case above, matters to the theology. It matters to how Christians are formed in worship—to how they know and love God. I tell my students that liturgical poetry is a way to access the heart of a people. When we put on our lips the words of a sixteenth-century or twenty-first-century poet, whether common or complex, foreign or familiar, we also access by grace the heart of God.

Conclusion

At its best, good poetry, like all good art, can make the familiar strange and the strange familiar; or as the American Wallace Stevens put it, in the presence of good poetry we find ourselves "more truly and more strange." But it bears repeating that all poetry is contextually meaningful. Its capacity to form a congregation at worship is directly related to how it is practiced in a particular context, the purposes to which it is employed, and how well it is understood by those who make use of the poetry. Every choice of language that we use about God opens up and closes down a way to know God.

Lots of majesty/solemnity language, for instance, may underscore a certain image of God as otherly, distant king; lots of intimacy/touch language may reinforce a sense of God as a romantic object or a divine pal like any other pal. Care is always needed. A wise worship leader will encourage a thoughtful engagement with language in general and with poetry

---

62. In J. Jefferson Cleveland and Verolga Nix, eds., *Songs of Zion* (Nashville: Abingdon, 1981), xvi, emphasis original.

in particular.[63] A wise poet will likewise choose to use language in charitable service of the people of God. Whether accessible or difficult, simple or complex, poetry, at its best, becomes a means to disciple a congregation, enabling them to say to God and to one another the good "words of eternal life" (John 6:68).

63. Helpful resources on this account include Debra Rienstra and Ron Rienstra, *Worship Words: Discipling Language for Faithful Ministry* (Grand Rapids: Baker Academic, 2009); John W. Cooper, *Our Father in Heaven: Christian Faith and Inclusive Language for God* (Grand Rapids: Baker Academic, 1998); and Ruth C. Duck, *Finding Words for Worship: A Guide for Leaders* (Louisville: Westminster John Knox, 1995).

Phaedra Taylor, *Untitled* (2019) (Photograph by author)

CHAPTER 7

Worship and the Narrative Arts

Scriptures provide the "narrative home" for the church. The church literally lives within the biblical narrative, whether it wants to or not! This is not our decision, but God's.

John W. Wright, Telling God's Story

Story isn't a flight from reality, but a vehicle that carries us on our search for reality.

Robert McKee, Story

We tell ourselves stories in order to live.

Joan Didion, The White Album

In the account of Luke 10:25–37, a lawyer approaches Jesus with a question: "Rabbi, what must I do to inherit eternal life?" Jesus answers his question with a question of his own: "What is written in the Law? How do you read it?" The lawyer answers by restating the twin commandment to love God and neighbor alike. Jesus affirms the lawyer's answer and tells him to live in light of it. But the lawyer remains unsatisfied. He persists: "But *who* is my neighbor?" At this point in the exchange the modern reader might expect a straightforward answer: your neighbor is X. But Jesus answers this second question with a story, and in doing so he offers the lawyer an opportunity to enter into true neighborliness *from the inside*.

If the philosopher Blaise Pascal is right in saying that the heart has reasons of which reason knows nothing, then Jesus cleverly addresses the lawyer's heart, his affective center, the seat of desire, by way of a narrative.[1]

---

1. Granted, the "heart," in the biblical register, is not simply to be equated with the emotions; it includes mental, volitional, and moral activities. But for biblical authors the heart certainly includes and in some cases revolves around emotional activities. For a careful

On this point James K. A. Smith writes, "It is stories that train and prime our emotions, which in turn condition our perception and hence our action."[2] A good story can retune the heart to the truth, make it possible to gain a feel for reality, and, as Susan Sontag puts it, "educate our capacity for moral judgment."[3] A good story enlarges and complicates our sympathies. It can show us another's pain in a way that we begin to feel it for ourselves. A good story reflects and shapes our deepest wants.

Storytelling in Jesus's ministry, then, functions as a primary vehicle for the re-formation of the heart. In telling his story, Jesus graciously draws his listeners into a narrative that subverts prevailing assumptions about a faithful life. He does so by pulling the lawyer affectively into a plot. The plot, in turn, involves an "aha" moment where the lawyer sees the answer vicariously but really. The lawyer not only *sees* the truth, as it is played out in Jesus's narrative, he also *feels* true neighborliness, as it is exhibited in the Samaritan protagonist. A twist occurs in the story, and the lawyer finds himself implicated in a role that he might never have imagined for himself: playing the "bad guy" instead of the "good guy."

With Jesus, the unimaginable becomes imaginable. But the point of the story is less about Jew versus Samaritan or even about human beings as such. It is about *God*. The story redirects the attention of the lawyer, and of the crowd listening in on the exchange, to the kind of mercy that describes the character of Yahweh. Jesus tells a story so that through this particular parable his hearers might acquire a feel for the things of God's kingdom, even as they feel *with* the Samaritan and *for* the stranger. "The story does what no theorem can quite do," writes C. S. Lewis. "It may not be 'like real life' in the superficial sense: but it sets before us an image of what reality may well be like at some more central region."[4]

This is a fundamental characteristic of story: to show us reality. In Jesus's story it is the reality of true neighborliness. Jesus tells the lawyer who

exposition of the relation between art and emotion, see Jeremy S. Begbie, "Faithful Feelings: Music and Emotion in Worship," in *Resonant Witness: Conversations between Music and Theology*, ed. Jeremy S. Begbie and Steven R. Guthrie (Grand Rapids: Eerdmans, 2011), 323–54.

2. James K. A. Smith, *Imagining the Kingdom: How Worship Works* (Grand Rapids: Baker Academic, 2013), 38. Cf. Iain McGilchrist, *The Master and His Emissary: The Divided Brain and the Making of the Western World* (New Haven: Yale University Press, 2009), 88.

3. Susan Sontag, "At the Same Time: The Novelist and Moral Reasoning," in *At the Same Time: Essays and Speeches*, ed. Paolo Dilonardo and Anne Jump (New York: Farrar, Straus and Giroux, 2007), 213.

4. C. S. Lewis, "On Stories," in *Of Other Worlds: Essays and Stories* (London: Geoffrey Bles, 1966), 15.

his neighbor is by *showing* him a narrated mercy. Stories in this way define reality; or as a proverb of the Hopi tribe says it, "Those who tell stories rule the world." Advertising agencies know this to be true—as do newspapers, victors of war, and the film industry. Families also have a story that inevitably governs their sense of reality. Not merely showing or defining, however, stories also constitute who we are as human beings. The sociologist Christian Smith says, "we not only continue to be animals who make stories but also animals who are *made* by our stories."[5]

Too often, especially for Protestant Christians, the biblical narratives are hastily turned into moral imperatives or abstract ideas. Tales become doctrine, parables are reduced to how-tos, and the story is plumbed for the kernel of truth, the "real point" of the story, while the husk, the story itself, is discarded. For many, the word "story" is associated with fairy tales. "You resort to stories," as Kendall Haven explains this view, "if you have a weak case or if you're hiding the truth."[6] But for Jesus, as for the authors of Scripture, the gospel lies *through* the narrative, not beyond it, not despite it. To be the people of God is not only to tell stories, then, but also to be constituted by the story of the Triune God.

This is no less true of the church at worship. The narrative arts are not only something a congregation employs—telling stories, using illustrations, narrating history, testifying to the faith. The narrative arts are also a way of understanding the very identity of a congregation: a people constituted by a particular story. How then do the narrative arts make sense of the work of the Triune God in the world? What are their singular powers? How do they serve a liturgical context? And how might specific practices of the narrative arts open up and close down formative possibilities for the people of God at worship? We take each of these questions in turn.

Theological Perspectives on the Narrative Arts

While conceptual and confessional summaries are necessary for a clear articulation of the Christian faith, they do not substitute for actual participation in the biblical narratives themselves and the ways in which our

---

5. Christian Smith, *Moral, Believing Animals: Human Personhood and Culture* (Oxford: Oxford University Press, 2009), 64, emphasis original.

6. Kendall F. Haven, *Story Proof: The Science Behind the Startling Power of Story* (Westport, CT: Libraries Unlimited, 2007), 16.

knowledge of the Triune God emerges *through* the narrative, not apart from it, and through our *retelling* of it, rather than in a one-off recounting of it. As George Lindbeck observes, "The stories [from the Gospels] in their narrative function unsubstitutably identify and characterize a particular person as the summation of Israel's history and as the unsurpassable and irreplaceable clue to who and what the God of Israel and the universe is."[7]

To enter into the community of the triune life, then, is to enter into the story of eternal fellowship between the Father, Son, and Holy Spirit. This is something the early church understood well. The historian Paul Blowers explains that, if the basic struggle of the ante-Nicene era (AD 100–325) revolved around the exact nature of "Christian" identity, then the "rule of faith," or the *regula fidei*, was to be understood as the church's identification *of* and *in* a narrative.[8] Both Irenaeus and Tertullian stressed not so much a complex of binding propositions but rather the arrangement of God's economy. What this economy exhibited, they believed, was a Trinitarian and christological plot.

The authority that the rule exercised in the first centuries of the church, Blowers writes, was "essentially the authority of a story, or a divine gospel (Gal. 1:11) enshrined within a grand story, with God himself as the primary narrator. It was a drama gradually unfolded with a coherent plot, climaxing in the coming of Jesus, who held the secret to the story's ending."[9] The error of heretics was not that they proposed a different idea of God. Nor did their error involve a lack of regard for Scripture. Their error lay in the fact that they were telling the wrong story of God. As Irenaeus insisted, the heretics had violated the integrity of the triune plotline that underlay all of Scripture.

To get the story of God wrong, as the ante-Nicene theologians saw it, was not just to get Scripture wrong. It was also to misconceive the meaning of the world and the shape of human life. N. T. Wright remarks that "the authority which God has invested in this book is an authority that is wielded and exercised *through* the people of God telling and retelling *their*

---

7. George Lindbeck, "The Story-Shaped Church: Critical Exegesis and Theological Interpretation," in *Scriptural Authority and Narrative Interpretation*, ed. Garrett Green (Eugene, OR: Wipf & Stock, 2000), 164.

8. Paul M. Blowers, "The *Regula Fidei* and the Narrative Character of Early Christian Faith," *Pro Ecclesia* 6 (1997): 199–228.

9. Blowers, "The *Regula Fidei*," 205. As Blowers explains, Tertullian reminded his readers that God had not arranged the Scriptures in this way by accident. God had arranged this narrative "argumentation" intentionally.

story as the story of the world, telling the covenant story as the true story of creation."[10] To receive the Scriptures, then, is to receive an invitation to discover one's identity within the narrative of both saints and sinners, both believers and doubters, both principal actors and bystanders to the revelatory actions of the Triune God.[11]

To encounter Jesus, as the chief protagonist of Scripture, is to encounter the one who recapitulates Israel's story, as the new Moses and the new David, the true Adam and the faithful Israelite. For Jesus, to tell stories is not simply a way for him to be a good first-century rabbi.[12] To tell stories is the way *by which* he shows us God. In telling his tales, of wise and foolish builders, of lost coins and errant sons, of sowers and nets and virgins, he also shows us our true humanity—with our singular beginnings, our long or foreshortened middles, with conflict throughout and the possibility of resolution here and there, and our certain ends, marked all the way through by the story of God's activity in our lives.

To join the body of Christ, accordingly, is to join the story of God the Father to form a one, holy, catholic, and apostolic people, and by the power of the Spirit to become a people who will bear the triune name in the world. "We call this new creation the church," writes Stanley Hauerwas. "It is constituted by Word and Sacrament, for the story we tell, the story we embody, must not only be told but be enacted."[13] It is a story that the church tells and enacts significantly in its corporate worship. In Smith's words, "Liturgies are compressed, repeated, performed narratives that, over time, conscript us into the story they 'tell' by showing" us a world yet to come and by inviting us to perform it here and now.[14]

To participate in corporate worship, then, is to participate in what Robbie Castleman calls a story-shaped liturgy. Such a "liturgy is outlined in Scripture, enacted in Israel, refocused in the New Testament community of the early church, regulated and guarded by the apostolic fathers, recov-

---

10. N. T. Wright, "How Can the Bible Be Authoritative?," *Vox Evangelica* 21 (1991): 18, emphasis original.

11. In the field of biblical studies, the discipline of narrative criticism most closely resembles the field of literary studies or the narrative arts. This particular discipline invites the reader to assess the biblical text in light of the tools and practices of literary criticism.

12. See Robert M. Johnston and Harvey K. McArthur, *They Also Taught in Parables: Rabbinic Parables from the First Centuries of the Christian Era* (Eugene, OR: Wipf & Stock, 2014).

13. Stanley Hauerwas, "The Church as God's New Language," in Green, *Scriptural Authority and Narrative Interpretation*, 185.

14. Smith, *Imagining the Kingdom*, 109.

ered in the Reformation and still shapes the liturgy of many congregations today."[15] Such a story-shaped liturgy is most fundamentally a participation in the story of Christ's life: to be called as he is called, to speak God's words as he speaks God's words, to be nourished by God even as he is nourished by the Father through the Spirit, and to be sent into the world in the Spirit's power even as Christ himself was sent.

Finally, the church patterns its worship to the biblical narrative, with all its textures and tensions, by reading it not only with the apostles but also with the saints throughout history. We cannot understand the full meaning of the narrative on our own. We need pilgrims who have gone before us and pilgrims who stand alongside us to discern the triune plotline of Scripture. Against an approach that privileges one generation's reading of the narrative or one single tradition's reading, I suggest that our ability to discern the truth of Scripture correlates to the time and energy that we spend reading the canon alongside fellow pilgrims, cross-historically and cross-culturally.

The Singular Powers of the Narrative Arts

With these theological perspectives in mind, we transition now to an identification of the singular powers of the narrative arts. By "narrative arts" I simply mean the art of storytelling. A story may be fact or fiction—or somewhere in between like certain novels might be.[16] It may be told orally or in print. It may be shared from memory or recited in strict adherence to an established tradition of storytelling. Photographs tell a story. So do the media of drama (like Chinese shadow puppetry), dance (like hula), and music (like hip-hop)—each in their own way. A story may be tragic and epic (like *The Odyssey*) or mundane and trivial (like the ones we tell around the proverbial water cooler).

A story takes shape by way of the principal and secondary characters, the role of the narrator, the texture and tone of the dialogue, what is said and what is left unsaid, its peculiar rhetorical traits, the context or setting in which the story is told, and its plot. The plot of a story is one power of the narrative arts. A plot describes the sequence of incidents or events that move the story

---

15. Robbie Castleman, *Story-Shaped Worship: Following Patterns from the Bible and History* (Downers Grove, IL: IVP Academic, 2013), 14.

16. Examples of this might include Philip Roth, *The Zuckerman Bound Trilogy*; Sandra Cisneros, *The House on Mango Street*; Jeanette Winterson, *Oranges Are Not the Only Fruit*; Jack Kerouac, *On the Road*; and James Frey, *A Million Little Pieces*.

forward. A plot is "what happens" in a story. "What happens" may happen to a place or a time or a thing as much as it will to a person or a people. As Frederick Buechner describes the opening passage of Luke's Gospel, the biblical text that significantly has informed his vocation as preacher and novelist:

> "In the sixth month the angel Gabriel was sent from God to a city of Galilee named Nazareth, to a virgin betrothed to a man whose name was Joseph, of the house of David; and the virgin's name was Mary," and that is the beginning of a story—a time, a place, a set of characters, and the implied promise, which is common to all stories, that something is coming, something interesting or significant or exciting is about to happen. And I would like to start by reminding my reader that in essence this is what Christianity is. If we whittle away long enough, it is a story that we come to at last.[17]

The plot of a story usually defines its characters, a second power. A character may be primary or secondary, human or nonhuman, friendly or antagonistic, important or not to the plot, but a character is always in some sense an "actor" in the story. In Numbers 22, for example, the angel of the Lord, Balaam, Balak, *and* his donkey are all central characters in the story.

A third power is theme. This describes the controlling idea or central insight of a story. This might include, for instance, good and evil, power and corruption, injustice and vengeance, heroism and courage, friends and enemies. The primary themes in Ruth, for instance, are family and loyalty, and the book is thus about what it means to be a faithful people of God.

Point of view is a fourth power. This involves the perspective from which a story is told. How involved is the narrator? In Genesis, for example, the narrator is very involved, while in Ruth the narrator is minimally involved. In some cases the perspective will be omniscient. In other cases the narrator will be semi-omniscient or first-person. A perspective may also aim to be objective or subjective. While Exodus is told principally in the third person, the book of Nehemiah and the book of Acts, unusually, use a first-person perspective. In the book of Ezra we get a combination of narratorial intrusion and shifts between third- and first-person narration.

Dialogue is an additional power. According to Robert Alter, "Dialogue is made to carry a large part of the freight of meaning."[18] Setting is equally

---

17. Frederick Buechner, *The Magnificent Defeat* (New York: Seabury, 1966), 58–59.
18. Robert Alter, *The Art of Biblical Narrative* (New York: Basic Books, 2011), 37. Steven D.

powerful to a story. "In the Book of Ruth," for example, as Steven Mathewson explains, "the movement of the setting from Israel to Moab and back to Israel is significant. By leaving Israel for Moab, Elimelech abandons the covenant community in search of a solution to his hunger."[19] In 2 Samuel 11–12, the narrator tells the reader that it is springtime. To the original readers this meant "the time when kings go to war." To find King David still in Jerusalem, then, signals to the reader that something is not right about this story.

Rhetorical devices represent a final power of the narrative arts. These include such things as similes ("like drops of blood"), metaphors ("bread of life"), images (serpent), signs and symbols (doves and trees), and motifs (such as the journey motif where particular characters, like Moses or Jacob, experience growth as they move from one place to another), repetition (as, for example, the recurrence of the term "loving-kindness," or *hesed*, in 2 Sam. 9), and ironies (which we witness in the speeches of Job or the exchanges between Jesus and the Pharisees). Such figures of speech infuse the story with a particular intensity.

On the Power of a Narrative

What power does a narrative possess to shape our sense of what it means to be human? In his essay "Pastors and Novels," Eugene Peterson draws our attention to five ways in which narratives are powerful.

First, narratives remind us of the storied shape of existence. All human beings have beginnings, middles, and ends. Stories as such remind us of basic things: the importance of history, of persons, of place. "Out of the chaos of incident and accident, story-making words bring light, coherence and connection, meaning and value."[20] Adds Hauerwas: "descriptively the self is best understood as a narrative, and normatively we require a narrative that will provide the skills appropriate to the conflicting loyalties and roles we necessarily confront in our existence. The unity of the self is therefore more like the unity that is exhibited in a good novel."[21]

Mathewson: "One of the functions of speech by the characters [in the Old Testament] is to provide insight into their traits." *The Art of Preaching Old Testament Narrative* (Grand Rapids: Baker Academic, 2002), 65.

19. Mathewson, *The Art of Preaching Old Testament Narrative*, 69.

20. Eugene Peterson, "Pastors and Novels," in *Subversive Spirituality*, 187.

21. Stanley Hauerwas, *A Community of Character* (Notre Dame, IN: University of Notre Dame Press, 1981), 144.

Second, story re-forms us after we have been de-formed by false stories and the broken worlds we inhabit. Daily we are de-formed, Peterson writes, by injury from another's carelessness, meaningless routines, disappointments, discrimination, accidents, and the reduction of our lives to labels, rules, and formulae. Good stories invite us into an experience of wholeness, where things are held together in ways that provoke us to say, "That's my story. That's the story I want to be a part of."

Third, story reminds us never to depersonalize people in the cause of efficiency. Story, Peterson argues, reminds us that the work of God is always personal, never generic. Story jogs our memories and draws our eyes to see the holy in the ordinary, the particular as the locus of God's saving work. Who am I? What's my purpose? Where am I headed? Good stories answer these questions especially well. The writer Jeanette Winterson remarks, "when we start to read literature . . . we start to understand life as a quest and ourselves as serious players. . . . As the conversation develops, so do you. And so the old question 'Who am I?' begins to shape itself into an answer."[22]

Fourth, story reminds us that salvation is always material, geographic, particular. Good stories remind us that humans cannot be separated from the earth, the *humus*, and that God works redemption from the places that have shaped us and brings salvation into the places in which we now live. "You can see now from my comments," Peterson writes, "that my gut feeling is that the most mature and reliable Christian guidance and understanding comes out of the most immediate and local of settings. The ordinary way. We have to break this cultural habit of sending out for an expert every time we feel we need some assistance. Wisdom is not a matter of expertise."[23]

Fifth, story pulls us vicariously into the dramatic center of a problematic situation in order to offer us a taste of the responsibility that is necessary for genuine transformation. In this way, Peterson explains, stories are subversive. They evoke emotions that potentially lead to holy living. Stories, unlike most classroom lectures, do not impose facts upon us, leaving us largely passive in our response. Instead they invite us into a narrative that places us in an active role. And as Stanley Hauerwas has observed, "The test of each story is the sort of person it shapes."[24]

---

22. Jeanette Winterson, "What Is Art For?," in *The World Split Open: Great Authors on How and Why We Write* (Portland, OR: Tin House Books, 2014), 178–79.

23. Eugene Peterson, *The Wisdom of Each Other: A Conversation between Spiritual Friends* (Grand Rapids: Zondervan, 1998), 69.

24. Stanley Hauerwas, with Richard Bondi and David B. Burrell, *Truthfulness and Trag-*

The Narrative Arts in Service of Liturgical Activities

How might the narrative arts, then, serve specific purposes of corporate worship? Let me suggest the following ways.

The Order of Worship

For some congregations the entire order of worship will be marked by the narrative of Christ's life or by the story of Israel's worship. The liturgy of congregations that follow the so-called Fourfold Order of Worship, whether Presbyterian or Lutheran, for instance, will hew closely to Christ's experience of calling, speaking, feeding, and sending—or, in liturgical terms, Gathering, Word, Table, Blessing. In Pentecostal congregations the liturgy will often reflect the story of Israel's temple worship: as a narrative that moves from outer courts to inner courts to holy of holies.

The Sermon

Another way in which the narrative arts serve worship is through the practice of storytelling in the sermon. This might include brief stories or illustrations as well as lengthy narratives that occupy a large part of the sermon. Some preachers will imaginatively retell the story of a character in Scripture or in church history.[25] "Narrative preaching" represents, one could say, an intensification of this practice. Ronald Allen identifies four forms of narrative preaching: sermons that are stories; sermons that develop in a fashion akin to stories; sermons that teach theology by telling stories and reflecting on them; and sermons that seek "to narrate the congregation into the larger and ongoing biblical story."[26]

---

edy: Further Investigations in Christian Ethics (Notre Dame, IN: University of Notre Dame Press, 1977), 35.

25. Jeff Barker includes examples of this practice in his book The Storytelling Church: Adventures in Reclaiming the Role of Story in Worship (Cleveland, TN: Webber Institute Books, 2011).

26. Ronald J. Allen, "Theology Undergirding Narrative Preaching," in What's the Shape of Narrative Preaching? Essays in Honor of Eugene L. Lowry, ed. Mike Graves and David J. Schlafer (St. Louis: Chalice Press, 2008), 27–28. In his book How to Preach a Parable (Nashville: Abingdon, 1989), Eugene Lowry defines narrative preaching as any sermon that has a narrative shape. The narrative sermon is chiefly a narrative and the point of the sermon is discovered through the story. Cf. Aaron Perry, "The Form of Narrative Preaching," Seedbed, April 19,

With Anna Carter Florence's sermon "At the River's Edge," for example, the listener is carried along the Nile of Moses's peril, into the floodwaters of the California depression, merging with the Ganges, and finally coursing into one's hometown, "where a crisis must be faced and decisions made."[27] In Frederick Buechner's sermon "A Sprig of Hope," the hearer encounters images of "Noah's vacant face, flickering with bewilderment; his dusty feet, dragging a little as they turn toward the lumberyard; the ark, staggering like a drunk; the heart of the dove, thrumming in her breast; and, above all, the face of one who weeps like a clown or a fool over the world's darkness and light."[28]

Reading Scripture

The narrative arts can form a congregation through the reading of big chunks of Scripture. N. T. Wright argues that church leaders should always look for ways to "make it possible for our congregations to try creative experiments for how to experience the whole Bible."[29] This would include reading larger chunks of Scripture in corporate worship. It would include preachers reading larger chunks in their sermons and trusting that the time taken for this reading will accomplish its own unique, irreducible formative effect on a congregation. It would also include special worship occasions where the whole Bible is read cover to cover in one continuous time framework.

The Liturgical Calendar

Keeping the liturgical calendar is an additional way to be formed by narrative. The liturgical calendar is a way for the Christian to be trained to

---

2016, https://www.seedbed.com/the-form-of-narrative-preaching/; John Holbert, "Narrative Preaching: Possibilities and Perils," *Preaching.com*, https://www.preaching.com/articles/narrative-preaching-possibilities-and-perils/.

27. Anna Carter Florence, "At the River's Edge," in *A Chorus of Witnesses: Model Sermons for Today's Preacher*, ed. Thomas G. Long and Cornelius Plantinga (Grand Rapids: Eerdmans, 1994), 171.

28. Frederick Buechner, "A Sprig of Hope," in Long and Plantinga, *A Chorus of Witnesses*, 225. Cf. Buechner, *Telling the Truth: The Gospel as Tragedy, Comedy and Fairy Tale* (New York: Harper & Row, 1988).

29. N. T. Wright, "Sign and Means of New Creation: Public Worship and the Creative Reading of Scripture," Calvin Institute of Christian Worship, January 2017, http://ntwrightpage.com/2017/01/30/sign-and-means-of-new-creation-public-worship-and-the-creative-reading-of-scripture/.

become a christomorphic human being. To be a Christ-formed human is to be a human who waits in often-painful expectancy (Advent). To be such a human is to be one who chooses to participate in the mystery of God Incarnate (Christmas). It is to be one who seeks to be a light in places of darkness (Epiphany), who practices the discipline of mortification (Lent) and resurrection in the light of God's good future (Easter), and who daily welcomes the empowering presence of the Holy Spirit (Pentecost) in all aspects of one's ordinary life (Ordinary Time).

The particular narrative that the church recounts through the liturgical year is the one that enables a congregation to participate through symbol and story in the re-membering work of the Spirit of God to conform the church to the image of Christ. As Rowan Williams describes it, "The rhythm of the Christian year was not just a matter of ecclesiastical convenience but a map of the soul's seasons; to grow up as a Christian involved the passage through darkness and light, hope and fulfillment, over and over again, letting the one story of God's action in Jesus become your own."[30] With this calendar the Christian looks not just to Jesus's example but also to the example of saints who have beautifully embodied Christ's life.

The Liturgical Calendar and Liturgical Art

When liturgical art is coordinated to the liturgical calendar, an intensification of its formative power occurs. As liturgical art rehearses the congregation in the meta- and micro-narratives of the gospel, which recapitulate the narrative of Christ's life, these rehearsals become counterforces to the false narratives that surround us through our week, usually tempting us to believe, as Iris Murdoch would say, that we are "monarchs of all we survey."[31] The point of such a rehearsal is to allow the essential metaphors and narratives of the Christian faith to work their way deep into our skin. Over time the hope is that the contours of our imaginations might become distinctively as well as instinctively Christlike.

In an example from the early church, we see how catacomb art formed the way Christians perceived what went on above ground. They saw images

30. Rowan Williams, foreword to *Strengthen for Service: 100 Years of the English Hymnal, 1906–2006*, ed. Alan Luff (Louisville: Westminster John Knox, 2005), viii.

31. Cited in Stanley Hauerwas, *Vision and Virtue: Essays in Christian Ethical Reflection* (Notre Dame, IN: University of Notre Dame Press, 1974), 32.

of Christ the Good Shepherd and of Jonah being regurgitated by the whale's belly. Such images functioned as counternarratives to the cult of the emperor. They reinterpreted reality as Christians daily experienced it. And while the images could not prevent the community from suffering, they charged the community's imagination with a prophetic vision that sustained it in the face of death. There was an Emperor, seated at the right hand of the Father, the images said, who would put the world to rights once and for all.

The Creed

Reciting the Nicene Creed, for example, is an ancient way for the narrative arts to form a congregation. When we confess belief in one God, the Father Almighty, and in one Lord Jesus Christ, born of the virgin Mary, crucified under Pontius Pilate, rising to life on the third day, with a kingdom that shall have no end, and a Spirit who has spoken through the prophets, even as we anticipate the resurrection of the dead and the life of the world to come, we repeatedly define ourselves by a particular narrative. For the Christian to recite the creed is to engage in a profound internalization of a cosmic story. To recite it is to enter into a "thick" time, where past, present, and future co-inhere in "narrated time."

Testimonies

Giving testimonies is a practice intimately related to the narrative arts. Scripture is full of testimonies: in the psalms and the prophets, in the Gospels and the book of Acts. The witness of John of Patmos is definitive for a Christian vision of "the end."[32] So is the witness of martyrs and missionaries. Anna Carter Florence describes a testimony as the act whereby "through *confession* (of what one believes) and *narration* (of what one has

---

32. Examples of testimony in Holy Scripture include Pss. 22:22; 35:18; 40:9–10; 68:26; 89:5; 107:32; 111:1; Acts 4:33; 5:32; 7:2–60. In his book *Thinking in Tongues: Pentecostal Contributions to Christian Philosophy* (Grand Rapids: Eerdmans, 2010), 51, James K. A. Smith argues that for Pentecostal believers, the testimony is a fundamental way to *be* Christian. Steven Land makes a similar argument in *Pentecostal Spirituality: A Passion for the Kingdom* (Cleveland, TN: CPT Press, 2010), 65. Grant Wacker, in *Heaven Below: Early Pentecostals and American Culture* (Cambridge, MA: Harvard University Press, 2001), 69, adds this: "Each person's private struggles somehow soared above the merely private and reappeared in a framework that spanned the millennia."

seen), believers *testify* to their faith in Jesus Christ."[33] Historically the practice of testimony has represented "the leading edge of witness" and "the dominant form of speech to outsiders," whether for women, the black church, or the persecuted church.[34]

Storytelling

Storytelling, while closely related to the practice of testimony, is distinguishable by its peculiar *function*. Whereas a testimony is usually focused on bearing witness to the gospel, storytelling is employed to discover meaning through the narration of a life. Storytelling is conspicuous at key moments in a Christian's life: at one's baptism, confirmation of the faith, ordination, or marriage, and around the time of one's death. Storytelling will often accompany tragic events, like the church shooting that occurred at Emanuel African Methodist Episcopal Church in Charleston, South Carolina, in 2015, the occasion of South Africa's "Truth and Reconciliation Commission," and the martyrdom of saints like Oscar Romero, Manche Masemola, Wang Zhiming, and Dietrich Bonhoeffer.

On the Formative Possibilities of the Narrative Arts in Worship

How then might specific practices of the narrative arts open up and close down possibilities for the formation of our lives in a corporate worship context? If every congregation has a story that defines its character, which is itself composed of a collection of specific stories, along with a practice of storytelling that serves to reinforce its life together, how do these stories form a congregation? How might they misshape a congregation? Which stories are primary and visible? Which stories are marginal and invisible? And, to borrow from the title of Robert Webber's final published book, who gets to narrate a congregation's story?[35]

---

33. Anna Carter Florence, *Preaching as Testimony* (Louisville: Westminster John Knox, 2007), xx, emphasis original. She contrasts this idea with the notion of testimony as a matter of "telling your story" or "using personal illustrations."

34. Carter cites here the work of Ronald E. Osborn, *Folly of God: The Rise of Christian Preaching*, vol. 1 of *A History of Christian Preaching* (St. Louis: Chalice, 1999), 413, 424.

35. Robert E. Webber, *Who Gets to Narrate the World? Contending for the Christian Story in an Age of Rivals* (Downers Grove, IL: InterVarsity, 2008).

Every congregation has its visible and invisible stories. The visible stories are the ones that define a congregation's primary identity and that remain conspicuous in the words, actions, symbols, and spaces of corporate worship. *Who is God?* Is the dominant story about "God the Holy Other One" or "God the Gentle Loving One"? *Who are we?* Are we the elect saints in exile? Soldiers for Christ? The broken beloved? *What is our relationship to people outside the household of faith?* Are they the damned, the strangers, the other, our neighbors? *What is our relationship to Christian history, to creation, or to the seven days of the week?* Are we intimately and integrally related to these or separate and opposed to them in some fashion?

Whose voices get heard most frequently in a gathering of corporate worship? Male or female? One voice or many? Is it the voice of the contemplative types or the activists? Is it the voice of the victorious narrative of faith or the narrative of those who died in faith, not having received the things promised? Is it the voice of the highly educated or the highly capable? Is it the voice of "our" generation or of the "Great Tradition"? Is it the voice of one skin color and one tongue or the voices of many tongues and nations? Do the voices of the poor, the disabled, the simple, the doubters, and the old folks get heard? What voices are prominent in the songs that are sung and the images that are seen week after week?

Infertility, divorce, shame, mass murder, astrology, injustice, and doubt: these are a few of the topics that appear in the birth narratives of Matthew and Luke. But it is unlikely that they will feature in many sermons or pageants that occur around the month of December. One would scarcely know, moreover, how utterly bizarre these narratives are by the activities of artists and advertisers, along with plenty of churches, during the Christmas holidays. Artists will often extract portions of the story, tidy them up, set them to music, and then allow radio stations to play them to death. Grocery stores will play them to a second death. Gas stations will complete the cycle by turning the songs into dismissible clichés.

Sermons, for their part, may rehash the stock details of the Gospels, with the hope that parishioners will feel the "magic" or "mystery" of Christ's birth. Church pageants will trot out the children in bathrobes, a pretty girl will play Mary, an awkward Joseph will remain forgettable, and an angel-child will belt out the good news to shepherd boys dragging their broom-sticks, eyes wandering over to the cookie table, even as the violins reach their sentimental climax. Phones will record the whole business for posterity so that parishioners will remember how cute and sweet the drama was, even if the actual stories that surround the birth of Christ are decidedly troubling and disorienting and patently incredible.

What happens when the *actual* stories of Christ's birth become invisible to the people of God at worship? It allows, I suggest, for the birth narratives of Matthew and Luke to become all too familiar and functionally innocuous. The story of Jesus loses its bite. A tame "baby Jesus" makes his annual, heartwarming appearance and leaves the people of God largely unbothered and, worse, unchanged. Yet when we read the two Gospel accounts closely, we quickly discover how strange these stories are, unsettling and fantastical at every corner, yet good news for all types of people—the too old, the too young, the social outcasts, the strangers to the faith, the faith filled, and the failures of faith.

As God has it, however, it is *through* this disturbingly odd narrative that we encounter the incarnate Son of God, born of the Virgin Mary, by the Spirit's power, and that we witness God's redemptive and revelatory work in the world. The Father announces the arrival of his beloved Son to a people for whom the good news almost immediately turns to bad news, or unpredictable news, or simply signals a return to the difficult and tedious condition of their lives. Things do not turn out as people thought they would. God offers hope, instead of good cheer, in the face of personal disappointment and systemic evil. God grants joy, rather than happiness, because joy can account for suffering, while happiness cannot.

God draws his people into a kind of love that bears all things, including death and the loss of privileges, so that the faithful might become agents of the kind of shalom that Jesus exhibits in his life, death, resurrection, and ascension. Is there, then, not a better way forward for the church? Is it not possible for Christians to bear witness to the terrifying yet life-giving news of Christ's birth? Are there stories that could be told and *should* be told so that the people of God might become more deeply faithful? And might the arts play a crucial role in refreshing our imaginations with a vision of peace on earth, the kind of hard-won, hard-edged peace that Jesus himself announces?

All sorts of possibilities can be imagined, I suggest. What if a visual artist rendered Elizabeth and Zechariah's experience of infertility as a way to open up insight not just into actual stories of infertility but into all sorts of experiences of barrenness? What if a theater artist wrote a Christmas pageant that highlighted the Middle Eastern and peasant aspects of Christ's birth? What if a group of filmmakers made a movie that represented the refugee status of Jesus, Joseph, and Mary as a way to illumine the refugee crisis in our world? What if a company of modern dancers cast a light, through the choreography of their bodies, on the experience of shame that the biblical characters experienced?

What if a poet called attention to the extraordinary, though often quiet, stories of the elderly, like Anna and Simeon, who remain faithful to God in this particular season of their life? What if a musician wrote a song that narrated the themes of injustice in the songs of Mary and Zechariah as a way to prepare the congregation for the prayers of the people, for a people who face injustice in their own lives? What if a worship leader created space for select members of the congregation to bear witness to the presence of God in the middle of unrelieved experiences of pain? What if a digital installation depicted a contemporary analog to the shepherds of Jesus's day, with its accompanying social stigma?

If any number of these things were done, even in simple fashion, I believe we would experience a renewed exposure to the gospel as radically *good* news. I believe we would experience a transformative encounter with the God of Jesus Christ. I believe such artworks would provide us with the capacity to live more faithfully in the actual conditions and contexts of our lives. I believe they would enable the birth narratives of Christ to become fresh again with insight and sharp with tension, for the sake of an experience that captured both the wild, terrifying nature of God's entrance onto the world stage and the gentle, intimate nature of God's care for each person.[36]

Every story that we tell in our corporate worship, through any of the media of art that mark our liturgies, thus opens up specific opportunities to be formed in the triune life. But it is also every story that we fail to tell that may malform us. It is every story that remains on the margin of a congregation's life that may rob a people of the true knowledge of God. It is every story that remains invisible to a congregation that might lead to damaging stereotypes. "The problem with stereotypes," remarks the Nigerian novelist Chimamanda Ngozi Adichie, "is not that they are untrue, but that they are incomplete. They make one story become the only story. . . . The consequence of the single story is that it robs people of dignity."[37]

It is important to stress, finally, that a congregation should preserve their defining stories. They should seek every opportunity to bear witness

36. A version of this material appeared in W. David O. Taylor, "Biblical Birth Narratives Are Weird and Incredible: We Can Stop Sanitizing Them," *Washington Post*, December 24, 2015, https://www.washingtonpost.com/news/acts-of-faith/wp/2015/12/24/biblical-birth -narratives-are-troubling-weird-and-incredible-we-can-stop-sanitizing-them-now/.

37. Chimamanda Ngozi Adichie, "The Danger of a Single Story," TED Talk, July 2009, https://www.ted.com/talks/chimamanda_adichie_the_danger_of_a_single_story.

to the good work of God in their life together. Telling and retelling their story is a way to remind a congregation that they have a narrative that *matters*—that they come from somewhere, that they are likewise headed somewhere, and that God in Christ by his Spirit is with them, here and now. But it is equally important to stress that a congregation should seek opportunities to tell the stories that bear witness to the whole counsel of God, the whole history of the church, and all the ways that God remains faithful to a broken people living in a broken world.

Around the time of Christmas, this would involve telling the stories of human beings whose lives have been marked by infertility, injustice, violence, abandonment, and strange dreams—and also astonishing joy, irrepressible song, humble faith, and miraculous rescue. Around Lent, it would involve telling stories of extraordinary courage and embarrassing episodes of doubt. Around Eastertide, it would involve telling the story of the God who saves the world as a suffering servant, victorious king, liberator, healer, and sacrifice. And in the season of Pentecost, it would involve a fantastical story of many tongues become one in the Spirit, along with ordinary stories of faithful living under ordinary circumstances and conditions of duress, whereby God's people seek to be faithful in small and large ways.

Conclusion

In his commentary on Luke's Gospel, Joel Green writes that the lawyer's aim in his question to Jesus was "to calculate the identity of those to whom he need not show love."[38] In his tale of the Samaritan man, however, Jesus cleverly subverts this aim. "Stripped of his clothes and left half-dead," Green comments, "the man's anonymity throughout the story is insured; he is simply a human being, a neighbor, in need."[39] And the Samaritan, unlike the prior two characters, "is not portrayed as a holy man at all, but rather as a traveling merchant."[40] It is the unlikely protagonist of a rabbi's story who exhibits the exaggerated compassion of God for a nameless person in need.

38. Joel B. Green, *The Gospel of Luke*, New International Commentary on the New Testament (Grand Rapids: Eerdmans, 1997), 426.
39. Green, *The Gospel of Luke*, 429.
40. Green, *The Gospel of Luke*, 431.

Rather than telling the lawyer, then, that his idea about neighborliness reflected a faulty notion of Yahweh, Jesus shows him the way forward *through* a narrative. Jesus takes the lawyer's original question ("Who is my neighbor?") and turns it into a better question ("Who acted as a neighbor?"). He takes the lawyer's presumed narrative about neighbors and replaces it with a narrative that shows the lawyer an image of true neighborliness as an image of the true character of God. Jesus, finally, invites the lawyer to become implicated in the story and to live his life in light of the story. A "Thou shalt not" may have addressed the lawyer's head, but it was a "Once upon a time" that one hopes reached his heart.[41]

"I think fiction may be, whatever else," writes the novelist Marilynne Robinson, "an exercise in the capacity for imaginative love . . . for people we do not know or whom we know very slightly."[42] This is certainly what we see at work in Luke's story of the compassionate Samaritan. As it pertains to a central feature of Jesus's ministry—namely, storytelling—N. T. Wright offers this observation: "Where a head-on attack would certainly fail, the parable hides the wisdom of the serpent behind the innocence of the dove, gaining entrance and favor which can then be used to change assumptions which the hearer would otherwise keep hidden for safety."[43]

This, to be sure, is one of the great powers of the narrative arts. But it is not the only power. Stories can show us reality. They can define and govern our reality. They can show us "the fathomless mystery" that characterizes our lives, as Buechner once put it.[44] They can "enlarge and complicate— and, therefore, improve—our sympathies."[45] They can show us what God is like. They can reveal to us what it means to be truly human, conformed to the image of the one whose story defines all human stories. And by God's grace, they can become an especially fitting servant of the church's worship, conscripting us into a story that makes good sense out of all our stories.

---

41. This is how Philip Pullman describes the power of stories: they "work secretly, and almost never in ways we can predict. And certainly never for the whole class at once. They work in silence." "The Moral's in the Story, Not the Stern Lecture," *The Independent*, July 18, 1996, https://www.independent.co.uk/news/education/education-news/opinion-the -morals-in-the-story-not-the-stern-lecture-1329231.html.

42. Marilynne Robinson, "Imagination and Community," *Commonweal Magazine*, February 27, 2012, https://www.commonwealmagazine.org/imagination-community.

43. N. T. Wright, *The New Testament and the People of God* (Minneapolis: Fortress, 1992), 38.

44. Frederick Buechner, *Now and Then* (New York: HarperCollins, 1983), 87.

45. Sontag, "At the Same Time," 213.

Performance of children's drama by Susanna Banner at Hope Chapel, Austin, Texas (Photograph by author)

CHAPTER 8

Worship and the Theater Arts

The story of God is theatrical. Every part of it could be its own play.

Alison Siewert, *Drama Team Handbook*

The theater of God in which the drama of Jesus Christ was played out was already in existence before the church fathers began to exhort the Christians to go to the theater of God: Christian drama had begun with the memorial act of the breaking of bread of the Last Supper.

Christine C. Schnusenberg,
The Mythological Traditions of Liturgical Drama

I'm baptizing you here in the river, turning your old life in for a kingdom life. The real action comes next: The main character in this drama—compared to him I'm a mere stagehand—will ignite the kingdom life within you, a fire within you, the Holy Spirit within you, changing you from the inside out.

Matthew 3:11 (*The Message*)

In his introduction to *Improvisation: The Drama of Christian Ethics*, Samuel Wells suggests that the disciplines and practices of improvisation "resemble the disciplines and practices of Christian ethics sufficiently closely."[1] Improvisation, he explains, is a matter of steeping oneself years "in a tradition so that the body is so soaked in practices and perceptions that it trusts itself in community to do the obvious thing."[2] What does this have to do with corporate worship? Wells answers: "For Christians the principal

---

1. Samuel Wells, *Improvisation: The Drama of Christian Ethics* (Grand Rapids: Brazos, 2004), 17. By ethics, Wells means "imitating God, following Christ, being formed by the Spirit to become friends with God" (31).
2. Wells, *Improvisation*, 17.

practice by which the moral imagination is formed, the principal form of discipleship training, is worship."[3]

In worship "Christians seek in the power of the Spirit to be conformed to the image of Christ—to act like him, think like him, be like him."[4] Our formation into the image of Christ through worship does not, in point of fact, happen spontaneously or effortlessly. It happens instead through careful, intentional effort. Through our disciplined participation in preaching and prayer, in baptism and the Lord's Supper, in confession of faith and of sin, in the sharing of song and blessing in the triune name, the church learns over time how to act like Christ. Corporate worship, on this dramatic analogy, becomes essential to the formation of Christlike virtue.

Wells's use of the practices of theater to illuminate the work of Christian worship is far from unusual. Christians throughout history have found the medium of theater to make good sense not just of the church's liturgical life but also of God's revelation in creation, the incarnate mission of Jesus, the biblical canon, the dramatic activity of the prophets, and the Spirit's work to transform God's people. The New Testament Greek term for "tabernacle," *skena*, is, as Todd Johnson points out, for example, "etymologically related to the classical Greek word *skene*, the scene house of the ancient Greek theater."[5] Under this light, one could argue that God in Christ not only tabernacles on earth; he also plays out a re-creative role in his life, death, resurrection, and ascension.

Like the medium of dance, however, the theater arts have received an uneven welcome in the church. Saint Augustine in *The City of God* argued that theater "feeds our passivity and narcissism."[6] In *Christians and the Theater*, published in 1876, J. M. Buckley felt that few things were more "unfavorable to the practice of religion than the practice of Theater-going."[7] An actor—in Greek, a *hupokrite*, a "mask-wearer"—takes us *away* from reality, it is argued, not nearer to it.[8] An undated tract from the American Tract

---

3. Wells, *Improvisation*, 82.

4. Wells, *Improvisation*, 84.

5. Todd E. Johnson and Dale Savidge, *Performing the Sacred: Theology and Theatre in Dialogue* (Grand Rapids: Baker Academic, 2009), 26.

6. Cited in Jonas Barish, *The Antitheatrical Prejudice* (Berkeley: University of California Press, 1981), 54.

7. Cited in Johnson and Savidge, *Performing the Sacred*, 34.

8. The Puritan critique of the theater was that it fell under the same judgment that Jesus leveled against the Pharisees: that they were hypocrites (cf. Matt. 6:2, 5, 16). What else

Society calls the theater "a seminary of vice" and "a sinful waste of TIME."[9] About the often vulgar, gory, cultic *ludi*, "plays," Tertullian declared, "We renounce all your spectacles."[10]

All such comments, of course, have a context. That context always requires careful attention. In Tertullian's time, for instance, as E. K. Chambers describes it in his book *The Medieval Stage*, "The Roman taste for bloodshed was sometimes gratified by mimes given in the amphitheater, and designed to introduce the actual execution of a criminal."[11] Christians are right to reject such evils. But to fault the theater for its "contagion" powers, exciting audiences to imitate actors, may say more about poor understandings of art than about inherent defects of art. No doubt the dangers of excess and distortion are real for the theater arts. But the abuses of art do not automatically delegitimize a work of art.[12]

People often argue that theater is incarnational—but so is dance. Scholars will say that a play makes the invisible visible.[13] But so does a work of sculpture. So what exactly is unique about the medium of theater? How does it make sense of the work of the Triune God in the world? What are its singular powers, what the Shakespeare scholar Bernard Beckerman calls "the quintessential conditions that govern its character"?[14] How do they serve a liturgical context? And how might specific practices of the theater arts open up and close down formative possibilities for the people of God at worship? It is these questions that the present chapter seeks to answer.

---

is a hypocrite, asked William Prynne, "but a stage-player, or one who acts another's part, as sundry authors and grammarians teach us?" Cited in Max Harris, *Theater and Incarnation* (Grand Rapids: Eerdmans, 1990), 70.

9. "The Christian and the Theater," American Tract Society, republished at https:// www.gracegems.org/ATS/theater.htm, emphasis original.

10. Cf. Christine C. Schnusenberg, *The Mythological Traditions of Liturgical Drama: The Eucharist as Theater* (New York: Paulist Press, 2010), ch. 9, "Roman Cosmogonies and the Roman Theater."

11. E. K. Chambers, *The Mediaeval Stage* (New York: Dover, 1996), 5n4. Cf. Schnusenberg, *The Mythological Traditions of Liturgical Drama*, 258–62.

12. Cf. W. David O. Taylor, "Hooker's Architectural *Via Media*," *The Living Church* 240, no. 6 (February 7, 2010): 10–14.

13. This is how Peter Brook describes what he calls the "holy theatre" in Peter Brook, *The Empty Space* (New York: Touchstone, 1996), 42–44.

14. Bernard Beckerman, *Dynamics of Drama: Theory and Method of Analysis* (New York: Drama Book Specialists, 1979), 10.

Theological Perspectives on Theater

One of the peculiar contributions of the theater arts to Christian faith is to remind us of the dramatic nature of God's work in the world. Some might even go so far as to say that we cannot fully appreciate the nature of triune economy apart from the language of the theater arts.

In understanding the nature of the universe, for instance, theologians have used the metaphor of the theater to characterize God's creation. In his commentary on Hebrews 11:3, John Calvin writes, "The world was no doubt made, that it might be the theater of divine glory."[15] About Psalm 104:31, Calvin insists that we are not only to be "spectators of this beauteous theater" but also to savor and to enjoy the abundance and variety of God's spectacular work.[16] In a comment on Genesis, Calvin argues that, after creating the cosmos, God placed the human creature "in a theater" so that wherever the human creature looked, it might behold the wonder-filled works of God and adore this God.[17]

It is not only, however, that the Creator makes a theater of the world and then leaves the stage to the creature to act as it pleases in the drama of human history. It is also that God enters the stage of the world himself. As Wesley Vander Lugt and Trevor Hart put it in their introduction to *Theatrical Theology*, "God created this cosmic theater, but he also performs the lead role. He does this not merely by speaking from offstage, but by entering into the action, preeminently by becoming flesh and dwelling among us as Jesus of Nazareth."[18] God remains in the play, so to speak, through the lively presence of the Holy Spirit. For the Christian, all of life is a "theater of sin and grace, death and life."[19]

Kevin Vanhoozer makes a similar argument about Holy Scripture. In the *Drama of Doctrine*, he writes, "the Bible is not merely a record of reve-

---

15. John Calvin, *Comm.* Heb. 11:3, in vol. 12 of *Calvin's New Testament Commentaries*, ed. David W. Torrance and Thomas F. Torrance, 12 vols. (Grand Rapids: Eerdmans, 1959–72). Cf. *Institutes of the Christian Religion*, I.5.5. See also Taylor, *The Theater of God's Glory: Calvin, Creation, and the Liturgical Arts* (Grand Rapids: Eerdmans, 2017), ch. 2.

16. Calvin, *Comm.* Ps. 104:31, in vol. 6 of *Commentaries of John Calvin*, 46 vols. (Edinburgh: Calvin Translation Society, 1844–55; reprint, Grand Rapids: Baker Book House, 1979).

17. Calvin, *Comm.* Gen., "The Argument," in vol. 1 of *Commentaries of John Calvin*.

18. Wesley Vander Lugt and Trevor Hart, eds., *Theatrical Theology: Explorations in Performing the Faith* (Eugene, OR: Cascade, 2014), xiii.

19. George Lathrop, *Holy Ground: A Liturgical Cosmology* (Minneapolis: Augsburg Fortress, 2003), 45.

lation but the means by which God, in and through the human authors, has an ongoing speaking part."[20] On this account, the divine author is not a teacher of propositional truths, nor a detached narrator of history. The divine author is instead "a dramatist who does things in and through the dialogical action of others."[21] How then should we regard the biblical texts in this theatrical image? Vanhoozer proposes that we view them as "the script (and the program notes) without which the church could neither understand nor participate in the drama of redemption."[22]

To view the Bible through this theatrical lens enables us, I suggest, to reenvision the role of Scripture in worship. In the same way that an actor internalizes a script—by reading and rereading it, by memorizing it, by saying it out loud, by chewing on it and analyzing it and absorbing it into her bones—so too the church at worship is to internalize the canonical script. The goal is not to read for the sake of reading—what the topic of the day or the lectionary requires. The goal rather is to immerse ourselves in the biblical text so that we can hear the voice of the divine author speaking to us. The goal is to be inspired and empowered by the Spirit to act like Christ in the divine drama, played out on the stage of our personal and public lives.

The Singular Powers of Theater

With these theological perspectives in mind, we transition now to an identification of the singular powers of the theater arts. In doing so we begin to discover the ways in which God works *through* the medium of theater, not despite it or beyond it. For the purposes of this book, I shall focus on the term "theater" rather than the more general term "drama." I will assume that theater involves human beings purposefully performing a story for a live audience on a stage, in an isolated time and space, in a relatively unmediated fashion. I will also assume that this definition includes tragedy, comedy, skit, serious drama, farce, melodrama, musical play, opera, documentary, and choral recitations.[23]

What, then, are the singular powers of the theater arts? Allow me to propose five.[24]

20. Kevin J. Vanhoozer, *The Drama of Doctrine: A Canonical-Linguistic Approach to Christian Theology* (Louisville: Westminster John Knox, 2005), 177.
21. Vanhoozer, *The Drama of Doctrine*, 179.
22. Vanhoozer, *The Drama of Doctrine*, 149.
23. Cf. Beckerman, *Dynamics of Drama*, ch. 1.
24. Plenty of other powers could have been considered here—such as the director,

A Live Performance

In contrast to a movie, a play is a live event. In the theater one gets a real audience *that sees what it sees*: actors acting in the flesh. It is of course what makes the experience of theater volatile. Anything could go terribly wrong. With a movie, one gets to watch digitally mastered humans, re-presented on a silver screen. In a play, human beings perform before us, here and now. Thornton Wilder remarks, "The supremacy of the theater derives from the fact that it is always 'now' on the stage."[25]

What occurs "now" for an audience is a multisensory experience. As Max Harris, in *Theater and Incarnation*, describes it, "Of all the arts, the theater alone accosts all the senses. While sight and sound ordinarily predominate, touch, taste and smell may at times play a deliberate and significant part. Actors may reach out to touch the audience; food may be shared; and, along with the unavoidable 'smell of the greasepaint,' there may be the soothing aroma of incense or the pungent stench of smoke accompanying battle and the melodramatic entry of the villain."[26] Though all the senses may be engaged in a play, a play is only suggestive of reality rather than an attempt at verisimilitude.[27] A play is more often about the appearance of, say, flying or eating, rather than the actual act of eating or flying, which a movie may seek to represent far more realistically. In a live performance an audience sees everything. In movies, by contrast, a cinematographer controls the point of view of the audience with a collection of lenses, while an editor cuts and pastes together the audience's perspective. With a movie we get to wind and rewind to all our favorite parts; we get to watch the exact same thing over and over. With a play we get to witness the story once, and that is all. If we watch it again, it will never be the exact same performance.

Among other things, a live performance underscores the importance—and the risk—of enfleshed presence. Live theater reminds our virtual age of the first order knowledge that our physical bodies afford us. Tina Packer, the founder of Shakespeare & Company, a theatrical company in Lenox, Massachusetts, says this: "It's only through people gathering together—which is what theaters do—that you can actually feel the human-

---

the costumer, make-up artists, and the light and sound design—but for reasons of space cannot be given the proper due.

25. Cited in Louis E. Catron, *The Elements of Playwriting* (Prospect Heights, IL: Waveland Press, 2000), xiii.

26. Harris, *Theater and Incarnation*, 2.

27. Beckerman, *Dynamics of Drama*, 19.

ity. It's a palpable, visceral feeling—a collective feeling. You can't feel it on Facebook, you can't feel it on television, and you don't get the truth in any of these places, either."[28]

Adds playwright Adam Rapp: "At our core, we are animals. And we need something from each other that we can't get from a screen."[29] This is similar to what the literary critic William Deresiewicz said once: "People are hungry to restore their connection to the physical world, the sensual world, the world of objects that display the marks of time and of the human touch."[30] In putting real human beings on stage, theater artists remind each of us of our own physical humanity. And by being a live event, a play makes possible, I argue, a kinesthetic connection that God has made us to need in order to flourish and that is central to Christian worship.

A Stage

In theater the play is written for the stage. It is not written to be literature, except in secondary ways. As Louis Catron insists, the "one test of any script is simple: Is it stageworthy?"[31] Whatever the nature of the stage, it is the place where the action happens. The theater arts remind us, accordingly, that our faith is fundamentally played out on a stage—not in a book, not in our heads. Our faith is not chiefly played out in the privacy of our homes. Nor is our faith played out in the enclosures of our church life, behind closed doors, as much as they matter.

Our faith is chiefly played out on the stage of the world.[32] Eugene Peterson, in *The Message*, translates 1 Corinthians 4:9 this way: "It seems to me that God has put us who bear his Message on stage in a theater [because we have become a spectacle (a *theatron*) to the world, to angels, and to mor-

---

28. As cited in Craig Lambert, "The Future of Theater," *Harvard Magazine*, January–February 2012, https://harvardmagazine.com/2012/01/the-future-of-theater. Accessed September 15, 2018.

29. "Theatrical Software" in *Harvard Magazine*, January–February 2008, https://harvardmagazine.com/2008/01/theatrical-software.html. Accessed September 15, 2018.

30. William Deresiewicz, "Commencement Address," Oregon College of Art and Craft, Portland, OR, May 13, 2017, https://ocac.edu/commencement-address-2017.

31. Cited in Catron, *The Elements of Playwriting*, xviii.

32. Trevor Hart develops this world-stage metaphor in his book *Between the Image and the Word: Theological Engagements with Imagination, Language and Literature* (Surrey: Ashgate, 2013), ch. 8, "Unfinished Performances."

tals] in which no one wants to buy a ticket." If we wish to know the nature of Christian experience, theater artists will tell us: It is like a stage upon which actors play a role, and they either play it well or they play it poorly.

The image of a world as a stage in Shakespeare's play *As You Like It* is not, as some might suppose, a mere metaphor for human life. It is instead a determinative metaphor: a metaphor that explains the true character of human experience. When the bard of Avon writes that "All the world's a stage. / And all the men and women merely players; / They have their exits and their entrances, / And one man in his time plays many parts, / His acts being seven ages," this is, again, no mere figure of speech.[33] It is a figurative way of speaking that enables us *to figure out* reality.

Theater artists remind us that the physical creation is not mute to the work of God to establish his kingdom on earth as it is in heaven. It, too, plays a role. Nor is the stage of our daily lives outside the domain of God's rule. Our work and our play, our politics and our entertainments, our relationships and our communities, our grocery shopping and our traveling, and our struggle for justice and mercy—all of these are ways by which we play out our role as citizens of Christ's kingdom.

The Script

Poetry, like theater, draws our attention to the significance of words. But the theater arts may be said to go further, reminding us that certain things can only be discovered through the *spoken* word. Whereas in film images and showing are everything, in the theater the words are king and the speech is everything.

> Rosencrantz: "What are you playing at?"
> Guildenstern: "Words, words. They're all we have to go on."[34]

The theater arts remind us of the power of the spoken word. In contrast to novels, which can be thoroughly enjoyed by reading them silently, in theater the power of words resides in their audibility. While the written word means one thing on the page of the script, it means another thing when it is a vocalized by actors. It takes on flesh and sense. It becomes idio-

---

33. Shakespeare, *As You Like It*, act 2, scene 7.
34. Tom Stoppard, *Rosencrantz and Guildenstern Are Dead* (New York: Grove, 1967), 41.

syncratic and hence dramatically consequential. "Theatrical dialogue is an artistic reproduction of the way particular characters speak, designed for actors to speak and aimed at the audience's ear, in contrast to literary writing which is more formal, written for an individual's eye."[35]

In the theater it is through monological and dialogical speech that meaning is discovered. The script becomes speech, and the speech in turn becomes the way *by which* human identity and relationship are constituted. Or as my father used to say to me when I was young, *Hablando se entiende la gente*: "People are more likely to understand each other if they have a chance to talk with each other." Words on a page are powerful but will not suffice. The thoughts in one's head only go so far. The spoken word is needed, the theater arts remind us, in order for something distinctive about the nature of reality to be apprehended.

The Audience

In contrast to movies, the audience in a theater performs a much more consequential role. In the theater an audience exercises a power *over* the actors and in some cases speaks back to the actors, while the actors in turn feel and respond to the audience. In theater, unlike novels, the actors remain vulnerable to their audiences. As Peter Brook describes it, an audience is always needed. "The onlooker is a partner who must be forgotten and still constantly kept in mind."[36] The Irish playwright Conor McPherson observes it this way: "Theater, as a much less inflected medium, really works when you are sitting in the audience and you realise that you are all feeling the same. The crowd laugh together, reassuring each other that it is OK to enjoy the experience. They respond as a group, each person having a subtly different but somehow unified experience."[37]

In contrast to sports and games, the theater requires an audience to fulfill its purpose.[38] In theater the audience is "in" on the story, not outside of it. In theater an audience "makes itself heard," unlike an audience in a performance of classical music, where the requirement to remain utterly

---

35. Catron, *The Elements of Playwriting*, 125.

36. Brook, *The Empty Space*, 51.

37. Conor McPherson, "Stage v Screen," *The Guardian*, May 2, 2003, https://www.theguardian.com/culture/2003/may/02/artsfeatures.

38. Playing football or a game of hide-and-go-seek with one's friends needs no audience for it to feel fully satisfying. This is not the case, in the main, for theater.

quiet is, as my mother reminded me as a child, indispensable to the right experience of the work. The theater arts, under this light, might help us to understand what it means to be a true audience to the words of Holy Scripture, as active rather than passive participants in the drama of God's revelation.

Too often our congregations have no sense of the dynamic story of Scripture. The laity's experience is often a passive one—words are read *at* them. They feel like outsiders to the narrative. For them, the story belongs "out there," not here, "to others," not to us and certainly not to me. But theater artists are especially suited to help the church get a feel for Scripture—how it sounds, how it tastes, how it smells and moves and enables us to be in touch with reality. Theater artists can help us to feel the textures and tensions of Scripture, *from the inside.*

For the people of God at worship, the theater arts can teach us how to be a proper audience to the biblical narrative. As a theater-like audience, we listen attentively to the words. Sometimes we shout back our responses, like "Amen!" or "God is good!" At other times we lean in with quiet but focused attention to the preacher's exposition of the biblical text. At all times we enter vicariously into the stories of Scripture and begin to resee our lives more faithfully in the light of the actions and words of the people who populate Holy Scripture.

Theater artists can likewise put us on the inside of the text so that we see it played out in our own lives, not just in our heads. Historically the church has done this through the mystery plays (which dramatize the ministry of Christ during the feast of Corpus Christi), the miracle plays (which were dramas based on the lives of saints), and morality plays (which were dramas intended to communicate moral choices through typological characters).

Actors

In the theater, the performance of actors is always fresh. This means that their performance is ever so slightly always morphing. Unlike a movie, in a play there is no such thing as a perfectly identical performance. There is only a faithful performance—faithful to the character in context. Theater artists remind us, I offer, how to be true actors in the divine drama, not playing the perfect role of Christ in the world but playing it faithfully— faithful to Christ in our respective contexts.

Theater artists also remind us of the importance of a "full, conscious and active" role that all Christians should be playing in corporate worship.[39] Todd Johnson, in *Performing the Sacred*, writes, "Worship is never a final performance but a rehearsal of our faith. Our life as disciples is an ongoing rehearsal of our faith, constantly reinterpreting the Scriptures in our lives as a part of the community of faith to which we belong.... The lesson one learns from theater is that participation is vital to the full formation of our faith and its ongoing rehearsal of our life as disciples."[40] This applies, for example, to the reading and hearing of Scripture. As Richard Carter and Samuel Wells imagine it, "Rather than the familiar 'This is the word of the Lord' or the somewhat tame 'Here ends the reading,' the announcement after the reading might better be, 'Lord, fulfill this Scripture today.'" In reciting such a thing, the church would be imitating Jesus's manner of reading (Luke 4:21). It is a manner that helps us remember that the words of God are always "living and active" (Heb. 4:12).

Carter and Wells suggest an additional remark by the reader: "And make our lives and our deeds a scripture for the blessing of your people in days to come."[41] To declare this is to invite the people of God into an active rather than a passive mode of hearing Scripture. It is a way to let our "Amens" become dynamic, self-involved, self-implicating declarations.[42] It is a way of declaring, "Let your word, oh Lord, change us here and now so that we may more readily become what we confess."

---

39. The Constitution on the Sacred Liturgy, or the *Sacrosanctum Concilium*, uses this language to describe the nature of the ideal participation of the laity in corporate worship. See http://www.vatican.va/archive/hist_councils/ii_vatican_council/documents/vat-ii_const _19631204_sacrosanctum-concilium_en.html.

40. Johnson, *Performing the Sacred*, 94.

41. Richard Carter and Samuel Wells, "Holy Theatre: Enfleshing the Word," in Vander Lugt and Hart, *Theatrical Theology*, 225.

42. In my own Anglican tradition, we say the same things week after week—prayers and confessions and benedictions. We likewise perform the same actions every time we gather for worship: we kneel, we bow, we stand, we open our hands to receive the bread and the wine, we turn our bodies toward the center as the Gospel is read in our midst. But like a skilled actor who performs the same play night after night, the recitation of these words and the performance of these actions always feel fresh. The words remain vibrant. The actions continue to feel full of tension, infused with possibility, because we ourselves, like actors on a stage, are never the same each time we gather. We know that we get to put on our lips, like the words of Shakespeare, good words, words that deserve to be said, to be memorized, to be internalized, and to be declared out loud in the midst of the assembly.

"An actor is someone who remembers," writes Charles Marowitz.[43] An actor remembers not only his lines, his cues, his entrances, and his exits; he also remembers what it means to feel hunger, to be lonely and proud, to be like a child, to have a history, and to be named by others. In Uta Hagen's words, an actor's job is to figure out who he "really" is, or as Stanislavsky saw it, the *truth*.[44] This too is the work of Christians in worship: to remember who they are so that they might be re-membered in Christ. It is the active role that the people of God perform by the power of the Spirit.

The Theater Arts in Service of Liturgical Activities

How might the theater arts, then, serve specific purposes of corporate worship? For certain traditions, the theater will serve to frame the very nature of the liturgy.[45] In such traditions, the liturgy will be seen as a dramatic setting where the faithful *do* theology.[46] We perform our Christology, not simply think about it. We enact our ecclesiology, not only talk about it. We rehearse our eschatology, not merely postpone it to a future date.[47] We learn rather how to become our "already / not yet" true selves, in Christ, *through* worship, dramatically anticipating today our destiny at the end of the age.

43. Charles Marowitz, *The Act of Being: Towards a Theory of Acting* (New York: Taplinger Publishing Company, 1978), 26.

44. Uta Hagen, *Respect for Acting* (New York: Macmillan, 1973), 26. Konstantin S. Stanislavsky, "The Evolution of My System," in *Actors on Acting: The Theories, Techniques, and Practices of the World's Great Actors, Told in Their Own Words*, ed. Toby Cole and Helen Krich Chinoy (New York: Crown Publishers, 1949), 494.

45. See Schnusenberg, *The Mythological Traditions of Liturgical Drama*, 262–69; Gordon Graham, "Liturgy as Drama," *Theology Today* 64, no. 1 (2007): 71–79; Richard D. McCall, *Do This: Liturgy as Performance* (Notre Dame, IN: Notre Dame University Press, 2007); Patricia Wilson-Kastner, *Sacred Drama: A Spirituality of Christian Liturgy* (Minneapolis: Fortress, 1999). Cf. Christopher Irvine and Anne Dawtry, *Art and Worship* (Collegeville, MN: Liturgical Press, 2002), 73–74.

46. "Built into the very warrant for sacramental worship is a verb of performance. Hidden in that performance is a vision of life in Christ that is not a state of being but rather an act, an act of the worshippers who *enact* a cosmos and a community that is nothing less than God's act of creation." McCall, *Do This*, 2, emphasis original.

47. Aristotle's ideas about practical reason are key here; see *Nicomachean Ethics*, 2nd ed., trans. Terence Irwin (Cambridge: Hackett Publishing Co., 1999), 86–98. See also Alasdair MacIntyre, *After Virtue: A Study in Moral Virtue*, 3rd ed. (Notre Dame, IN: Notre Dame Press, 2007), 23–24, 45–46, 161–62, 222–25.

Another way that the theater arts might serve corporate worship is through the dramatic pageant. This would include, for many, a Christmas or an Easter pageant. For some this might include a public performance of a feast of the church or a reenactment of the life of a saint.[48] Done rightly, a pageant becomes not a mirror of the contemporary congregation's vision of the Christian life, simply telling the people what they already know about God and about themselves. Done rightly, a pageant becomes a window through which the congregation perceives afresh the story of Scripture or the story of church history, and through these stories the story of the Triune God.

In seeker-friendly churches like Willow Creek Community Church in Barrington, Illinois, a dramatic sketch may become a way to serve the sermon and to prepare the congregation to hear it with attentive ears. Such a practice is also intended to appeal to those who find themselves on the margin or beyond the margins of Christian faith. This practice would be kindred to the use of skits to serve a particular announcement. It would also be akin to the so-called evangelistic drama, whose primary purpose is to present the good news of Jesus to those who are strangers to it.

In other churches, pastors might enact their sermon. Instead of giving topical or expository treatment of a text like Judges 4–5, about Deborah, the preacher will memorize a script that "brings to life" the story of the biblical character. This is similar to the phenomenon of the dramatic first-person monologue. In my years as a pastor in Austin, I worked with actors who brought to life, in five-to-ten-minute monologues, the lives of Bathsheba, John the Baptist, Anna and Simeon, Joseph, the Magi, and a particular angel who announced the good news of Jesus's birth from the back of the angelic host (from Luke 2). As we witnessed the performances, it was as if the biblical characters were with us, in flesh, bearing witness to us.[49]

Jerusha Matsen Neal, an actress and a playwright, has written a book comprising a series of one-woman monologues, *Blessed: Monologues for Mary*. Each monologue engages the narratives surrounding the mother of Jesus, refracted through the experiences of contemporary women. As Neal describes the project, "The pieces take this title [of Mary as the mother of

---

48. Cf. Harris, *Theater and Incarnation*, 86–89, 112–18; Jennifer Herdt, *Putting on Virtue: The Legacy of the Splendid Vices* (Chicago: University of Chicago Press, 2007), ch. 5, "The Jesuit Theatrical Tradition: Acting Virtuous."

49. Jana Childers, *Performing the Word: Preaching as Theater* (Nashville: Abingdon, 1998).

the Word] seriously—reinterpreting Mary's story to refer, not only to the experience of childbirth and mothering, but also to the very real labor of creative, scientific, word-driven work. What does Mary's choice to make space for the Word in her body—and her literal struggle to find space to give birth in the crowded streets of Bethlehem—have to teach women who are pregnant with creative life?"[50]

In similar fashion, certain churches may replace a standard sermon with an entire drama. The aim of the drama will remain consonant with the aim of the sermon: to elucidate the character of God so that the people might respond faithfully to God. But the drama will accomplish things that the art of oratory and rhetoric cannot. In the fall of 2001, I wrote a drama based on Matthew's Gospel. Forty-five minutes long, involving multiple translations, and making use of the entire sanctuary space, the drama used three actors to tell the gospel story afresh. It also enlisted the congregation as a player in order to implicate it in the story.[51] The result was an immersive dramatic experience that allowed the congregation to experience the story of Jesus "on the inside," to see it played out "on the stage" of our public worship.

This use of drama is common with children's ministries. It is unfortunate, however, that children's capacity to comprehend theology, Scripture, or even arts is often underestimated, and they are frequently given cutesy, dumbed-down, or even "childish" dramas rather than substantial ones. C. S. Lewis is right to chide such an attitude: "a children's story which is enjoyed only by children is a bad children's story."[52] Would that more congregations took children more seriously and trusted their capacities to understand serious art and to do serious art themselves.[53]

---

50. Jerusha Matsen Neal, *Blessed: Monologues for Mary* (Eugene, OR: Cascade Books, 2013), 1.

51. Toward the end of the drama, an actor playing the role of Pilate asks the congregation what they wish to do with Jesus called the Messiah. Two actors, standing amid the congregation, rouse the congregation to call for Jesus's crucifixion. By this point in the play, the congregation has immersed itself so thoroughly in the story that, when the Pilate character asks for their verdict, the congregation fully commits to the role of angry crowd and bellows over and over again, "Crucify him!" It was a bit of a chilling moment. One saw how easily a group of people could go from friend to foe.

52. C. S. Lewis, "On Three Ways of Writing for Children," in *Of Other Worlds: Essays and Stories* (London: Geoffrey Bles, 1966), 24.

53. Christ Church Anglican in Austin, Texas, wrote a Christmas pageant for children that underscored the Middle Eastern aspects of the story. It was quite a thing to behold, and it was remarkable to see the children take to the story so eagerly.

The Formative Powers of the Theater Arts in Worship

How then might specific practices of the theater arts open up and close down possibilities for the formation of our humanity within the context of corporate worship? Let me suggest two practices here: the practice of testimonials and the practice of Scripture reading.

A Live Testimony

How a testimony is given at a worship service makes a considerable difference in how it is received and in how it forms a congregation. That difference is most pronounced in the comparison of a live testimony with a filmed testimony. If we watch an interview that has been filmed, say by World Vision or by the small-groups ministry, we watch a sequence of moving images that have been edited just so, framed by a particular point of view, and backed by a carefully chosen musical track. A live interview can scarcely compete with the power of a filmed testimony. Nor should it try to.

A live interview is a more immediate experience of a human being. A person's facial expressions, vocal intonations, emotional temperature, physical idiosyncrasies, public reputation—all of these things add up to a communicative potency. It is the potency of this person's *unedited* life, not a photoshopped or edited life. What the congregation witnesses in hearing a person's testimony is an embodied presence. This is one of the formative possibilities that a live testimony opens up: the possibility of encountering a fellow member of Christ's body in the flesh, warts and all.

In contrast to an edited video, this person's in-the-moment actions include the possibility that things could go awfully wrong. Her testimony may not "come off" right. Even if the testimony is written out and vetted by the pastoral leadership, she may not connect with anyone in the room. Unlike with video, where she can do multiple takes, standing in front of the congregation she gets one shot "to get it right." She will get no help from an editor to erase her mistakes and no music to make her sound better. In this way, a live testimony may close down possibilities: it entails the risk that things might "go sideways" and therefore this testimony may become off-putting to the congregation.

Again, Conor McPherson writes, "In the theater, there is nowhere to hide." That is also the case with a live testimony. The act of courage and the vulnerability that is involved in such a testimony is itself a grace that becomes a gift to the members of the congregation, who themselves are always in need of that same grace—the grace to be fully themselves, unafraid, unhidden, alongside others, before a gracious God. The point here is not that a videoed testimony could not accomplish a similar goal. The point is that a live testimony opens up the possibility of a more immediate human encounter whose capacity to acutely affect a congregation is directly related to the real-time, physical presence of the person bearing witness to God.

A Dramatic Reading of Scripture

There is no one way that Christians historically have read Holy Scripture within a corporate worship context. What Scripture is read, how much of it is read, the place from which it is read, the manner in which it is read, and who gets to read it—all these factors vary from tradition to tradition, and from congregation to congregation. No practice of Scripture reading is neutral, either. Might there then be a benefit to reading Scripture dramatically? Might there be something gained by memorizing the reading of Scripture and looking a congregation in the eye rather than only reading it from the page? Might it form a congregation in a manner that remains integral to liturgy rather than an interruption to it?

The Dramatized New Testament, for example, invites readers to hear the distinctive voices in the drama of the biblical narrative.[54] The text of Mark 10:46–52, for instance, is divided into five voices: a narrator, Bartimaeus, Jesus, and two voices from the crowd. Read by five members of a congregation, as a form of readers' theater, the text will likely *sound* differently. Its sound will more closely approximate the original exchange between Jesus and the blind man. Read well, a congregation may hear, perhaps for the first time, the tension, the pathos, and the sense of anticipation that characterize the story. Read poorly, whether melodramatically or stiffly, they will fail to hear "the Word of the Lord" to them.

In a talk given at Calvin College in 2017, N. T. Wright addressed the question of Scripture reading in public worship.[55] One of his proposals was

---

54. *The Dramatized New Testament: New International Version*, ed. Michael Perry (Grand Rapids: Baker, 1993).

55. N. T. Wright, "Sign and Means of New Creation: Public Worship and the Cre-

for congregations to welcome an "actual performance" of individual books or long passages. As Wright saw it, the results could be "spectacular." Such a practice may be rare, but it is not unheard of.[56] What does such a practice open up? It opens up the possibility of a "thick hearing" of Scripture: *both* hearing big chunks of Scripture *and* hearing the larger flow of Scripture in a sensory-rich fashion. What does it close down? Few actors possess the skill to devote to the practice; it may be cost-prohibitive for many congregations to invite such actors to perform; and the time required to perform large blocks of Scripture may be difficult for most churches to fit into their public worship.

An Antiphonal Reading of Scripture

A final way that the theater arts might form a congregation is by reading two kindred biblical texts in antiphonal fashion.[57] By this I do not simply mean reading two texts back and forth. I mean interpolating texts. Take Genesis 1 and Matthew 28, for example. Linguistically and thematically the texts echo each other. Using two readers, the two texts are brought into conversation with each other. So, for instance, a portion of the reading might include this pairing:

Genesis: "In the beginning God created the heavens and the earth."

Matthew: "And Jesus said, 'All authority in heaven and on earth has been given to me.'"

Another pairing might include these two verses:

---

ative Reading of Scripture," Calvin Institute of Christian Worship, January 2017, http://ntwrightpage.com/2017/01/30/sign-and-means-of-new-creation-public-worship-and-the-creative-reading-of-scripture/. For a video of his talk, see https://worship.calvin.edu/resources/resource-library/public-worship-as-sign-and-means-of-new-creation/.

56. Max McLean, Bruce Kuhn, and Alison Siewert are a few of the actors who have performed entire books of the Bible for congregations around North America. For details on each actor, see https://fpatheatre.com/about/; http://www.brucekuhn.com; https://www.alisonsiewert.com/about-alison/.

57. Congregations that already use the Revised Common Lectionary might find this practice to be readily accessible because of the way in which the lectionary brings Old Testament, Psalms, Gospel, and Epistolary texts into sympathetic relation to each other.

Genesis: "And God said, 'Let us make humanity in our image, according to our likeness.'"

Matthew: "Therefore go and make disciples of all nations."

Reading Scripture this way becomes a way to accent the resonances in the biblical canon.[58] Doing so might help a congregation hear how Scripture is always talking to itself—always developing the conversation, always mutually interpreting itself. No particular scholarly or literary skill is required to do this well. All that is needed is a careful attention to the text. What this practice opens up formatively is, among other things, an opportunity for a congregation to see how Scripture *does* theology: how it talks about God and the things that God cares about. What it closes down is the opportunity to read a single biblical text all the way through, in a way that is perhaps more commonly useful.

What is the ultimate goal with any of these dramatic practices? The ultimate goal is to read Scripture in a way that a particular community in a particular place hears something fresh about a particular passage and therefore something fresh from the Holy Spirit, the particular author of Scripture, so that the words of God might bear good fruit in the people of God.[59]

Conclusion

In the theater, the term "play" involves a double meaning. A play is a thing done (a "work") and it is the manner in which the thing is done (playfully). Said otherwise, to put on a play is to be at play before an audience who chooses to enter into the play. This playful dynamic, or what the philosopher Paul Thom calls "playful beholding," goes in both directions: for a play to work, both actors and audiences must choose to be play-full.[60]

This idea of play also describes, I suggest, God's own creation. It is how "Wisdom" conceives herself, "playing" in God's presence (Prov. 8:30–31). It

---

58. Genesis 1 could just as easily be paired with Psalm 8 or with John 1.

59. "When [Max McLean] read the Gospels, I [Warren] felt as if I was right there, hearing them read for the first time. I felt the emotion and pulse of each situation as it unfolded." Max McLean and Warren Bird, *Unleashing the Word: Rediscovering the Public Reading of Scripture* (Grand Rapids: Zondervan, 2009), 13.

60. Cited in Jim Fodor, "The Play of Christian Life," in Vander Lugt and Hart, *Theatrical Theology*, 130.

is how God's creatures are formed in their earliest years: in play, which is to say, reveling in the sheer gratuity of life. It is how the universe comes into being, as an expression of "God's sheer delight in play."[61] And it is how Christians ought to regard the work of worship, I argue: as a work of play, which is itself a manifestation of wonderment, delight, and adoration. In Joseph Cardinal Ratzinger's words:

> Children's play seems in many ways a kind of anticipation of life, a rehearsal for later life, without its burdens and gravity. On this analogy, the liturgy would be a reminder that we are all children, or should be children, in relation to that true life toward which we yearn to go. Liturgy would be a kind of anticipation, a rehearsal, a prelude for the life to come, for eternal life, which St. Augustine describes, by contrast with life in this world, as a fabric woven, no longer of exigency and need, but of the freedom of generosity and gift.[62]

If Wells is right that the principal form of discipleship for the Christian is corporate worship, then the medium of theater becomes an invaluable aid to this discipling work. As Christians clothe themselves "in Christ" through the practices of worship, the hope is that these practices might actually shape and symbolically inform the way they play out their faith in the world—what it means to work, to befriend neighbors and strangers, to serve neighbors, to laugh and celebrate, to feel pain and face death, and, as Ratzinger suggests, to act by grace like a child of God.

61. Fodor, "The Play of Christian Life," in Vander Lugt and Hart, *Theatrical Theology*, 145.
62. Joseph Cardinal Ratzinger, *The Spirit of the Liturgy*, trans. John Saward (San Francisco: Ignatius Press, 2000), 14.

Prostration of priests (Photograph by William D. Taylor, used with permission)

CHAPTER 9

Worship and the Kinetic Arts

They cut me down
And I leapt up high;
I am the life
That'll never, never die;
I'll live in you
If you'll live in me—
I am the Lord
Of the Dance, said he.

Sydney Carter, "Lord of the Dance"[1]

The life of faith does not go in a straight line but turns, falls, sinks, pulls, pushes, releases, clings, pauses, leaps, and dances.

Celeste Snowber Schroeder, *Embodied Prayer*

Sing a little, dance a little, exhort a little, preach a little, pray a little and a good many littles will make you a great deal.

Shaker saying

Our physical bodies are a gift. They may not feel like a gift at times, but, like all the gifts of God's creation, our bodies represent tangible evidence of the grace of God, evidenced supremely and definitely in the flesh of Christ Jesus, graced beyond measure (John 1:14). Because they are a gift, our bodies are to be stewarded rather than to be possessed, cherished as a microcosm of God's glory, not manipulated like machines. Our bodies are to be seen

---

1. The chorus is key to the theology of Carter's hymn: "Dance, then, wherever you may be / I am the Lord of the Dance, said he / And I'll lead you all, wherever you may be / And I'll lead you all in the Dance, said he." See https://hymnary.org/text/i_danced_in_the_morning_when_the.

as essential, not secondary, to our God-given humanity. For to be human is not to have a body and a soul as if they were self-contained departments; to be human is to be some*body*.[2] In our *somebodyness* we love and work and play. In our *somebodyness* we harm others and hide ourselves. In our *somebodyness* we worship.[3]

When we move our bodies within a liturgical context, whether formally or spontaneously, individually or communally, it is a way of saying, "with my body, I Thee worship," to borrow language from the Anglican Book of Common Prayer. In worship, the body *gets* to join creation's praise; this is the body's pleasure and its duty. But it also true that the body *needs* to join creation's praise, for that is the proper context for all creaturely worship of God. At times the body will follow the movements of a sanctified mind and a vivified heart. At other times it will lead the movements of a broken heart and a forgetful mind back into alignment with the good will of God. It is always, of course, the hope that the body will work in concert with the heart and mind, so that the whole self is offered in praise to the whole Godhead.

Ultimately, I argue that we move our physical bodies in the context of corporate worship not for the sake of movement alone. We move our bodies because we wish to be caught up in something bigger than ourselves. What is that exactly? It is the movement of angels who bend their gaze before the ascended Christ. It is the movement of rivers that clap their hands and of mountains that skip for joy. And it is the movement of stars in their heavenly course and of the entire cosmos, which by the power of the Holy Spirit assumes an orbit of love around the Lamb on his throne, in whom all things hold together. "Could there be anything more blessed," asked Saint Basil of Caesarea, "than to imitate on earth the dance of angels and saints? To join our voices in prayer and song to glorify the risen creator?"[4] Surely not, is the presumed answer.

---

2. "After some attempts to program such a machine, it might become apparent that what distinguishes persons from machines, no matter how cleverly constructed, is not a detached, universal, immaterial soul but an involved, situated, material body." Hubert L. Dreyfus, *What Computers Still Can't Do: A Critique of Artificial Reason* (Cambridge, MA: MIT Press, 1972), 236. Cf. Gabriel Marcel, *Creative Fidelity*, trans. Robert Rosthal (New York: Fordham University Press, 2002), 18–20; Clarence W. Joldersma, "Incarnate Being and Carnal Knowledge," in *Ways of Knowing in Concert*, ed. John H. Kok (Sioux Center, IA: Dordt College Press, 2005), 25.

3. "Since the beginning of things, no flesh has come into being without touch." Paul J. Griffiths, *Christian Flesh* (Stanford, CA: Stanford University Press, 2018), 7.

4. Cited in Ronald Gagne, Thomas Kane, and Robert VerEecke, *Introducing Dance in Christian Worship* (Washington, DC: Pastoral Press, 1984), 47.

The fourth-century theologian John Chrysostom wrote, similarly, "Of those in heaven and those on earth, a unison is made, one General Assembly, one single service of thanksgiving, one single transport of rejoicing, one joyous dance." But he also said, "where dancing is, there is the evil one."[5] This sounds a more sober, and seemingly contradictory, note, but it is not an uncommon sentiment. Basil the bishop of Caesarea chided the believers when he asked, "Do you move your feet . . . when you ought to bend the knees in prayer?"[6] Or, more bluntly, even coldly, as Western missionaries once told the Papuan people of New Guinea: "Dancing is not good. In front of God you have to be polite."[7] Such comments simply remind us of the complicated relation that exists between the kinetic arts and the corporate worship of the church, in both the East and the West.[8]

How then might we construe the role of the kinetic arts in the economy of the Triune God? What are their singular powers? What, more specifically, are the unique powers of the physical body? How might posture, gesture, and movement, as representative of the kinetic arts, serve the purposes and activities of corporate worship? And how might any instance of kinetic art open up and close down the possibilities for the formation of our humanity in a liturgical context? It is these questions that our present chapter seeks to answer.

Theological Perspectives on the Kinetic Arts

In his book *The Trinitarian Faith*, the Scottish theologian Thomas Torrance writes, "far from God being inactive in his inner being, it belongs to the essential and eternal nature of his being to move and energise and act."[9] The charismatic Anglican Thomas Smail elaborates on this idea when he

5. Cited in Gagne, Kane, and VerEecke, *Introducing Dance in Christian Worship*, 50.

6. Cited in Janet Randell, *In Him We Move: Creative Dancing in Worship* (Carlisle, UK: Solway, 1999), 23.

7. Charles E. Farhadian, "Worship as Mission," in *Christian Worship Worldwide: Expanding Horizons, Deepening Practices* (Grand Rapids: Eerdmans, 2007), 189.

8. On the virtual absence of dance in the worship of the early centuries, Frank Senn writes, "dance played a prominent role in many pagan cultus, such as the orgiastic cult of Dionysius. Because early Christians did not want to be associated in any way with such rites, they most likely avoided dancing in house-church meetings." *Embodied Liturgy: Lessons in Christian Ritual* (Minneapolis: Fortress, 2016), 323.

9. Thomas Torrance, *The Trinitarian Faith: The Evangelical Theology of the Ancient Catholic Church* (London: Bloomsbury T&T Clark, 2016), 73–74.

describes the inner life of the Triune Community this way: "The Spirit has his origin in the outward movement of the Father's love out to the Son, but he has his destination in the inward movement of the Son's love back to the Father."[10] This movement that occurs within the Godhead continues on the stage of human history. In the story of the incarnation, the Father sends the Son, the Spirit hovers over Mary's womb, and the good news is cast abroad by angels.

At the baptism of Jesus, the Spirit alights upon the Son and the sound of the Father's voice breaks through the cloud. At the end of the gospel story, the Son ascends to the Father, while the Spirit "like a gale force" (Acts 2:2, The Message) moves about the disciples. As Eugene Rogers vividly captures this double movement, "Just as the Son rises like fire into the heavens on Ascension Day, so the Spirit descends like fire upon the disciples at Pentecost."[11] Our participation in the Lord's Supper, to use one example of a common practice of worship, also involves movement. As John Calvin describes it, Christ descends to us by the Spirit in our partaking of the body and blood, so that we might ascend in faith by that same Spirit into fellowship with the Father.[12] In the beginning of God's works there is movement (Gen. 1:1). In the end there is also movement (Rev. 22:17, 20).

Angels and the host of heaven likewise find themselves in movement. Revelation 5:11 says, "Then I looked and heard the voice of many angels, numbering thousands upon thousands, and ten thousand times ten thousand. They encircled the throne and the living creatures and the elders" (NIV). In Dante's fourteenth-century work *Paradiso*, as illustrated by the French artist Gustave Doré in 1868, a circle of angels swirls in perpetual movement around the divine light (see page 16, above). Dante describes the imagined host of angels this way:

> That other host—who, as they fly, behold
> And sing His glory, which enamors them,
> His goodness, which has given them such glory
> Just like a swarm of bees, which at one time
> Alight upon the flowers, and then again

---

10. Thomas A. Smail, *The Giving Gift: The Holy Spirit in Person* (London: Hodder & Stoughton, 1988), 160.

11. Eugene J. Rogers, *After the Spirit: A Constructive Pneumatology from Resources outside the Modern West* (Grand Rapids: Eerdmans, 2005), 200.

12. Calvin, *Institutes of the Christian Religion*, IV.17.8–11.

Return to where their savory toil is stored,
Descended to the heart of that vast flower,
So bright with leaves, thence rising up again
To where their love eternally abides.[13]

The Dutch poet Joost Van den Vondel (1587–1679) envisions the heavenly scene similarly:

As air through many organ-pipes is guided,
One spirit is to many tongues divided,
In equal time through field of equal sound,
Where Church and God together dance the round.
The angel hosts from heaven's height descending
Dance deeply down, our sacrifice attending,
About Christ's body on His altar-stone.[14]

Like the host of heaven, the people of God move in praise on earth. Miriam dances (Exod. 15:20). Jephthah's daughter dances (Judg. 11:34). So do David (2 Sam. 6:5–23) and the Shulammite woman (Song 7:1–4). The psalmist enjoins the faithful to dance (Pss. 30:11; 149:3; 150:4), while Ecclesiastes describes "a time to mourn and a time to dance" (3:4 NIV; cf. Lam. 5:15). Following the exile, the people of God also dance (Jer. 31:4, 13).[15] Holy Scripture is full of movement language: for example, *hagag*, "to dance in circles" (Ps. 42:5); *sabab*, "to encircle, turn about" (Jer. 31:22); *raqad*, "to skip" (Ps. 29:6); *qippus*, "to jump" (Song 2:8); *kirker*, "to whirl, pirouette" (2 Sam. 6:14); *pizzez*, "to skip" (2 Sam. 6:16); *pasah*, "to limp dance" (1 Kings 18:26); and *siheq*, "to dance, play" (2 Sam. 6:14).

The faithful "revolve in a circle" (Exod. 15:20). They "bow and sink down" (Pss. 5:7; 29:2; 45:11; 66:4). They stand (Ps. 33:8) and they kneel (Ps. 95:6). There is the raising of hands (Ps. 88:9), just as often as there is clapping (Ps. 47:1) and rising (Ps. 119:62) and falling (Ps. 72:11). This rich vocabulary does not by itself prescribe a particular way for the church to

13. Dante Alighieri, *The Divine Comedy*, trans. Lawrence Grant White (New York: Pantheon Books, 1948), 183: *Paradiso*, Canto 31.

14. Cited in Gerardus van der Leeuw, *Sacred and Profane Beauty: The Holy in Art* (New York: Holt, Rinehart and Winston, 1963), 31.

15. The NIV renders the text this way: "I will build you up again / and you, Virgin Israel, will be rebuilt. / Again you will take up your timbrels / and go out to dance with the joyful."

worship God in a new covenantal context. But it does suggest a determinative pattern and a default way of being in the world before God in praise. Pentecostal and African traditions of worship understand this kinetic habit intuitively.[16]

"What Christians presently do with their bodies matters, matters eschatologically," writes N. T. Wright in *The Resurrection of the Son of God*.[17] It matters precisely because our bodies have been caught up in the physical body of Christ. Through Christ's ascended flesh, his *sarx*, as the Gospel writer testifies, the purpose of all flesh—namely, communion with God—is apprehended. Just as in Christ's body we discover the true extent of the human body's brokenness, so too in Christ's body do we discover its unqualified belovedness. As a temple of the Holy Spirit, moreover, the body becomes a "place" in which the glory of God is witnessed. The double entendre expressed in the phrase "the body of Christ" in fact highlights the somatic and ecclesial nature of the redemptive work that the Spirit accomplishes in God's people.

By the Spirit's animating power the human body is both a *corpus Christi* and a *corpus ecclesiasticus*: a body of Christ and an ecclesial body.[18] In Pauline terms, "there is no crucified One (Rom. 7:4) or exalted One (Phil. 3:21) without his body, just as, conversely, participation in the body of Christ is not imaginable without the glorification of God in the *soma* of the believer."[19] If the human body discovers its right orientation by being conformed to the *body* of Christ, then, the *body* of Christ (the church) in worship becomes a primary place where physical bodies are rightly formed. It is in the church's *corporate* worship that our *corporeal* worship discovers its *telos*.

Saint Jerome (AD 340–420) declares, "In the church the joy of the spirit finds expression in bodily gesture and her children shall say with David as they dance the solemn step: 'I will dance and play before the face of the Lord.'"[20] This positive estimation of the body's worth stands over against

16. "In many cultures, the integral connection between the behavior involved in making music and the sound itself is clear. . . . In these settings, to make music is to dance, to move." Mary E. McGann, *Exploring Music as Worship and Theology: An Interdisciplinary Method for Studying Liturgical Practice* (Collegeville, MN: Liturgical Press, 2002), 22.

17. N. T. Wright, *The Resurrection of the Son of God* (Minneapolis: Fortress, 2003), 290.

18. This phrase intentionally plays off of Robert W. Jenson's language in his essay "*Anima Ecclesiastica*," in *God and Human Dignity*, ed. R. Kendall Soulen and Linda Woodhead (Grand Rapids: Eerdmans, 2006), 59–71.

19. Udo Schnelle, *The Human Condition: Anthropology in the Teachings of Jesus, Paul, and John* (Minneapolis: Fortress, 1996), 59.

20. Cited in Gagne, Kane, and VerEecke, *Introducing Dance in Christian Worship*, 47.

all confused thoughts about the enfleshed nature of Christian worship. It stands over against all forms of metaphysical mind-body dualism.[21] It stands opposed to the idea that the body-soul relation is unidirectional, where only the soul affects the body, not vice versa. It resists the idea that the physical body is the autonomous property of the individual, to do with as he or she pleases rather than being interdependent to other "members" of Christ's body.

To affirm the role of the body in worship is not about legalism: it is not a matter of *having* to use our bodies, it is about *getting* and *needing* to use them. To affirm the place of the kinetic arts in our liturgies is not about automaticity: the act of bowing to the cross does not automatically make us humble, nor does the act of raised hands in itself indicate maturity. Nor is this a matter of personality types. The kinetic arts are not for extraverts only, nor for charismatic sorts, nor for the "emotionally expressive" in our midst. They are for all types. While we seek to worship God authentically, "just as we are," our personalities do not have the last word in our acts of praise and prayer—the gospel does.

To sum up the argument thus far, to worship well corporately requires that the faithful worship well corporeally. This is for several reasons. Because our humanity is a gift of God, it is our whole humanity that we offer to God in worship, not just parts of our humanity. Because the Second Person of the Trinity has assumed human flesh and, in his life, death, resurrection, and ascension, has offered that flesh in praise to the Father by the Spirit's power, our flesh too is to be offered in praise to the Father with the Spirit's help.

Because a primary purpose of corporate worship is the discipleship of the Christian, a primary task of corporate worship is the discipline of the physical body. Because corporate worship is an act of the will, not just of the heart and mind, we choose to offer our bodies to God, often despite our feelings. Self-expression that follows the urgings of the heart matters, but so does formative expression that leads the passions of the heart. Finally, because the body participates in creation's ongoing praise of God, the physical world becomes a tutor for the physical body; a grammar of postures, gestures, and movements; and a source of inspiration.

---

21. Cf. James K. A. Smith, *You Are What You Love: The Spiritual Power of Habit* (Grand Rapids: Brazos, 2016); and *Desiring the Kingdom: Worship, Worldview, and Cultural Formation* (Grand Rapids: Baker Academic, 2009).

What Are the Kinetic Arts?

With this theological perspective in mind, how are we to understand the kinetic arts? I use the term "kinetic arts" in this chapter to include three things: posture, gesture, and movement. Postures include such things as standing, sitting, and kneeling. Gestures involve bowing, prostration, crossing oneself, the kiss of peace, the joining of hands, and the laying on of hands, as well as the turning of the body in a particular direction. Movement entails lifting of hands, clapping, jumping, leaping, stomping, processing, and choreographed dance proper. With all these things the physical body communicates itself. It communicates openness or resistance. It conveys an active or a passive demeanor.

In sitting, the body may signify a willing attention to the words of the preacher or it may represent a passive disinterest in whatever is being said. A person may cross himself as a sign of the cruciform life he wishes to live or in superstitious fear that evil might come to him if he does not. Hands open say one thing, while an anxious brow and slumped shoulders say another. As Nathan Mitchell explains, the body "is intrinsically polyphonic."[22] In its capacity to speak several languages simultaneously, the physical body represents a unique contribution to our participation in worship. It also suggests a reason for why the proper use of the body in worship has generated so much misunderstanding in church history.

The Singular Powers of the Kinetic Arts

What then are the singular powers of the kinetic arts? I wish to answer this question in two parts. First, briefly, I shall identify the singular powers of the kinetic arts. Second, at greater length, I shall identify the singular powers of the physical body. To understand how the kinetic arts form us, we need to have a clear sense of how our physical bodies form us. First, however: the powers of the kinetic arts. The body itself, as a biological organism, is the most fundamental power of the kinetic arts. The body involves breath, heartbeat, muscles, bones, organ, reflexes, and balance. The body may be still or in motion, upright or folded in on itself, opened out and closed in.

22. Nathan Mitchell, *Meeting Mystery: Liturgy, Worship, Sacraments* (Maryknoll, NY: Orbis Books, 2006), 180.

Action is a second power of the kinetic arts. This answers the question, What is the body *doing*? Is it posturing? Is it gesturing? Is it moving? A third power is space. Where is the body placed? Is it in a large or small space? Is it near others or far away? Time is a fourth power. This answers the question, When? This includes such things as pulse, tempo, accent, and rhythmic pattern. Time likewise describes one of the unique characteristics of dance. Like drama and music, dance cannot be fixed in time and hung on the wall, as a painting can. It can only be experienced in the moment.[23] As Judith Rock and Norman Mealy observe, "Dance is a time art. A dance cannot be framed or preserved in a museum; it lives and breathes for us only in the moment of performance. In its brief incarnation, a successful dance creates a momentary relationship with us by drawing us into the temporal and physical reality that it is and presents."[24]

Energy is a fifth power of the kinetic arts. Is the movement still or rapid, sharp or smooth, sudden or sustained, flowing or tight? The last power is people. With whom is the body engaged? With nobody? With one other person? With multiple people? Alone a person can communicate one thing through movement; with others a different "conversation" can take place through the interaction of bodies. In all these ways, the kinetic arts exercise their powers through the physical body. In kneeling, a posture of humility is adopted. With the body low to the ground, we become vulnerable, and in this posture of physical weakness we signal to ourselves and to others our desire for a humble heart.

In jumping during a song of praise, we abandon a measure of self-possession. In allowing our bodies to move up and down, in hops and leaps, we practice what it means to be self-abandoned to God in all of life, rather than self-protective. In the gesture of open hands, palms facing upward, the pastor prays for the congregation. It is not a gesture for proclamation or instruction; it is a gesture of petition, a request of God on behalf of the people of God.[25] David Abram offers this observation about the power of gesture and hereby helps to elucidate the power of all the kinetic arts:

23. When a dance is captured on camera, as it is often, it becomes a different thing; it morphs into a different medium, the medium of film.

24. Judith Rock and Norman Mealy, *Performer as Priest and Prophet: Restoring the Intuitive in Worship through Music and Dance* (San Francisco: Harper & Row, 1988), 1. A similar point is made in Gagne, Kane, and VerEecke, *Introducing Dance in Christian Worship*, 126.

25. Cf. Kimberly Bracken Long, *The Worshiping Body: The Art of Leading Worship* (Louisville: Westminster John Knox, 2009), 77–88.

The gesture is spontaneous and immediate. It is not an arbitrary sign that we mentally attach to a particular emotion or feeling; rather, the gesture *is* the bodying-forth of that emotion into the world, it *is* that feeling of delight or of anguish in its tangible, visible aspect. When we encounter such a spontaneous gesture, we do not first see it as a blank behavior, which we then mentally associate with a particular content or significance; rather, the bodily gesture speaks directly to our own body, is thereby understood without any interior reflection.... Communicative meaning is always, in its depths, affective; it remains rooted in the sensual dimension of experience, born of the body's native capacity to resonate with other bodies and with the landscape as a whole.[26]

The Singular Powers of the Physical Body

With these powers of the kinetic arts in mind, how might we describe the singular powers of the physical body? Whatever else the physical body may communicate through posture, gesture, and movement, it communicates so much more on account of the fact that the body has "a mind of its own" and that it functions as a sociocultural signifier. Scholars in the field of embodied cognition remind us that our knowledge of the world occurs through our bodies.[27] "Grasping something with the hand," writes Clarence Joldersma, "is central for the bodily agent's way of knowing the world."[28] A jovial person is "light on his toes" and "bright-eyed." Confident persons carry themselves in an "open" manner.[29]

When imagining the future, we lean forward; when remembering the past, we dip back. "The body never lies," we say; or, "I know it in my bones," we insist. These figures of speech describe the ways we figure

26. David Abram, *The Spell of the Sensuous* (New York: Vintage Books, 1996), 74–75, emphasis original.

27. John A. Sloboda and Patrik N. Juslin, "Psychological Perspectives on Music and Emotion," in *Music and Emotion: Theory and Research*, ed. Patrik N. Juslin and John A. Sloboda (Oxford: Oxford University Press, 2001), 86.

28. Joldersma, "Incarnate Being and Carnal Knowledge," 25.

29. Cf. Jeremy Begbie, "Faithful Feelings: Music and Emotion in Worship," in *Resonant Witness: Conversations between Music and Theology*, ed. Jeremy S. Begbie and Steven R. Guthrie (Grand Rapids: Eerdmans, 2011), 342–44.

out the world through our bodies. The body also signifies itself in culturally particular ways. Asian cultures, where the elderly are honored, perceive elderly bodies differently than American culture. The color of skin signifies different things in different cultural contexts. The meaning of male and female bodies is inevitably conditioned by our social location. Whatever powers the kinetic arts may exercise in corporate worship context, then, will reside in the fundamental powers of the physical body itself.

Body Knowledge

The first power of the body is *body knowledge*. This is a kind of knowledge that athletes and farmers know a great deal about. An athlete acquires a form of kinetic intelligence after a lifetime of repetitive physical exercises. A farmer obtains a sense for the weather after a lifetime of smelling the air.[30] With farmers, the nose knows what it knows. Our bodies frequently have "a mind of their own" when it comes to food, sex, or drugs. When our bodily responses become disordered, the re-ordering of our responses occurs *through* the body, as art therapists and victims of post-traumatic stress disorder (PTSD) might testify from firsthand experience.[31]

When Christians open their hands to receive the minister's benediction, it is a way for them to know that all of life requires an open-handed reception of God's blessing. When a congregation marches from the parking lot into the sanctuary on Palm Sunday, it is a way for Christians to get a "feel" for the pilgrimage quality of their life on Monday through Saturday. When a multiethnic congregation holds each other's hands during the passing of the peace, it is a way for their bodies to signify the reconciliation that ought to characterize their whole lives. In doing these things a congregation gains *body knowledge* of the body of Christ.

---

30. Farmers, in fact, can often smell the specific quality of rain before it arrives. When lightning within storm clouds splits oxygen apart into separate atoms, those atoms recombine to form ozone instead of oxygen. As the storm winds blow, the ozone is blown out ahead of the storm.

31. Cf. Celeste Snowber Schroeder, *Embodied Prayer: Harmonizing Body and Soul* (Liguori, MO: Triumph Books, 1995), ch. 10. See also https://adta.org.

Muscle Memory

A second power of the body is *muscle memory*. A pianist's fingers, for example, acquire memory of a piece through repetition, such that it can eventually be played without conscious thought. When members of a multigenerational congregation lay hands on one another during the prayer ministry, it becomes a way to physically signify the congregation's unity across the ages. The hope is that this repeated action, as a tactile sign of the re-membering work of the Spirit, might generate holy *muscle memory* in moments when members might be tempted to judge and find wanting persons older or younger than themselves.

Nonverbal Communication

A third power of the body is *nonverbal communication*. Our bodies are always talking whether we realize it or not.[32] We may say one thing with our mouth ("I trust you") but a contrary thing with our eyes ("I don't trust you"). Within a context of corporate worship, there are two kinds of congregations: those whose body language communicates joyful welcome to fellow members of the congregation and warm hospitality to visitors and those whose body language communicates just the opposite, despite whatever words may be said to the contrary. The difference between the two is night and day. The difference is fundamentally theological, not cultural.

Sign

A fourth power of the body involves its capacity to function as a *sign*. A hand with two fingers extended in a V-shape is widely recognized as a sign of peace. A soldier who salutes the commanding officer needs no words to signify his willing submission to authority. The idea of the church "raised to the things above" can be signified in different ways in worship. For some, the spontaneous act of raising hands high above

---

32. Cf. Joe Navarro, *What Every BODY Is Saying: An Ex-FBI Agent's Guide to Speed-Reading People* (New York: HarperCollins, 2008). The author boasts, "Read this book and send your nonverbal intelligence soaring."

one's head signifies a desire to yield one's heart fully to God in heaven. For others, the formal act of raising hands high above one's head signifies a desire to honor the authority of God over all things. Whatever the movement, it will never be a generic thing; it will always be context and culturally specific.

Body Image

A fifth power is *body image*. This refers to the relative worth that individuals place upon their body in relation to others' bodies. Images of a willowy female liturgical dancer, dressed in a flowing satin costume, twirling sparkly ribbons, may readily come to mind for some. "This is what *such women* do: they dance like *this*," some might say stereotypically. But to allow this image to predominate is to succumb to a sinful mind-set.[33] Men *do* dance, as both biblical and church history remind us. And far from being the thing of "fair and fragile" female bodies, women's bodies are strong in *many* different ways.[34] For both men and women the "ideal" image of the body is the same: a body fully yielded to God.

An Enculturated Body

Body image is closely related to a sixth power of the body: the *enculturated body*. This includes the ways in which different cultures perceive each other's bodies. It includes ideas about who is "in" and who is "out."[35] It in-

33. On this point, see Heidi Schlumpf, "In Defense of Liturgical Dance," *National Catholic Reporter*, April 14, 2017, https://www.ncronline.org/blogs/ncr-today/defense-liturgical -dance.

34. For women to dance "in the spirit of Miriam," for instance, is to dance in the strength that characterizes a biblical tradition of liberation. On this point, see Angela Yarber, *Dance in Scripture: How Biblical Dancers Can Revolutionize Worship Today* (Eugene, OR: Cascade, 2013), ch. 2. For both men and women, the "ideal" image of the body is the same: a body fully yielded to God.

35. "If you knew the steps," choreographer Camille Brown says in a 2016 TED Talk, in which she presents a visual history of social dance in twenty-five moves, "it meant that you belonged to a social group." To know a particular "move" is to belong to a specific group. https://www.ted.com/talks/camille_a_brown_a_visual_history_of_social_dance _in_25_moves.

cludes ideas about "who my people are." For many African churches, it is in "dance that the African can best be himself."[36] To be an African Christian, on this understanding, is to be a Christian who moves freely in worship. For Sarah Pack, as a Korean-American, to raise her hands in worship meant that she fell out of step with the cultural expectations of the Presbyterian Korean-American churches of her childhood, which valued postures of dependence and deference before God.

As an adult Pack chose to lift her hands in a symbol of solidarity with victims of injustice. "I literally reach out to God," she writes. "*Do something with your power. Be who you say you are. Show us your mercy and deliver justice, God.* Hands low challenged me to offer everything to him. Hands high in this powerful, physical posture emboldens my prayers as I continue to explore unfamiliar ways of encountering a Savior. With my body, I not only submit myself to God's authority—I confront it."[37] For Pack, to turn her palms out to God became a way to turn her face outward, too. To use her body in all these ways became a way to embrace a different culture of the body, a culture of strength and of hope.

Embodied Presence

A final power is the power of *embodied presence*. Politicians, for instance, know that there is no substitute for the tireless travel that takes them on the campaign trail from town to town, shaking hands, sharing meals, and listening to stories, rather than communicating only by way of print, radio, television, or internet. And while a pastor may call sick parishioners over the phone in order to pray for them, a unique power is experienced when the pastor visits them at the hospital and prays with them in person—holding their hand, looking them in the eye, remaining near at hand. This also holds true for ministries of prayer in corporate worship: it is one thing to pray for one's congregation at a distance; it is another thing to lay hands on a person and to pray for them in an enfleshed, face-to-face manner.

---

36. Cited in Roberta King, with Jean Ngoya Kidula et al., *Music in the Life of the African Church* (Waco, TX: Baylor University Press, 2008), 57.

37. Sarah Pack, "How Lifting My Hands in Worship Became My Protest to God," *Christianity Today*, January 16, 2007, emphasis original, http://www.christianitytoday.com /ct/2017/january-web-only/how-lifting-my-hands-in-worship-became-my-protest-to-god .html.

All the singular powers of the body add up in the end to the experience of bodily inertia. This describes a certain way of being in the world in our physical bodies that we take for granted and that we assume and do not readily or consciously question, unless and until our bodily inertia itself is questioned and re-ordered.

The Kinetic Arts in Service of Corporate Worship

To get a sense of the ways in which the kinetic arts might serve corporate worship, it will be helpful to clarify our use of terms. The term "sacred dance" usually denotes the broadest category for dance in the service of God.[38] "Praise dance" is a term often used by Pentecostal and charismatic traditions,[39] while "liturgical dance" represents movement that is performed in service of the corporate worship and tends to be the preferred nomenclature of mainline denominations.[40] Some postures, gestures, and movements may be simple, others more complex.

The styles of dance may be folk, classical, modern, or otherwise. They may be representational or impressionistic. If accompanied by text or words, the power of the dance will be one thing. If unaccompanied by text or words, the power of the dance will be another thing. In some cases, a congregation will play an active role, as in the practice of liturgical gestures or spontaneous outbursts of clapping. In other cases, a congregation will play a more passive role, as in the observance of a festival procession or a performance by dancers.

One general function of the kinetic arts is *aesthetic*. A Messianic Jewish circle dance, for example, may be done for the sake of delight. A hip-hop performance may be done for the pure joy that a community experiences in the presence of God.[41] Another function is *didactic*. Sandra Organ-Solis, a former ballerina for the Houston Ballet, has created a choreographed version of the Nicene Creed that she has often performed for congregations in the middle of a worship service. She speaks a phrase from the creed and

---

38. See, for instance, http://sacreddanceguild.org; http://www.balletmagnificat.com.

39. See, for instance, http://www.musiclyric4christian.com/praise-dance.html; https://www.youtube.com/watch?v=oqD4i7gkj3I; https://hillsong.com/college/dance-stream/.

40. See https://www.umcdiscipleship.org/resources/the-work-of-liturgical-dancers.

41. See, for instance, https://www.youtube.com/watch?v=fYvdLqPKL7M and http://breakfree2024.com.

accompanies that phrase with interpretive movement. This serves not as a substitute for the verbal confession of the creed but as a way to perceive the kinetic contours of faith.

Another general function of the kinetic arts is *devotional*. Walking a labyrinth, for instance, is a way for the body to move in prayer.[42] As the body moves through the spiral of lines, the heart contemplates the things of God and is kindled with affection for God. The posture of stillness is another way for the body to serve the purposes of devotion. Stillness is an underrated but sorely needed practice for Christians, who cannot know certain things about God apart from a quieting of the body as a way for the heart and mind to attend to God (Ps. 46:10).

The kinetic arts may also serve a particular *activity* of the liturgy. At Church of the Servant in Grand Rapids, Michigan, for example, liturgical dancers carry the elements of the Lord's Supper from the back of the sanctuary to the front. This is done to symbolize the movement of gift of bread and wine *from* God *to* the people of God—from the raw materials of earth and the cultural goods of human making to the table of God. In doing so, the dancers represent the actions of the people and invite their whole humanity to be caught up in worship.[43]

The kinetic arts may be enlisted, lastly, for *missional* purposes. In fourth-century Jerusalem, a procession of Christians moved through the city streets during major holy days, testifying thereby of the expansive scope of God's reign on earth.[44] A similar thing occurred with the March for Jesus movement in the late twentieth century.[45] This included processions of Christians, singing and praying, carrying festive banners, lifting joyful shouts into the air, through the streets of a given city—of Melbourne, Australia, in 1983; of São Paolo, Brazil, in 2016; and, in 1994, of over ten million Christians from over 170 nations who covered every time zone on the planet.

42. See https://labyrinthlocator.com.

43. Cf. "Common Questions About Our Worship," https://www.churchoftheservantcrc.org/worship/worship-at-cos-frequently-asked-questions/.

44. Lester Ruth, Carrie Steenwyk, and John D. Witvliet, *Walking Where Jesus Walked: Worship in Fourth-Century Jerusalem* (Grand Rapids: Eerdmans, 2010), 23–24. This might also describe the experience of Christians during the Feast of Fools, Children's Festival, and the Dance of Death.

45. See https://en.wikipedia.org/wiki/March_for_Jesus.

The Formative Powers of the Kinetic Arts in Worship

SATB and Raised Hands

Recalling our example from the introductory chapter, where our imagined congregation is split up into soprano, alto, tenor, and bass voices (in technical terms: SATB), a particular image of the body of Christ is evoked. Each individual voice joins to other similarly tuned voices in order to sing as a subgroup. The tenors, for example, or what we might call the tribe of tenor-like voices, occupy a specific sonic space. Comprising various clans— leggero, spinto, lyric, and so on—they generate a fullness of sound, from C_3 to A_4 on the musical scale. But they are not alone. They are joined and in-filled by other tribes of voices: the basses, the altos, the sopranos, each with their own clans.

The work of the tenor tribe is not only to remain attuned to itself, one to another. Its work is also to attend to these other voices, to press up against them *just so*—not too loudly, not too softly, not too forcefully, not too timidly. Together these four tribes, each possessing their own logic, their own resonances, their own way of being in the sonic world, interanimate each other in order to produce a distinct song. Together, they occupy a common musical space, saturating one another without overwhelming or suppressing each other.

Singing this way generates a distinctive manner of being *together*. Each individual voice occupies a particular space, existing in co-inherent relation to the other sonic spaces. And the fullness of sound generated by one voice does not diminish the fullness of sound produced by any of the other voices. The particularity of each voice is secured; each voice inhabits other particular voices, too. A congregation that sings in this way is *actually together*, musically speaking, but it also opens up a metaphorical way of being together both within and outside of the context of the liturgy.

Whereas the sound of many voices may generate an image of togetherness, there is another way in which the liturgical arts can generate a particular metaphor of unity: through the use of physical bodies, particularly with the use of raised hands. Here bodies, raised upward, are fully extended. From a posture of contraction, physical bodies are opened out and in this way become vulnerable, exposed to one another. With hands raised upward, whether in spontaneous or prescriptive fashion, the church honors God with its bodies—each body a unique temple of the Holy Spirit.

At its best, the worshiper in this setting gives visible and commensurate expression to the expansive reach of the heart for God.

Unlike the sounds of voices that absorb and saturate one another, raised hands exist side by side. The boundaries of bodies are clearly delineated: my body *here*, your body *there*. The particularity of human persons is also more marked. While it may be possible to hear the particular characteristics of the voices of those standing nearest to you, usually what you hear is a blended whole. But with physical bodies, it is possible to distinguish a whole range of unique skin colors, shapes of hands, the angle of joints, the length of fingers—in short, the very things that make an individual one of a kind and, as the case may be, the things that turn us on, turn us toward, or turn us off to each other.

A congregation that worships this way is, again, *actually together*, lifting up holy hands in prayer and praise to God (cf. 1 Tim. 2:8). But they also offer a kinetic and visual metaphor for the kind of togetherness that Jesus prays for in John 17 on behalf of his disciples. Each of these practices of kinetic art, then, opens up and closes down possibilities for the formation of unity in a given congregation at worship. Each practice signifies a particular way of being the body of Christ. Each practice enables a congregation to *see* and to *feel* its common life in an irreducible manner.

Expressive Movement versus Pre-scripted Movement

Expressive movement is the kind of movement that is oriented around a spontaneous, expressive response to God. Charismatic, Pentecostal, and nondenominational churches, along with plenty of congregations in the Global South, might favor this sort of movement in corporate worship. The mission of St. Gregory of Nyssa Episcopal Church in San Francisco, for example, is to invite people "to see God's image in all humankind, to sing and to dance to Jesus's tune, and to become God's friends." Each Sunday, congregants are encouraged to kick up their feet as they circle the altar in celebration of God. Worship at St. Gregory's is deliberately physical and participatory, intended to evoke ancient Byzantine practices of kinesthetic worship.[46]

In contrast to this, pre-scripted movement is oriented around a formal, choreographed response to God. Performance-based movements are like-

---

46. See https://www.saintgregorys.org/more-about-our-services.html.

wise pre-scripted.[47] Examples of pre-scripted movement include bowing to the cross to signify one's reverence to Christ. At the reading of the gospel, bodies are turned to the center as a sign of a gospel-oriented life that would mark the community at all times. Some may kneel to pray in a posture of humility, signifying the supplication of the heart, while others may stand to pray as a reminder that the Christian has been "raised with Christ" (Col. 3:1 NIV). With hands open, a person *receives* rather than *takes* the elements of the Lord's Supper. In sharing the peace of Christ, a kiss or a handshake becomes a tangible sign of the reconciliation that Christ makes possible.

Both spontaneous and the choreographed movement, I maintain, form people's bodily experience in worship in important ways. Each performs its own distinctive role in discipling the people of God into the image of Christ. What does expressive movement open up formatively? It allows our bodies to be led by our minds and hearts so that we might offer our whole self to God in worship. What does pre-scripted movement open up? It allows our bodies to lead our hearts and minds in the way of faithful discipleship. With the first it is an outflow of the emotions; with the second it is a sacrifice of praise, frequently despite our emotions. With the first we exhibit an intimate relationship between body and heart; with the second we exhibit a willing relationship between the body and heart. In both cases we affirm the integrity of our person; in both we offer bodies in humility to God.[48]

Seating Arrangement

No seating arrangement is ever neutral. Three seating arrangements, I suggest, become most determinative for the posture of the physical body in a congregational context. The first seating arrangement is what might termed "side by side." Such an arrangement evokes associations with processions and marches. Here we recall the marches of Israel (Ps. 68:24–27)

47. Mainline churches might favor such movement, though free churches often encourage the creation of dances for worship. See, for example, Carolyn Deitering, *The Liturgy as Dance and the Liturgical Dancer* (New York: Crossroad, 1984). See also Bethel Music, "Seas of Crimson" (Synesthesia), https://www.youtube.com/watch?v=fMPinCNZnbo.

48. Barry Liesch, in *People in the Presence of God: Models and Directions for Worship* (Grand Rapids: Zondervan, 1988), 213–17, matches a set of accessible movements to specific hymns as a way for a congregation to take "baby steps" toward the inclusion of movement in worship.

and the processions of saints on pilgrimage (Ps. 48:12–14). In processions human beings walk side by side, shoulder to shoulder, eyes forward, marching in step. In spaces like the Gothic style of Salisbury Cathedral or the Italian Renaissance style of St. James Cathedral in Seattle, Washington, a longitudinal architectural plan invites the physical body to move from back to front, from outside ("world") to inside ("sanctuary").[49]

What does such an arrangement open up formatively? It underscores the idea of worship as pilgrimage: from life as it is lived now to life as it is envisioned in the eschaton.[50] A longitudinal plan invites people to stand side by side and in this way to say, "This is how we are together: our bodies face forward, our faces turned to a common end, our strength anchored in the joy set before us." What does such an arrangement close down? In such an arrangement the experience of congregational song involves the act of singing to the back of another person's head. What captures the gaze is, at best, the imagined host of our song, Christ himself, or, perhaps at worst, whatever stands at the front of the space—a wall, an organ, a painting, a person, or a screen, however helpful or distracting they may be.

A second determinative seating arrangement is what might be called "circling up." This includes both actual circle arrangements, like the central-plan design that typifies much of Byzantine architecture, or half-moon arrangements, such as St. John's Abbey, in Collegeville, Minnesota.[51] Here the primary association might be one of camaraderie. Human bodies stand side by side but slightly angled toward other bodies. Like children on the playground, human bodies are huddled up or arm in arm. "We are together in this way," we might say, "tuned in toward several 'one anothers.'" Jean N. Kidula describes the common experience of distinctively African

49. See, for example, https://www.salisburycathedral.org.uk/visit-about-building/glance-floor-plan and http://www.stjames-cathedral.org/Tour/default.aspx.

50. "In Santa Maria Maggiore itself . . . forty-three mosaic scenes above the nave colonnade narrate 'structural' episodes of Judeo-Christian faith: the stories of Abraham, Moses, Joshua. Thus believers, as they advance toward the altar, perceive themselves inserted in a historical and meta-historical process that leads them toward the 'city founded, designed, and built by God' (Heb. 11:10). At the end of this journey—at the right and left of the wall closing the nave—two cities are in fact represented: 'Jerusalem' and 'Bethlehem' as they are identified in inscriptions." Timothy Verdon, *Art and Prayer: The Beauty of Turning to God* (Brewster, MA: Paraclete, 2013), 73.

51. See https://www.visitcambridge.org/things-to-do/church-of-the-holy-sepulchre-the-round-church-p506881; https://en.wikipedia.org/wiki/Byzantine_architecture; http://www.saintjohnsabbey.org/your-visit/abbey-church/.

worship this way: "Creating a circle means that members of the performance group are visible to everybody, but each member can really be seen properly by the few that are close by, especially when there is a big group performing. This rather ambiguous placement ensures community and anonymity while promoting individuality and particularity."[52]

Such an experience is possible for worship spaces whose seating arrangement is circular or semicircular. What does such an arrangement open up formatively? In such an arrangement the experience of congregational song involves singing in a way that attends more closely to persons on either side and on down the line. Here we glimpse the eyes of others. Here we *sense* that we are not alone in our song and the sighting of other faces inspires our own song. What does such an arrangement close down? Not all spaces can be easily amended to make a circular arrangement possible.

The third determinative seating arrangement is "face to face." Here human bodies exist in close proximity. Here direct attention is given to the bodies of others. Here the expressiveness of the face is consequential. Sitting across from one another, as parishioners do at St. Gregory's Episcopal Church in San Francisco or as individuals may do in monastic choir stalls or even in house churches, means that what is done with one's physical body affects others in the most direct fashion.[53] A "face-to-face" encounter is what the faithful are promised in glory (1 Cor. 13:12) and what Saint Paul wishes he could obtain with the saints (2 Cor. 10:1).

What does such an arrangement open up formatively? A face-to-face arrangement of seats evokes associations with an experience of intimate table fellowship, with echoes of the disciples gathered around the table at the Last Supper. "We are together in this way," we might say, "as we look across at each other." In such an arrangement the experience of congregational song involves singing one to another, face-to-face, and becomes thereby a prompt to worship. What does such an arrangement close down? With no place to hide, the bodies and faces of others may prove to be obstacles to worship.[54]

---

52. Jean Ngoya Kidula, "Music Culture: African Life," in King with Kidula et al., *Music in the Life of the African Church*, 45.

53. See https://en.wikipedia.org/wiki/Choir_(architecture); https://www.saintgregorys.org/worship.html.

54. Working around existing seating arrangements is often difficult. Few congregations have the freedom to modify their liturgical spaces. The Anglican Diocese of London offers some helpful perspective on things that could be done in the document "How to

Admittedly, while most congregations are not able easily to change their seating arrangements, it is helpful, I believe, to know how our arrangements form our life together. And there might be micro-changes that a congregation might explore as they address each other with songs, hymns, and spiritual songs to God.

Conclusion

While fitting bodily behaviors may vary from culture to culture and from liturgy to liturgy, one might expect there to be basic kinetic actions that befit specific activities of worship: the condition of humility corresponding to a deferential posture; the condition of celebration corresponding to an expansive movement; the condition of receptivity corresponding to a gesture of welcome. Whatever the signification of the particular kinetic action, we form our bodies in corporate worship and are formed by our bodies.

We train our bodies to desire the things of Christ and are trained by our bodies to continue desiring them. We encourage or discourage one another by our bodily acts of worship. We employ our bodies mindlessly or mindfully, self-indulgently or hospitably. We bring to worship healthy and whole bodies or we bring broken and dispirited bodies, bodies burdened by insecurity, self-hatred, sickness, loneliness, fears of disapproval, failure, rejection, and being out of control. We worship God with bodies that have been scarred by touch and with bodies that have been starved of touch.

The hope, of course, is that however we use our bodies in worship, our bodies might form in us a deeper sense of our fellowship in Christ's broken body and of our participation in the power of Christ's resurrected body. The hope is that our bodies will be both faithfully free and faithfully shaped in worship. The hope is that we will get a feel for the Word made flesh and a sense of the Spirit's work in the world that God so loves. Just as the life of God is far from static, then, so too the life of faith is far from sedentary, and in corporate worship we get to present our bodies as living sacrifices so that they might be renewed and refreshed in Christ by the Spirit.

Replace and Reorder Church Seating," https://www.london.anglican.org/kb/replace-re order-church-seating/.

With our bodies, in the end, we get to join all of creation's praise and, in our respective liturgical contexts, to discover thereby the ways in which we might cling to God and release to God, stretch out to God and retreat from God, turn and return to God, fall before and rise again in faith before a God who reaches out to us in grace and turns our wailing into dancing, and our tentative gestures of faith into full-fledged movements of love and adoration.

Stations of the Cross, Chapel of St. Basil, University of St. Thomas, Houston, Texas (Photograph by author)

CHAPTER 10

Mother Tongues and Adjectival Tongues

God speaks to a man's heart in the language he has sucked from his mother.

> Maurice Leenhardt, "Letter to the
> Pastors of Nouvelle-Calédonie"

Each mortal thing does one thing and the same:
Deals out that being indoors each one dwells;
Selves—goes its self; *myself* it speaks and spells,
Crying *What I do is me: for that I came.*

> Gerard Manley Hopkins, "As Kingfishers Catch Fire"

One of his Majesty's chaplains preached; after which, instead of the ancient, grave, and solemn wind music accompanying the organ, was introduced a concert of twenty-four violins between every pause, after the French fantastical light way, better suited to a tavern or playhouse than a church.

> John Evelyn[1]

If music making is an emblem of identity, as many scholars hold, and a means to preserve the integrity of a community, what happens, for instance, to a traditional Anglo-Catholic church in Boston, Massachusetts, if it were to sing the doxology in Swahili rather than in the native language of its congregation, English?[2] How is the identity of such a congregation

---

1. Cited in Carl Engel, *Researches into the Early History of the Violin Family* (London: Novello, Ewer & Co., 1883), 149–50. Evelyn's comment was written in London, on December 21, 1662, and refers to the introduction by King Charles II of a consort of twenty-four violins into the liturgy of the Chapel Royal, which Evelyn termed "his four-and-twenty fiddlers" and which, he felt, violated the "spirit" of the liturgy.

2. Mark P. Bangert, "Dynamics of World Musics: A Methodology for Evaluation," in

changed if it sings the doxology in Swahili *regularly* rather than only occasionally? And how is its peculiar identity further refashioned if it substitutes the pipe organ for electric guitars and the use of professional choirs for the practice of extemporaneous singing, along with the occasional invitation to "sing in the Spirit"?[3]

In his book *Musicking*, Christopher Small argues that the act of "musicking" is a way to establish a set of relationships "and it is in those relationships that the meaning of the act lies."[4] If this is so, how has our imagined congregation, by dint of these musical modifications, reconfigured its unique identity? If black gospel songs are added to the liturgical repertoire and the practice of syncopated singing is accompanied by lively kinetic activities, has the singular character of our Anglo-Catholic church fundamentally changed? On what terms should it retain and resist certain musical practices in order to remain *fully* itself? And what musical practices might it add as a way to be more *richly* itself?

Similar questions can be asked of other congregations. At what point, for example, is a traditional Lutheran congregation no longer recognizably itself if it adopts the poetic and rhetorical practices of Baptist preachers? If a congregation in the Orthodox Presbyterian Church (OPC) swapped its official hymnal for the use of songs by Bob Dylan, the Indigo Girls, and Kendrick Lamar, is it still OPC in any meaningful way? When is a Vineyard congregation no longer truly itself if it replaces a bare stage with an altar adorned with candles, incense, and holy icons? And can an Indian Pentecostal congregation remain truly Pentecostal if it exchanges musical instruments for long stretches of silence and a subdued physicality?

The question that this chapter seeks to address is a familiar one to many congregations around the world: At what point have they lost their singular identity when certain practices of liturgical art are introduced or removed? Two extreme responses to this question might be: "This is who we are and we are never going to change," or, "It does not matter what we do, so long as our hearts are sincere." At best, the desire of the former is

---

Worship and Culture: Foreign Country or Homeland?, ed. Gláucia Vasconcelos Wilkey (Grand Rapids: Eerdmans, 2014), 116–17. Other helpful resources include James R. Krabill, ed., *Worship and Mission for the Global Church: An Ethnodoxology Handbook* (Pasadena, CA: William Carey Library, 2013); Teresa Berger and Bryan D. Spinks, eds., *The Spirit in Worship—Worship in the Spirit* (Collegeville, MN: Liturgical Press, 2009).

3. Simon Frith, *Performing Rites* (Cambridge, MA: Harvard University Press, 1996), 272.

4. Christopher Small, *Musicking: The Meanings of Performing and Listening* (Hanover, NH: University Press of New England, 1998), 13.

perhaps to stay true to its Spirit-constituted self, while the desire of the latter is maybe to be open to the new work of the Spirit. At stake with both is the nature of its unique identity as a worshiping congregation and the integrity of its life together.

My aim here is to make *theological* sense of a congregation's desire to remain true to itself through its practices of liturgical art and to be open to new things, too. Drawing on the thought of Colin Gunton, I propose a way in which the arts in worship can become instruments of the Spirit's work to accomplish this double goal.[5] My argument is, first, that the arts in worship should secure a congregation's particular way of praising God, what I will call its "mother tongue," in order to enable that congregation to be *more fully itself*; and, second, that when a congregation welcomes new practices of the arts in worship, what I will call "adjectival tongues," it enables that congregation to become *more richly itself*.[6]

The Work of the Spirit in Jesus's Life

In Gunton's book *The One, the Three and the Many*, the Holy Spirit plays a decisive role.[7] On the one hand, against a tendency where the "one" smothers the "many," Gunton argues that it is the Spirit who preserves the particularity of individual persons and things.[8] On the other hand, against a tendency where the "many" suppress the "one," Gunton contends that the Spirit frees the many to be in right relation to each other in order to be truly together. What the Spirit accomplishes in the life and ministry of Jesus, Gunton insists, can be seen as the decisive pattern of the Spirit's work in creation at large.

5. While the argument of the chapter may apply in some fashion to Eastern Orthodox public worship, the issues that arise in those variegated contexts require a measure of care that this essay cannot properly give.

6. A different version of this material appeared in W. David O. Taylor, "Mother Tongues and Adjectival Tongues: Liturgical Identity and the Liturgical Arts in a Pneumatological Key," *Worship Journal* (2018): 54–70.

7. Colin Gunton, *The One, the Three and the Many: God, Creation and the Culture of Modernity* (Cambridge: Cambridge University Press, 1993). Cf. Jeremy Begbie, *Resounding Truth: Christian Wisdom in the World of Music* (Grand Rapids: Baker Academic, 2007), esp. chs. 8–9.

8. Gunton, *The One, the Three and the Many*, 190.

The Spirit Deepens the Particularity of Jesus

A central thing that the Spirit accomplishes in Jesus is to establish his particularity. Gunton points to the pattern of the Spirit's work in the life and ministry of Jesus at pivotal moments: overshadowing him at his birth (Luke 1:35), moving him to visit the temple as a child (Luke 2:27), descending upon him at his baptism (Mark 1:10), driving him into the desert to be tempted (Matt. 4:1), empowering his teaching (Luke 4:18; John 3:34) as well as his works of healing and exorcism (Matt. 12:28; Luke 4:14–21), superintending his death (1 Pet. 3:18), raising him from the dead (Rom. 1:4; 8:11; cf. 1 Cor. 15:42–49), and partnering with him in the summons of the heavenly bride of Christ (Rev. 22:17).

At the dawn of the church, Jesus gives instructions to his apostles through the Spirit (Acts 1:2). At Christ's ascension a cloud hides him from his disciples' sight (Acts 1:9). This cloud recalls the cloud that envelops Jesus at his transfiguration (Luke 9:28–36), an event that in turn uses the same language of Luke 1:35, where the Spirit envelops Mary at Jesus's conception.[9] What the Spirit accomplishes in Jesus is to enable him to be *this particular* person, not a generic person; *this* kind of messiah, not any kind of messiah. Gunton borrows Duns Scotus's idea of *haecceitas* in order to capture the singular *thisness* of things.[10] The Spirit, under this light, deepens Jesus's own *thisness*, as it were—his unique personhood.

The Spirit Frees Jesus to Live in Nondeterministic Ways

A second function that the Spirit performs in Jesus's life is to free him to live in nondeterministic ways. Jesus goes to this village, not that one; he heals this woman, not that woman; he eats in this house, not that one. And he allows himself to be interrupted by people along the way, from demoniac to centurion, even as sets his face like flint toward the cross and to thereby fulfill the Father's will, yet in a way that cannot be described,

---

9. Eugene J. Rogers, *After the Spirit: A Constructive Pneumatology from Resources Outside the Modern West* (Grand Rapids: Eerdmans, 2005), 54. Gregory of Nazianzus says, "Christ is born; the Spirit is His Forerunner. He is baptized; the Spirit bears witness. He is tempted; the Spirit leads Him up. He works miracles; the Spirit accompanies them. He ascends; the Spirit takes His place." *A Select Library of the Nicene and Post-Nicene Fathers of the Christian Church*, ed. Philip Schaff et al., repr. ed. (Grand Rapids: Eerdmans, 1983), 7:327.

10. Gunton, *The One, the Three and the Many*, 198–204.

even retroactively, as mechanistic.[11] Inasmuch as the Spirit frees Jesus to be his own particular self, so Jesus is freed to live in nondeterministic, "novel" ways.[12] It is the Spirit who capacitates Jesus to be a particular person rather than a presumed or predictable thing.[13] And what the Spirit accomplishes in Christ's life, the Spirit accomplishes in all living beings.[14]

The Spirit Perfects the Son through a Mutually Constitutive Relationship with the Father

Gunton explains that the particular humanity of Jesus is constituted by his relationship to the Father, which is mediated by the Spirit.[15] As Gunton sees it, "trinitarian love has as much to do with respecting and constituting otherness as with unifying." What we witness then is not a spirit of homogenization "but of relation in otherness, a relation which does not subvert but establishes the other in its true reality."[16] And the fundamental inertia of the Spirit is an eschatological one. For it is the Spirit who "brings about the perfection of this particular sector of the created word—the humanity of Jesus Christ—as the guarantee and first fruits of the reconciliation of all things."[17]

The Work of the Spirit in Creation

If we can assume, with Gunton, that the Spirit's pattern in Christ's life offers us a way to make sense of the Spirit's work in creation, then the following may be suggested.

11. With Gunton, I would want to assert here that it is the Spirit who establishes the integrity of the human agency of Christ. On this reasoning the human life of Christ is enabled by the Spirit rather than (pre)determined or "wielded" by the Eternal Word.

12. Cf. Robert Jenson, *Systematic Theology*, vol. 1, *The Triune God* (Oxford: Oxford University Press, 1997), 159–60.

13. Relevant material in Barth includes *Church Dogmatics*, III.3, trans. G. W. Bromiley and R. J. Ehrlich, ed. G. W. Bromiley and T. F. Torrance (Edinburgh: T&T Clark, 1960), 42–43, 95, 103, 104, 107, 117, 118, 119, 138.

14. Jeremy S. Begbie, "Looking to the Future: A Hopeful Subversion," in *For the Beauty of the Church: Casting a Vision for the Arts*, ed. W. David O. Taylor (Grand Rapids: Baker Books, 2010), 182.

15. Gunton, *The One, the Three and the Many*, 205. Cf. Colin Gunton, *The Triune Creator: A Historical and Systematic Study* (Grand Rapids: Eerdmans, 1998), 223–24.

16. Gunton, *The One, the Three and the Many*, 39, 182.

17. Gunton, *The Triune Creator*, 171.

The Spirit Particularizes All Things in Creation

As the Lord and Giver of Life, the Spirit is the one who maintains the unique character of "the cabbages, mountains, statues and melodies that surround us."[18] What we witness in God's creation is not timeless ideals but rather a celebration of creation's particularity: Napa and Savoy cabbages, volcanic and plateau mountains, freestanding and relief sculptures, Celtic and sub-Saharan melodies.[19] This indeed is the mystery of existence: not that everything is the same but "that everything is what it is and not another thing."[20] The calling of the Christian, accordingly, to borrow the language of the essayist Cynthia Ozick, is "to distinguish one life from another; to illuminate diversity; to light up the least grain of being, to show how it is concretely individual, particularized from any other; to tell, in all the marvel of its singularity, the separate holiness of the least grain."[21] For Gunton, it is the Spirit who enables each thing in creation to be "its own thing."

The Spirit Frees Creation to Operate in Nondeterministic Ways

In the gift of particularity to creation, the Spirit also enables things in creation to unfold in novel and unpredictable ways. Jeremy Begbie, drawing on Gunton, puts the point this way: "With respect to creation at large, if the Son or Word through whom all things are created is associated with the dynamic stability of reality, the Spirit is active 'to enable new possibilities, to empower freedom to live in the abundance that is given.'"[22] It goes against the character of the Spirit of God, in fact, to deny the creature the freedom to be just what it is in its creaturely life. In the Spirit there is a "place" for each thing in creation. This place is a gift, and it is a grace. And it is a place for the creature to "go of itself" rather than to be governed by

---

18. Gunton, *The One, the Three and the Many*, 196.

19. Gunton, *The One, the Three and the Many*, 207. Alexander Schmemann makes a similar point in *For the Life of the World: Sacraments and Orthodoxy* (Crestwood, NY: St. Vladimir's Seminary Press, 1973), 76.

20. Gunton, *The One, the Three and the Many*, 206.

21. Cynthia Ozick, *Art and Ardor* (New York: Alfred A. Knopf, 1983), 248.

22. Jeremy S. Begbie, *Theology, Music and Time* (Cambridge: Cambridge University Press, 2000), 242; cf. 223–24, 241–45.

irresistible forces. It is a place for the creature to go anew, more fully and richly itself. This too is creation's true end.[23]

The Spirit Makes Possible a "Constitutive Relatedness" in Creation

To be a particular thing in creation, from the perspective of the Spirit's work, is to be relationally constituted.[24] This means that things in creation are not merely "connected"; it means that all things in God's creation "mutually constitute each other, make each other what they are."[25] As Gunton puts it, "Everything may be what it is and not another thing, but it is also what it uniquely is by virtue of its relation to everything else."[26] What Trinitarian love accomplishes, then, is a constitutive relationality whereby things and persons in creation are opened out to one another without any loss of particular identity. And it is because of the Spirit's work in creation that the "one" and the "many" need not be in competition with each other: the "one" can remain fully "one" while being richly related to the "many."[27]

The Work of the Spirit, Liturgical Identity, and the Liturgical Arts

If we take Gunton's theology of the Spirit and begin to apply it to the subject of this chapter, we might suggest the following as a set of working propositions toward a pneumatology of liturgical identity as it relates to the arts in worship.

First, to possess a unique liturgical identity is a gift of the Holy Spirit. In expressly pneumatological terms, the Spirit *deepens* the particularity of liturgical identity; the Spirit *opens up* liturgical identity to the possibility of genuine newness; and the Spirit *opens out* liturgical identity to others—to God, to each other, to cultural context, and to the physical geography. This work of the Spirit represents both *a way of being* as a particular congregation and *a way to orient oneself* as a particular member of Christ's body to other particular members.

---

23. Gunton, *The Triune Creator*, 86.
24. Gunton, *The Triune Creator*, 170.
25. Gunton, *The Triune Creator*, 169.
26. Gunton, *The Triune Creator*, 173.
27. Gunton, *The Triune Creator*, 161–62, 224.

Second, liturgical identity is marked by integrity. The corporate worship of a local congregation is a nameable, identifiable thing, constituted by particular individuals in Christ's body. Liturgical identity, on this account, has a coherent shape: a God-given, Christ-rooted, Spirit-graced shape. Said otherwise, a local congregation's worship has integrity. This integrity is both a gift and a constraint. A particular congregation's worship gets to be one thing and not everything or anything.

Third, liturgical identity is marked by semi-porosity. By this I mean that the corporate worship of a local congregation is not a hermetically sealed, calcified thing. It is instead a semipermeable thing, *opened up and opened out.*[28] Liturgical identity, on this account, is open to the re-forming Word of God; it is responsive to the reforming power of the Spirit; it is mutually implicated in the worship of the catholic and apostolic church; and it is fundamentally influenced by its cultural and geographic context.

Fourth, to be a member of Christ's universal body is to be willingly vulnerable to the mutually constitutive influence of other particular members of that body, whom the Holy Spirit unites, by faith and in fact, in God's love.[29] To welcome the insights of other members of Christ's body into one's own worship, to allow one's worship to be reshaped and refreshed by the practices of other members of the global church, to become humbly willing to learn from the worship of the people of God throughout history—to become vulnerable in all such ways is not easy, but the gospel requires it, and the grace of God makes it possible.

Fifth, the liturgical arts become an acute way to deepen the particularity of liturgical identity. Put colloquially and recalling the opening illustration of this chapter, a particular congregation might say, "This is our kind of music," or, paraphrasing the poet Gerard Manley Hopkins, "*Myself* this music speaks and spells, crying *What I sing is me: for that I came.*"[30] This kind of music represents a "who we are," "how God speaks to us," "how we speak to God from the heart." On the Holy

---

28. If there is "no God to give things space in which to be, we lose the space between one another and between ourselves and the world of particulars without which we are not truly what we are." Gunton, *The Triune Creator*, 71.

29. This idea is similar, perhaps, to Tertullian's idea that "whatever belongs to those that are of us, belongs to us," which Gordon W. Lathrop develops in his essay "Every Foreign Country a Homeland, Every Homeland a Foreign Country: On Worship and Culture," in Vasconcelos Wilkey, *Worship and Culture*, 10–25.

30. Gerard Manley Hopkins, *Poetry and Prose* (London: Penguin Classics, 1953), 51.

Spirit's terms, this kind of artistic particularity is to be preserved and celebrated.[31]

Sixth, the liturgical arts become an acute way to open up liturgical identity to genuine newness. Two sorts of newness are in view here. One sort of newness is "more of our kind of music." This involves the introduction of new kinds of liturgical art that correspond to one's particular tradition: new practices of song or uses of musical instruments, for example, "that remain consistent with who we have always been." A second sort of newness is liturgical art that can be described as foreign and, in some cases, difficult to a particular congregation. This is perhaps "your kind of music that we are trying on for size."

Seventh, the liturgical arts become an intentional way to allow one's practice of corporate worship to be influenced and reshaped by others. This may include liturgical art that responds to the particular time and place of a congregation—for example, art that makes use of local materials and resources or that responds to a tragic incident in one's city. Another sort may be art that involves a cross-cultural exchange, where the "right hand of fellowship" is extended to another congregation whose practice of liturgical art is occasionally welcomed. A third sort of liturgical art may be introduced for expressly theological reasons. This may include the practice of multicultural singing, a more intentional use of silence, or a more active exercise of the physical body.

Eighth, the language of "mother tongue" and "adjectival tongue" becomes a way of naming this instrumental activity of the liturgical arts in the economy of the Spirit. A mother tongue describes a native or primary language and therefore also a "heart" language for a given congregation in worship. An "adjectival tongue" describes a secondary or a foreign language for a given congregation in worship.

Ninth, a mother tongue is the way in which liturgical identity is particularly and therefore fully expressed. Although it is a complex subject in the fields of linguistics and anthropology, the idea of a mother tongue includes certain features that commend themselves to the argument here.[32] First, a mother tongue, in psychological terms, represents a deep-

---

31. I am, of course, using music here as shorthand for all liturgical art practices that characterize a given congregation.

32. On the nature and function of a "mother tongue," see, for example, Nigel Love and Umberto Ansaldo, "The Native Speaker and the Mother Tongue," *Language Sciences* 32 (2010): 589–93; M. Paul Lewis and Gary F. Simons, *Sustaining Language Use: Perspectives on Community-Based Language Development* (Dallas: SIL International, 2016); Lamin Sanneh,

est sense of self. For native speakers, a mother tongue marks them as a definable people, an *ethnos* with an identifiable ethos. Second, a mother tongue informs social patterns and cultural ties, identifying a community externally: "This is who we are in relation to everybody else." Third, one who speaks a mother tongue primarily possesses an intuitive, rather than a grammatical, understanding of the language. The "native" speaker is an authority because he or she has been immersed in the language by way of relationship to other native speakers. While a mother tongue is a complex, dynamic thing rather than a static, singular thing, it can nonetheless be described by observable patterns of communication—through verbal as much as through nonverbal means. The practices of liturgical art that comprise a congregation's mother tongue—including textual, linguistic, sonic, visual, and kinetic media—are the manner by which native speakers express themselves most deeply.

Tenth, an adjectival tongue is the way in which liturgical identity is more richly expressed. An adjective, according to the general rules of grammar, modifies a noun, qualifying or specifying it in some way. "She's a lady," describes one thing. "She's a little, old, spunky, Southern lady," describes a far more detailed thing. An adjective hereby invests a noun with richer meaning. Adjectives, we might say, are the ways in which the particularity of a thing or person is nuanced, clarified, concretized, enriched. A generic falcon becomes, in Hopkins's poem "The Windhover," "morning's minion, king- / dom of daylight's dauphin, dapple-dawn-drawn Falcon."[33] A generic song becomes, in the context of a Spirit-constituted liturgical body, a Sanctus, sung in four-part harmony, with heads bowed, knees bent, in the face of a linen banner hanging over the chancel, upon which an Indonesian artist has painted an abstract representation of the Trinity. Adjectival tongues, on the terms of this chapter, comprise new works and practices of liturgical art that open up and open out a liturgical identity. They are the ways in which particularity is more richly expressed.

Eleventh, the language of mother tongue and adjectival tongue captures an important aspect of a scriptural imagination. In Holy Scripture,

---

Translating the Message: The Missionary Impact on Culture (Maryknoll, NY: Orbis Books, 1989), 200; Alan Aldridge, "In Their Mother Tongue," *Modern Churchman* 29, no. 2 (1987): 12–18; Andrew Walls, *The Missionary Movement in Christian History* (Maryknoll, NY: Orbis Books, 2002); Anna Carter Florence, *Preaching as Testimony* (Louisville: Westminster John Knox, 2007), ch. 4, "True Speech in the Mother Tongue."

33. Hopkins, *Poetry and Prose*, 30.

the language of "tongues" is frequently used to indicate a particular people: for example, in Genesis 10:20 ("These are the sons of Ham, after their families, after their tongues, in their countries, in their nations" KJV) or in Revelation 7:9 ("a great multitude . . . of all nations, and kindred, and people, and tongues" KJV). Holy Scripture also points to the possibility of "new" tongues, whether in the figurative sense of a new *song* (as in Ps. 33:3 or Isa. 42:10 or Rev. 5:9) or an actual *tongue* (as in Acts 1–2), both of which point to a fundamental feature of the church as the temple of the Holy Spirit. While the New Testament underscores the importance of particularity in the church—of gifts, of callings, of peoples, of "members," and of "kinds"—it also describes the church as "a rich complexity rather than a warring Babel."[34] The church is a communion of the particular, each fully, richly itself, which by the power of the Spirit becomes a "final transfiguration of the cosmos."[35]

Twelfth, an eschatological perspective can never be far from a pneumatological reading of liturgical identity and the liturgical arts. Theologically, the goal of liturgical identity cannot be regarded as an end in itself. Its end instead is the perfecting work of the Spirit. On this understanding, the end of liturgical identity, grounded in the worship of Christ himself, in whom creation has already reached its eschatological goal, is not "more of the same." Its end is rather a capacity to be more fully, particularly itself. Its end is not "mere" predictabilities or "mere" development but rather the experience of "endless and surprising novelty." And it is not "each doing his own thing" but rather each mutually animating each other in an image of the co-inherent life of the Triune God.[36] The purpose of the arts in worship, on this thinking, is to deepen the unique and particular identity of a congregation, to enrich that congregation with Spirit-ordered newness, and to strengthen the bond of the many parts of Christ's body so that they might be one in the Spirit, in the name of the one God and Father of all.

---

34. Gunton, *The One, the Three and the Many*, 187.

35. Jeremy Begbie, "Christ and the Cultures: Christianity and the Arts," in *The Cambridge Companion to Christian Doctrine*, ed. Colin E. Gunton (Cambridge: Cambridge University Press, 1997), 116.

36. Begbie, "Looking to the Future," 182.

Conclusion

Without a proper understanding of the Spirit's work in corporate worship, the desire for the unique expression of a particular congregation's worship may be experienced as a threat by other members of Christ's body because it is felt to undermine the harmony of the universal church ("We've got to all be the same!"). The experience of genuine newness may likewise be experienced as a threat because it is felt to undermine the integrity of a congregation's identity in worship ("To do new things is to lose our identity!"). And Gunton's idea of "constitutive relatedness" might be experienced as a threat because it is felt to undermine the uniqueness of a congregation's worship ("If we choose to incorporate your art practices into our worship, we will lose who we truly are before God at worship!").

As it relates to the specific concern of this chapter, I suggest that God does not desire sameness or homogeneity in the church's worship. God desires for each congregation to offer up a particular worship through the arts, unique to *this* people, in *this* time, in *this* place, as a way to become more truly, more fully itself. This is the Spirit's work to secure the "mother tongue" of a congregation's worship. The Spirit also enables a congregation to welcome "adjectival tongues" into its corporate worship as a way to make that congregation more richly itself. God has constituted the church a body of many members. These members mutually animate each other, and across time and space they cross-pollinate each other with artistic riches. This too is the work of the Spirit to enable each member to become more richly itself.

On what terms should specific practices of art be introduced or resisted in corporate worship? What kinds of practices might be fundamentally incongruous to the "heart language" of a congregation's worship, such that they no longer feel that they can worship God faithfully, "from the heart"? At what point does the identity of a worshiping congregation strain under too much newness? Or how do we think about multigenerational, multicultural congregations that include many mother tongues? Whose heart language is privileged? Is none privileged and therefore no person ever sings from the heart? And what sort of pastoral wisdom, diligent work, personal character, and artistic knowledge is needed for good leadership in these matters? These are difficult questions and very real practical matters that require careful, communal discernment.

Returning to our original illustration, I might propose the following for our imagined Anglo-Catholic church in Boston: "The gift of a mother tongue is a gift of the Spirit to worship God with our pipe organ, our professional choirs, our Episcopal hymnal, our measured cadences and ritualized movements. With God's blessing, we say it is good to be who we are as this unique member of Christ's body in this city, at this time. But the Spirit also gives us the gift of adjectival tongues. On occasion we sing the doxology in Swahili. On occasion we sing extemporaneously, possibly even with lively physical movements. This, we believe, is the gift that opens us up to the new thing that God wishes to do here and now. With this gift we open ourselves to be implicated in the global church and possibly irrevocably changed. Worshiping in this way reminds us that we are neither alone nor self-sufficient. We need and we welcome other members of Christ's body into our liturgical life and, by God's grace, we become more richly ourselves."

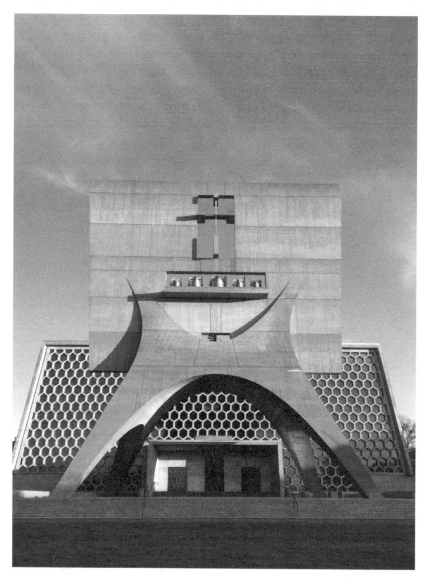

Saint John's Abbey Church and Bell Banner, Collegeville, Minnesota (Photograph by author)

CHAPTER 11

The Worship Arts and the Mission of the Church

> Whatever belongs to those that are of us, belongs to us.
>
> Tertullian, *On the Veiling of Virgins*

> God not only intends for seekers to *observe* our worship. God intends for seekers to *become* worshipers.
>
> Sally Morgenthaler, *Worship Evangelism*

> And thus it is the very joy of the Kingdom that makes us remember the world and pray for it. It is the very communion with the Holy Spirit that enables us to love the world with the love of Christ.
>
> Alexander Schmemann, *For the Life of the World*

Mission is the church's work of bearing witness in word and in deed to the good news of God before a watching world. But the church's mission is never its own to define; it is instead defined by the mission of the Trinity. As God the Father sends his Son, by his Spirit, into the world in order to announce and to embody the good news, to judge and to redeem the world, to heal and to transform it, and to enable it to become a transfigured image of the new creation, so the Father sends his people, in the name of Jesus, and by the empowering presence of the Spirit, to fulfill the divine mission in every place and in every time. The corporate worship of the church participates in this triune mission, and it does so in all sorts of ways. The purpose of this chapter is to suggest how public worship might participate in God's mission and how the arts in particular might serve God's mission through the church's public worship.

Public Worship Is a Public Witness

First, the act of corporate worship, excepting in places where the church is persecuted, is intrinsically missional inasmuch as it is a public event

223

rather than a private one. As a public event, the worship of the church is a public testimony to the world of the character of the Triune God. This is as true of Eastern Orthodox and Presbyterian worship as it is of Pentecostal and Baptist worship. The church at worship bears witness to God openly, not covertly. The good news, which the church acclaims in its prayers and praises, does not belong to a secret few; it is published instead for all to see. As Patrick Kiefert writes in *Welcoming the Stranger*, when the early Christians worshiped, they did so in public, always with the intent to show "hospitality to the stranger."[1] Just as the church is a recipient of the Lord's hospitality, then, so the church's worship is to be a hospitable act to a watching world, ever welcoming the stranger and the seeker to taste and to see that the Lord is indeed good.

In Hawai, in Papua, and on the island of New Guinea, a "Glory Hut" (*Pondok Kemuliaan*) is weekly filled with young Pentecostal believers engaged in acts of enthusiastic worship. The Glory Hut, as Charles Farhadian explains, is a temporary dwelling place, modeled on the indigenous Sentani huts made of thatched roofs and walls built from dried palm leaves. "What is most striking about the Glory Hut's worship space," he writes, "is its structural openness to the surrounding community. Worship, through music, testimony, preaching, and praying, pours out into the wider neighborhood."[2] Whenever the Christians worship in the Glory Hut, it is something that the inhabitants in the local area can see. The structure's open architecture is thereby formative. Curious passersby "are free to stay out-

---

1. Patrick R. Keifert, *Welcoming the Stranger: A Public Theology of Worship and Evangelism* (Minneapolis: Fortress, 1992), 71. On this view, I suggest that "high" liturgy is not intrinsically inhospitable, nor inimical to God's mission, in the same way that a "low" liturgy is not automatically hospitable, nor inevitably missional, to the visitor and stranger. While Eastern Orthodox practices of worship may seem utterly foreign to some, for example, and therefore inhospitable to outsiders, the elements of worship themselves and the manner in which the Divine Liturgy is led by a priest can become profound expressions of hospitality—and in this sense be regarded as a fulfillment of God's mission. Conversely, the practices of worship that characterize so-called nondenominational or progressive churches, with their (peppy or hip) radio-friendly songs and their relevant sermons, may be off-putting to visitors looking for the substance of Christ and may scarcely resemble the actual mission of Christ. It may simply look like another version of themselves, with the patina of Jesus. Context always comes into play, as does the manner in which worship leaders conduct themselves.

2. Charles E. Farhadian, "Worship as Mission: The Personal and Social Ends of Papuan Worship in the Glory Hut," in *Christian Worship Worldwide: Expanding Horizons, Deepening Practices*, ed. Charles E. Farhadian (Grand Rapids: Eerdmans, 2007), 180.

side or enter the fellowship space without feeling intimidated. And many do in fact stroll in and join the assembly inconspicuously."[3]

Whether a church's worship is architecturally "open" or "closed off" to the immediate neighborhood, it will always hopefully bear witness to its calling as a sent people: sent in Jesus's name to manifest the love of God to every tongue, tribe, and nation. When Christians gather in worship they also testify to their true identity that, like Jesus, is oriented outward to those who remain far from the love of God.[4] Robert Taft writes, "The purpose of baptism is to make *us* cleansing waters and healing and strengthening oil; the purpose of Eucharist is not to change bread and wine, but to change you and me: through baptism and Eucharist it is *we* who are to become Christ for one another, and a sign to the world that is yet to hear his name."[5] When worship is done for God's sake, it becomes not a centripetal movement, turning us further in on ourselves; it becomes, rather, a centrifugal movement, turning us upward and outward.

Public Worship Includes the Concerns of the World

Second, the act of public worship brings with it the concerns of the world and, in turn, inspires the people of God with a love for the world that resembles God's own love for the world. In his essay "Trumpets, Ashes, and Tears," the philosopher Nicholas Wolterstorff argues that the liturgy ought always to serve our life in the world rather than only be seen as an end in itself. The workweek is not just for the sake of Sunday; Sunday is for the sake of the week of work that lies ahead. The liturgy on this understanding is an instrument of grace, not only for heaven's sake but for earth's sake too. The goal of corporate worship includes the hope that it might guide and empower "us for our work as covenant partners with God in the coming

3. Farhadian, "Worship as Mission," 180.

4. "The church represents the presence of the reign of God in the life of the world, not in the triumphalist sense (as the 'successful' cause) and not in the moralistic sense (as the 'righteous' cause), but in the sense that it is the place where the mystery of the kingdom present in the dying and rising of Jesus is made present here and now so that all people, righteous and unrighteous, are enabled to taste and share the love of God before whom all are unrighteous and all are accepted as righteous." Lesslie Newbigin, *The Open Secret: An Introduction to the Theology of Mission*, rev. ed. (Grand Rapids: Eerdmans, 1995), 54.

5. Robert Taft, "What Does Liturgy Do? Toward a Soteriology of Liturgical Celebration: Some Theses," *Worship* 66, no. 23 (1992): 201, emphasis original.

of God's kingdom."[6] We do not leave behind all the events of our ordinary life—work, home, family, play, and so on—when we gather for worship. We do not escape our "normal life" when we "come to church." Instead, we bring into public worship all the cares of this world, all the vicissitudes of our lives, all the things we control, and all the things that lie beyond our control.

Worship in turn reorients our vision of the world and encourages us to live well in it as we return to it with new graces, with hope and faith renewed, with a fresh love for the people and the places that mark our lives. With "trumpets" we celebrate the joy of creation. With "ashes" we enact our confession of sin. With "tears" we lament for all that has gone wrong in the world. "The celebration of the liturgy," Wolterstorff writes, "does not represent our turning away from a so-called profane or secular world to a so-called sacred world. It is our response to our apprehension of *this* world as gift and glorious work of God."[7] This is what occurs, for example, when congregations around the city of Austin, Texas, join the homeless community in worship at Church Under the Bridge.[8] Gathered on Sunday mornings at the intersection of 7th Street and IH-35, disparate communities sing and pray in Jesus's name, share bread, and forge relationships in witness to a watching world to the healing power of God.

All Aspects of Public Worship Can Become Missionally Charged

Third, specific designs, activities, objects, and words of corporate worship can become missionally charged. For instance, how we enter and how we leave a church, architecturally speaking, can take on missional significance. "Beyond creating an environment that enables the liturgy and provides appropriate symbolic and typological resonance," Wolterstorff observes, the architect's "challenge is to create an environment that is both expressive of the unique character of those actions that comprise the liturgy and expressive of the fact that as we enter the place of the liturgy, we carry with us the thanksgivings, regrets, and laments of daily life, and the fact that, when we disperse, we in turn carry into daily life the guidance and

6. Nicholas Wolterstorff, "Trumpets, Ashes and Tears," in *Hearing the Call: Liturgy, Justice, Church, and World*, ed. Mark R. Gornik and Gregory Thompson (Grand Rapids: Eerdmans, 2011), 23.

7. Wolterstorff, "Trumpets, Ashes and Tears," 25.

8. "Church Under the Bridge" is a ministry of *Mission: Possible! Austin*. See https://www.mpaustin.org/church-under-the-bridge/.

strength, the courage and hope, that we have received."[9] The neo-Gothic architecture of St. John the Divine in New York City, for example, built on high ground in cruciform shape, can become a sign to the world that lies outside the walls of the church of the good news of the cross of Christ on behalf of a suffering world.[10]

Human beings do not learn how to regard their physical bodies rightly simply by moving them from place to place throughout their day. Healthy "body image" is a rare thing, especially as abuse and neglect of the body remain all too common. So when an Episcopal priest processes forward, with a crucifer before him, while the people bow their heads to the cross, this symbolic activity by the congregation is a way to testify, among other things, "This is what bodies are for, for humble adoration of the One who heals all bodies through his own broken body." Or when members of a high-church Methodist congregation cross themselves, they may do so as a public reminder of the cruciform life that marks their bodies at all times. Or when a Lutheran congregation walks through a Stations of the Cross exhibit, this might serve to reinforce the pilgrimage quality of their entire lives. Or, finally, when charismatic Christians lie prostrate in prayer, this can function as a sign of the humility that would mark their whole life.

All of Public Worship Can Become Mission

Fourth, the entire shape of corporate worship and the whole purpose of corporate worship can be oriented toward mission. With the so-called classic order of worship, employed by Episcopalians or United Methodists or even nondenominational churches, there is an intentional movement from "gathering" to "sending." This movement reminds the church that it has entered into worship *from somewhere* and that, at the end, it *goes somewhere*, too. It goes somewhere, not inconsequentially, with the summons and the blessing of God. That "somewhere" is for each person a specific place that they occupy in the world, a place that comes with signs, easily discerned or with difficulty, of the presence of the Spirit of Christ. For the missionally

9. Nicholas Wolterstorff, "The Theological Significance of Going to Church and Leaving and the Architectural Expression of That Significance," in Gornik and Thompson, *Hearing the Call*, 240.

10. Cf. Armand Léon van Ommen, *Suffering in Worship: Anglican Liturgy in Relation to Stories of Suffering People* (London: Routledge, 2016).

minded believer, that place is an occasion for the grace of God to be enacted by those who have been formed through worship: with psalms that acknowledge both darkness and light, with paintings that signify both the goodness and the disfigurement of our neighborhoods, with stories that highlight both the ordinary and extraordinary dimensions of life in the Spirit.

Other church traditions may shape their worship to become expressly intelligible and accessible to outsiders to the Christian faith.[11] For such traditions corporate worship is fundamentally evangelistic. Their goal will be a winsome presentation of the gospel to both "wanderers and the spiritual refugees."[12] Such an approach to worship is common to both free-church and mainline congregations: for example, the "camp meetings" of late nineteenth-century revival movements;[13] the "seeker friendly" churches like Willow Creek Community Church of the 1980s and early 1990s; the "emerging church" movement in the United States of the late 1990s and early 2000s; the "Fresh Expressions" movement in the United Kingdom in the early 2000s, geared to the "unchurched" or "dechurched," which includes things like "Messy Church" or "Cafe Church";[14] and the "stadium" worship experiences of Jesus Culture in the 2010s. With their goal to see "justice and worship go hand in hand," Hillsong's approach to musical worship is typical of many other congregations around the globe.[15]

---

11. "The essential discovery of the frontier churches was a form of worship for the unchurched, a need none of the other traditions had yet dealt with seriously." James F. White, *Protestant Worship: Traditions in Transition* (Louisville: Westminster John Knox, 1989), 171.

12. Worship is "a stage from which to present the gospel and reach out to the unchurched and irreligious." Thomas H. Schattauer, "Liturgical Assembly as Locus of Mission," in *Inside Out: Worship in an Age of Mission*, ed. Thomas H. Schattauer (Minneapolis: Fortress, 1999), 2. Cf. https://www.evolvingfaithconference.com.

13. "Camp meetings engendered their own characteristic music—popular, with simple harmonies, easy to sing and to remember. The crowds were largely illiterate and there were no hymn-books, so the songs or hymns often had a rousing, memorable chorus, the opening words of which frequently served as the piece's title. The leader would often yell the verses and the audience could respond with the chorus; singing could be accompanied with other physical responses such as clapping, shouting, and even dancing." Tim Dowley, *Christian Music: A Global History* (Minneapolis: Fortress, 2011), 179.

14. For more details, see http://freshexpressions.org.uk/about/what-is-a-fresh-expression/.

15. "Who Is Hillsong Music Australia?," http://archive.li/mpvJG. Accessed January 26, 2018. See also Joe Coscarelli, "'Hillsong' Casts a Secular Lens on an Evangelical Band," *New York Times*, September 14, 2016, https://www.nytimes.com/2016/09/15/arts/music/hillsong-united-church-documentary.html.

Practices of Art in Worship Can Participate in God's Mission

Fifth, the ethical manner by which the church engages its practices of liturgical art is a way for the church to participate in the mission of God. Because the church's mission is caught up in God's desire to restore all things, the church at worship bears witness to the world's belovedness and brokenness, its abundance and its scarcity, through its works of liturgical art. It does so for the common good, not its own good alone. It does so in a way that bears witness to the character of God and therefore also to the true character of human life, in both its individual and communal forms, in both its personal and institutional manifestations. One way in which liturgical art might accomplish this purpose is by building cathedrals in an ethically sound way. This of course may sound like the *least* obvious way. It might sound like a perversion of earth's resources and a corruption of the church's vocation. But perhaps by looking at the Cathedral of Our Lady of the Angels in Los Angeles, California, we can see how extravagant art might bear faithful witness to God in an ethically responsible, missionally vibrant manner.

Why spend millions of dollars to build a cathedral when one could use that money to feed the poor? When the project by the Catholic Archdiocese of Los Angeles was announced, both insiders and outsiders raised a host of concerns. The cost alone seemed absurd. General estimates in the project budget included, for instance, $5 million for the altar, $3 million for the main bronze doors, and $2 million for the wooden lectern. Pews were going to cost an average of $50,000. As one reporter put it, "The great costs incurred in its construction led certain critics to dub it the 'Taj Mahony' and the 'Rog Mahal.'"[16] According to the US Department of Health and Human Services, the poverty threshold for an individual adult in the United States in 2018 was $12,140. For $250 million, the price tag of the cathedral, one could care for approximately 20,593 poor persons. Was this not an egregious use of funds that could—and indeed *should*—have been used otherwise?

In response to charges such as these, Christians throughout the centuries have argued that a cathedral of this magnitude represents an ethically sound endeavor because the poor deserve something extravagantly beautiful, too. The massive resources that a cathedral represented could likewise become a massive source of generosity, both practical and social, to the "least of these" in society. "The cathedral," writes James Gillick, "is an enterprise that is, to

---

16. Chris Haslam, "Art Attack in LA," *Sunday Times*, February 24, 2008, 4; Jennifer Ordoñez, "The Catholics: A Cardinal's Campaign," *Newsweek*, April 10, 2006, 38.

every intent and purpose, a social security system of immense beauty designed to sustain a local people for upwards of a quarter of a millennium."[17] Abbot Suger, who served as the primary patron for the Basilica of St. Denis, completed in 1144, in what is now a northern suburb of Paris, offered a similar defense of his actions. Fellow monks, like his contemporary Bernard of Clairvaux, felt that the exorbitant cost of the basilica contravened the simple gospel of Jesus. The abbot responded by saying that all things ought to be done "with all inner purity and with all outward splendor."[18] Humility of character and lavish architectural beauty are not necessary rivals.

As far back as Saint Jerome's time, Christians in favor of cathedral projects have urged the church not to neglect the ministry to the poor while it goes about building sumptuous churches. Cheap offerings to the poor and a cold charity were just as much of an offense to Christ. Nothing in Scripture, they have argued, absolutely condemned projects of extraordinary splendor. The God who requires charity of all Christians accepts also beautiful churches as God-honoring work.[19] The example of the Cathedral of Our Lady of the Angels does not by any means resolve all the tensions associated with such an ornate work of church architecture. But it can perhaps become an occasion to consider how vast expenditures of money, labor, and time on behalf of an artistically extravagant church building might be consonant with the requirement of Christians to do justice, love mercy, and walk humbly with God—that is, to advance the mission of the church in the world in an ethically responsible fashion.

Practices of Art in Worship Can Forge Unity across the Church

Sixth, works of liturgical art can forge unity with members of Christ's body across physical and temporal, as well as cultural and theological, boundary lines. This, too, can strengthen the mission of the church. Singing another's song, for example, is a way to cultivate empathy for other members of the global church. The Lutheran church musician Mark Bangert says this: "Understanding ultimately means allowing the music to lead one to the people

---

17. James Gillick, "On the Economics of a Cathedral," accessed August 14, 2018, http://www.sacredarchitecture.org/articles/on_the_economics_of_a_cathedral.

18. Cited in Deborah Sokolove, *Sanctifying Art: Inviting Conversation Between Artists, Theologians, and the Church* (Eugene, OR: Cascade Books, 2013), 23.

19. Richard Hooker, *Of the Laws of Ecclesiastical Polity*, in *The Folger Library Edition of The Works of Richard Hooker*, vol. 2, ed. W. Speed Hill (Cambridge, MA: Harvard University Press, 1977), 60.

whose it is, to their joys and sorrows, their unique insights into God's love for them and for the part of the earth they inhabit."[20] Beyond singing the occasional foreign-language song, however, the practice of multicultural worship can forge a rich unity in the church.[21] Michael Hawn puts the idea in concrete terms: "Singing the *estribillo* (refrain) of a Spanish-language hymn in the original language by a majority English-speaking congregation may say more about hospitality to Latinos and Latinas within the community than handshakes by the ushers or words of greeting from the minister."[22] Key here is the idea of hospitality to the global body of Christ.[23]

The practice of multicultural or multiethnic worship takes the church into an even more costly, but equally more beautiful, experience of hospitality. Sandra Maria Van Opstal remarks that leading worship in a multiethnic context involves the gift of hospitality ("We welcome you"), solidarity ("We stand with you"), and mutuality ("We need you").[24] In such worship, she writes, the church seeks to include the underrepresented in the congregation, it aims to affirm unity around major events within the global church and around the world, and it welcomes opportunities to be led by other members of Christ's body. Beyond this specific instance, how might the worshiping church testify to God's hospitality if we offered good rather than mediocre coffee to our visitors? What if we saved up money to buy well-designed furniture rather than cheaply manufactured things? And what if we chose to put excellent art, instead of the leftovers, in spaces

---

20. Mark P. Bangert, "The Last Word? Dynamics of World Musics Twenty Years Later," in *Worship and Culture: Foreign Country or Homeland?*, ed. Gláucia Vasconcelos Wilkey (Grand Rapids: Eerdmans, 2014), 130.

21. "God desires [that] his people, from every nation . . . be unified around Jesus, worshipping together." Josh Davis and Nikki Lerner, *Worship Together: In Your Church as in Heaven* (Nashville: Abingdon, 2015), 16.

22. C. Michael Hawn, "Praying Globally," in *Christian Worship Worldwide: Expanding Horizons, Deepening Practices*, ed. Charles E. Farhadian (Grand Rapids: Eerdmans, 2007), 220.

23. What many contemporary Christians do not realize, perhaps, is that the very shape of their worship is already pluri-cultural. As Gordon Lathrop reminds us, "today, in the renewed liturgy, we keep a revised version of the ancient Asian Christian reworking of the Jewish Passover to become our Pascha, or Easter, the ancient Roman (and then northern European) Christian reworking of the pagan winter solstice has now become our Christmas, as well as the eastern Mediterranean (and perhaps ancient Spanish) creation of Epiphany and the ancient Egyptian and African creation of Lent." "Every Foreign Country a Homeland, Every Homeland a Foreign Country," in Vasconcelos Wilkey, *Worship and Culture*, 17.

24. Sandra Maria Van Opstal, *The Next Worship: Glorifying God in a Diverse World* (Downers Grove, IL: InterVarsity, 2016), 74.

where the children worshiped? Whatever practices of art we employ in our liturgical life together, faithful worship will always be marked by the hospitality of Christ himself.[25]

Practices of Art in Worship Can Extend beyond the Bounds of Public Worship

Seventh, works of liturgical art that have been created originally for one context—namely, corporate worship—can find themselves operating in a different context—namely, in the public square—and in this way function missionally. The film documentary about Hillsong Music, for example, titled "Hillsong: Let Hope Rise," takes what occurs within a primarily worship context and places it within so-called secular spaces—movie theaters, Netflix, and portable media players.[26] This is of course what has happened historically with "church music." Bach's liturgical cantatas, originally performed at St. Thomas Church in Leipzig, Germany, are now performed in the Musashino Academia Musicae in Tokyo, Japan. Black spirituals, originally sung by slaves in the cotton fields, are now sung by pop stars at the Grammy Awards. Gregorian chant, the music of medieval monasteries in France and Germany, turns up on sophisticated classical music radio stations. John Newton's hymn "Amazing Grace" is regularly used for auditions on the television show *The Voice*. Whether wittingly or not, works of liturgical art can transcend their original context and become heralds of

---

25. Mark Charles offers this example: "A church in Denver hosted a Navajo worship service about once a month. It included cooking, singing, sharing needs and concerns, retelling parables, feasting (fry bread, mutton, stew) and Communion with tortillas. The service lasted from about 2 p.m. to 10 p.m. This wonderful service valued the Navajo people and was the appropriate place for them to offer their traditional songs." "Contextualizing Worship: My Journey to Worship God as a Navajo Christian," Calvin Symposium on Worship, January 1, 2009, https://worship.calvin.edu/resources/resource-library/contextual izing-worship-my-journey-to-worship-god-as-a-navajo-christian/. See also the bilingual picture book in English and Spanish on the Lord's Supper, *En la mesa de Dios / At God's Table* (Grand Rapids: CICW Books, an imprint of Calvin College Press, 2017). Justo Gonzalez commends the book this way: "It has the rare virtue of being able to serve as a children's book and as a catalytic for many a profound adult conversation. And—an even rarer virtue—it is likely to provoke and sustain many a cross-generational discussion in which children can participate jointly with adults." https://calvin.edu/directory/publications/en -la-mesa-de-dios-at-gods-table.

26. See http://hillsongmovie.com.

the good news across the highways and airways, reaching audiences in a way that could scarcely have been imagined by the creators of these works.

Practices of Art in Worship Can Participate in Christ's Own Mission

Eighth, artists who create works for a corporate worship context enter into the calling of Christ the Chief Worshiper, and because Christ's calling involves the fulfillment of God's mission, liturgical artists participate in the fulfillment of this christological mission too. More specifically, in the same way that the mission of Christ has a priestly, prophetic, and kingly shape, so the mission of the liturgical artist has a priestly, prophetic, and kingly shape.

In their prophetic mission, artists bear witness to the world of the Word of God, both the enfleshed Logos and Holy Scripture. To bear witness to the incarnate God and to the Scriptures that testify to this particular God involves a witness, among other things, to God's justice. "From the jail at Philippi to the Birmingham jail," writes Mark Labberton, "God's people have known that worshipful singing, especially in the face of injustice, is one of the strongest acts of faith, hope and love available to us."[27] "Justice," adds Paul Westermeyer, "is not the only thing we sing about as Christians, but because we sing about this curious God in Christ who rescues all of us wounded and poverty-stricken folk, we sing about that too." He adds, "Justice sings because the gospel sings. If we don't sing it, the rocks will cry out."[28]

In their priestly calling, liturgical artists offer the life of God—the true, merciful, comforting, forgiving, hopeful, judging life of God—to the people of God for the sake of the world that God so loves. Likewise, liturgical artists offer the lives of the people—the confident and humbled, whole and broken, heartfelt and half-hearted, faithful and faithless lives—back to God himself, again for the sake of the world. Such is the work of ethnodoxologists, for example.[29] This is a group that helps (largely non-Western) peoples around the globe generate worship art that makes use of their own indigenous tongues and through their own indigenous styles

---

27. Mark Labberton, *The Dangerous Act of Worship: Living God's Call to Justice* (Downers Grove, IL: InterVarsity, 2007), 123. "Music can reawaken our voice, ignite our righteous anger, intensify our conviction, strengthen our resolve" (124).

28. Paul Westermeyer, *Let Justice Sing: Hymnody and Justice* (Collegeville, MN: Liturgical Press, 1998), 110.

29. See, for instance, the work of Heart Sounds International, http://heart-sounds.org.

and forms. The goal is "to see Christ-followers from every culture express their faith through their own arts."[30]

In their kingly vocation, recollecting the royal calling of Adam to exercise dominion over the earth, liturgical artists take the materials of creation, as Jesus does with bread and wine or with dirt and spit, and make something of them within the context of corporate worship. They do so in fulfillment of their calling "to farm and to take care" of the earth. Liturgical artists might make things that are both simple and complex, both playful and terrifying, both strange and familiar, both new and old, both big and small. Examples of this kingly calling might include the group Aradhna, which makes worship songs in the idiom of classic Indian music;[31] the electronic dance music utilized by groups like Jesus Culture;[32] a Stations of the Cross installation along the streets of Portland, Oregon;[33] and hymns that make direct connection to God's concern for the care of creation.[34]

The Spirit Can Send Us Outward through Practices of Art in Worship

Ninth, the work of the Spirit is to "uncurl" us before God and to "open us outward" toward our neighbor. This work of the Spirit stands over against

30. *Worship and Mission for the Global Church: An Ethnodoxology Handbook*, ed. James R. Krabill, Frank Fortunato, Robin P. Harris, and Brian Schrag (Pasadena, CA: William Carey Library, 2013), 1. See also Brian Schrag, *Creating Local Arts Together: A Manual to Help Communities Reach Their Kingdom Goals* (Pasadena, CA: William Carey Library, 2013); Joan Huyser-Honig, "All God's Children Have Gifts: Disability and Worship," https://worship.calvin.edu /resources/resource-library/all-god-s-children-have-gifts-disability-and-worship/.

31. See http://aradhnamusic.com.

32. See Zac Hicks, "Exegeting Sound: Hearing the Reverberations of the Gospel in EDM," June 16, 2014, http://zac.e24creative.com/exegeting-sound-hearing-the -reverberations-of-the-gospel-in-edm/.

33. The contemporary artist Scott Erickson created a Stations of the Cross exhibit/ pilgrimage, which he renamed "Stations in the Street." He did so as a way for the artwork to become public property to people who made regular use of a biker commuter path in Portland. In his words: "I wanted to offer this meditation of God's 'with-us-ness' to our neighbors . . . without the prerequisite of entering into our building." See here a video that explains the project: https://www.youtube.com/watch?v=7Ot3s5JUO1s. See also http:// scottericksonart.com/studio/.

34. See http://atyourservice.arocha.org/wp-content/uploads/2014/06/Songs-Hymns .pdf. Along these lines, see also the Yale Institute of Sacred Music conference, "Full of Your Glory: Liturgy, Cosmos, Creation," https://ism.yale.edu/event/conference-full-your-glory-lit urgy-cosmos-creation.

the work of sin that causes us to curl in on ourselves, away from God, and to "close us up," away from our neighbor.[35] An important instrument that accomplishes this work of the Spirit in service of the church's mission is liturgical art. The Spirit who makes faithful worship possible rescues us from all forms of self-absorption, manifested in racism, individualism, nationalism, consumerism, sexism, and so on, and frees us to love our neighbors as Jesus loves them. Whenever an inner or "heart" journey is made within the context of worship, the fundamental trajectory of such a journey is eccentric in the original sense of the term: *outside of oneself*. When such journeys are undertaken, the Spirit moves us up to God and outward toward our neighbor, where in faith we are enabled to love our neighbor in Christ even as we love ourselves in Christ.

Works of liturgical art have the power to derail the sinful inertias of our life in order to jolt us into seeing things that have all too easily gone unnoticed or into feeling things for others, in sympathy or empathy, as God feels for them. Examples of such work include the practice of corporate songs of lament on behalf of the sorrows of the world;[36] the practice of visual art like the sixteen-by-forty-foot banner portraying the resurrected Christ, which hung in the chancel space at the Church of the Resurrection in Wheaton, Illinois, reminding parishioners of the brown-skinned Messiah of Middle Eastern origin whom they worshiped;[37] and tattoo art that tells the story of the Stations of the Cross, of Christ's suffering, death, and resurrection, as artist Scott Erickson made for Ecclesia Church in Houston, Texas, training muscles of attentive perception to see our common human brokenness under the light of Christ's brokenness.[38]

When works of liturgical art accomplish this work of the Spirit, they help us to see how "the business of my neighbor is my business, too." At First Baptist in Edmonton, Alberta, three banners hang high above and behind the pulpit.[39] The one on the right, notably, represents an angelic

---

35. I borrow this phrase from Martin Luther's idea of *incurvatus se*, which describes the effects of sin to cause human beings to become self-obsessed rather than God-oriented.

36. See John D. Witvliet, "A Time to Weep: Liturgical Lament in Times of Crisis," https://www.reformedworship.org/article/june-1997/time-weep-liturgical-lament-times-crisis.

37. See http://www.churchrez.org/ministries/worship/visual-arts. See also W. David O. Taylor, "Discipling the Eyes Through Art in Worship," *Christianity Today*, April 27, 2002, http://www.christianitytoday.com/ct/2012/april/art-in-worship.html.

38. See Scott Erickson, "Cruciformity—Design and Invite," http://scottericksonart .com/cruciformity-design-and-invite/. Scott writes, "it's not just the victory over death that gets me. . . . It's that Jesus shared in some of the worst human experiences."

39. The banners can be glimpsed on the church's home page: https://fbcedmon

being enflaming the city. The leadership responsible for the commission of the art explains that its intent is to capture the church's commitment to the city. The congregation will be persistently reminded by what they see Sunday after Sunday that the Spirit of God desires to bring new life to the heart of the city, and that each member has a role to play in that work—a work that is grounded in the Lord's Supper, where bread is broken and wine is poured out for the sake of the world. In this way, fostering both sympathetic and empathetic love for their neighbors, the art enables the church to fulfill the mission of Jesus in the world.

Conclusion

Whether a congregation's worship emphasizes the praise of disciples of Jesus or aims to "reach" and "connect" with nonbelievers, all corporate worship that remains centered on the glorification of the Triune God is done so *for the sake of the world* that God so loves. "Worship, like mission," writes Ruth Meyers, "proclaims and celebrates the good news of God's love, and worship is offered for the sake of the world."[40] The Orthodox theologian Alexander Schmemann uses similar language to describe the sacraments: "The Eucharist is the sacrament of unity and the moment of truth: here we see the world in Christ, as it really is, and not from our particular and therefore limited and partial points of view. Intercession begins here, in the glory of the messianic banquet, and this is the only true beginning of the Church's mission."[41] With the arts in worship, the church bears witness to God's mission in physically, affectively, imaginatively, and metaphorically intensive and intentional ways.[42]

None of this, of course, comes without effort. Gordon Lathrop remarks, "For Christians to intentionally and willingly join these amphibians" (as he describes those who are "capable of swimming and walking in more than

---

ton.ca. I write about the banners in my article, "Discipling the Eyes Through Art in Worship."

40. Ruth A. Meyers, *Missional Worship, Worshipful Mission: Gathering as God's People, Going Out in God's Name* (Grand Rapids: Eerdmans, 2014), 5.

41. Alexander Schmemann, *For the Life of the World: Sacraments and Orthodoxy* (Crestwood, NY: St. Vladimir's Seminary Press, 1973), 44–45.

42. Don E. Saliers makes a similar point in his essay, "Liturgy and Ethics: Some New Beginnings," in *Liturgy and the Moral Self: Humanity at Full Stretch Before God*, ed. Byron Anderson and Bruce T. Morrill (Collegeville, MN: Liturgical Press, 1998), 3–35.

one culture") "to find 'every foreign country a homeland,' to treasure other cultures in whatever way is possible, bit by particular bit, and to learn more and more from them, indeed, to seek to hold more than one idea about how to live at one time—none of this is easy."[43] Adds C. Michael Hawn, "Creating a culturally conscious worshiping community is potentially so difficult that many may decide that such an experience is neither practical nor perhaps even desirable."[44] If the hard work of making liturgical art in service of the church's mission is done, it will be because people are committed to each other relationally. In Douglas Brouwer's words, "it's less about the rhythms, and more about the relationships."[45] Making liturgical art for the sake of God's mission is hard work. Working with other people in this important task is hard work. But it is the work that Christ gives us.

As Christians clothe themselves "in Christ" (Col. 3:9–10), then, through the activities of corporate worship, the hope is that these practices will form in them the kinds of relational habits that make them Christ-like wherever they may find themselves. The hope is that these practices will symbolically form how each of us sees the world—what it means to work, to play, to eat, to love, to feel pain, to pursue justice and peace, to face death, and so on. In our songs and images, our rhetoric and poetry, our stories and movements, the church worships for the life of the world. It is in this sense that we can say that corporate worship is a dimension of mission, directly or indirectly. Whatever the shape of our corporate worship may be, then, and however we may include the arts, the hope is that our liturgical art practices will make it possible for "all the families of the nations" (Ps. 22:27 NRSV) to know and love the Trinity.

43. Gordon Lathrop, "Every Foreign Country a Homeland, Every Homeland a Foreign Country," in Vasconcelos Wilkey, *Worship and Culture*, 12–13.

44. C. Michael Hawn, *One Bread, One Body: Exploring Cultural Diversity in Worship* (Herndon, VA: The Alban Institute, 2003), 141.

45. Douglas J. Brouwer, *How to Become a Multicultural Church* (Grand Rapids: Eerdmans, 2017), 143. Gerardo Marti, in *Worship across the Racial Divide: Religious Music and the Multiracial Congregation* (Oxford: Oxford University Press, 2012), 195, adds this observation: "Music alone is not sufficient; it is relationships and a sense of belonging that bind people to their church.... So it is not about the performance, but the relationships signified and reinforced through musical performance that help sustain the diversity of a multiracial congregation. Even if the music is bad, even 'terrible,' the cross-racial unity comes out of caring relationships people share together."

Chapel of St. Basil, University of St. Thomas, Houston, Texas (Photograph by author)

Conclusion

See how elastic our stiff prejudices grow when love once comes to
bend them.

Herman Melville, Moby-Dick

But love will best judge what may hurt or edify; and if we let love be
our guide, all will be safe.

John Calvin, Institutes of the Christian Religion

[Christians] do not constitute a house of God unless they are cemented
together by love.

Saint Augustine, Expositions of the Psalms

If the arts in worship can form God's people into the image of Christ, it is only because the Spirit of God enables them to be fit for such a task. The liturgical arts are not *intrinsically* spiritual. They are not *inherently* charged with divine electricity. They do not *magically* make human beings more whole and holy like Christ, nor do they possess *automatic* capacities to mediate divine grace, and they are certainly not to be seen as *self-sufficient* vehicles of God's glory in and through creation. They are instead, as the Latin puts it, *capax Dei*: that is, enabled *by* God to serve the praise of God on earth as it is in heaven.[1]

---

1. To argue this is to argue, with Trevor Hart, against a "free-for-all in which any and every material form may be appealed to as a likely site of encounter with" God, and instead emphasize what God chooses to do—and indeed *wishes* to do when the people of God gather for worship. "Unseemly Representations," in *Between the Image and the Word: Theological Engagements with Imagination, Language and Literature* (Surrey: Ashgate, 2013), 178. Cf. Peter Leithart: "Grace is not a thing or energy but God's attitude of favor toward us, manifested in his coming near to us through his Spirit to form and renew covenant friendship, to have personal communion with us, and to offer us the gifts and blessings of Word and Sacrament." "Embracing Ritual: Sacraments as Rites," *Calvin Theological Journal* 40 (2005): 9.

At a fundamental level, then, a Trinitarian theology must always govern our understanding of the liturgical arts.

This means, among other things, that the arts in worship are caught up in the movement of Christ to enable creation to become a dynamic theater of God's glory by the power of his Spirit. It means that the liturgical arts are caught up in the priestly movement of Christ himself—by the Spirit, offering in love the things of God to humanity and, by the Spirit again, the things of humanity to God. It means that the worship arts do not "merely exist" but are rather caught up in a movement of divine love, enabling the faithful to "lift their hearts" in love to God, rather than remain entrapped in self-absorbed concerns, and to love the world as God so loves it, rather than remain unmoved by the ethical realities that mark human life.

With this Trinitarian orientation in mind, I offer the following final affirmations.

Corporate worship is a context for substantial formation.

While corporate worship is not the only place that individual Christians are formed (they are no doubt profoundly formed at home and at work, in nature and in relationships, on retreats and on the go), corporate worship is in fact one of the more substantial, consequential places in which the people of God are formed. To the extent that the weekly practice of public worship constitutes a common and constant practice for Christians throughout all ages, what Christians see and smell, taste and touch, feel and imagine through their experiences of art in worship will inevitably form a way of being human in the world. Said otherwise, since there is always an artistic and aesthetic shape to the experience of corporate worship, however minimalist it may be, the liturgical artistic practices of corporate worship inevitably perform both positive and negative formative work for the Christian, opening up and closing down a way of being in the world under the light of the Triune God.

In corporate worship we acquire a sense for God's sense of things.

Along these lines, since corporate worship is a primary place where discipleship occurs, the liturgical arts, by God's grace, become an occasion for Christians to acquire faithful disciplines of looking and hearing, sensing and tasting, in order to perceive the world as God perceives it. Such a formative view of the liturgical arts would mean that it is never impossible, only perhaps difficult, for a congregation to learn a new practice of art in worship. This would require right training, patience, and a humble willingness to learn. As church history testifies repeatedly, new practices of art in worship *can* in fact be learned and become intelligible over time, and in this way they can serve to edify the church.

However it is that each medium of art may perform its formative work in worship, I argue that all the liturgical arts can, somehow, someway, disclose the true knowledge of God, train the church in the worship that marks the praise of the physical creation, awaken desire for God through the beauty of the cosmos, foster obedience and love, chide ingratitude and pride in our failure to acknowledge God's abundant provision, summon the faithful to the praise of God in their common life of worship, and acquire a sense for God's sense of things.

Regular learning about our practices of art in worship is essential.

Regular learning about why we do any given practice of liturgical art is essential for the formative effect of that particular practice to become fully fruitful for the people of a given congregation. It is difficult to overestimate the value of regular teaching, regular reminders, and regular encouragement by the senior leadership of a given congregation to engage the worship arts in a thoughtful and careful manner. Plenty is learned, of course, through the routinized practice of art in worship over time, generating habits and instincts that cause us to imagine the world a certain way. But reflective thinking on our practices of liturgical art is necessary and invaluable. James K. A. Smith offers this helpful reminder: "For the sake of the community of practitioners, worship planners and leaders need to take on the responsibility of reflexive evaluation of our practices in order to ensure that the imaginative coherences of worship are consistent with the vision of God's kingdom to which we are being habituated."[2]

Art in worship is chiefly a get-to, not a have-to (but it is also a need-to).

The experience of art in corporate worship is chiefly a *get-to*, not a *have-to*. We *get to* make music; we don't *have to* make music. We *get to* tell stories; we don't *have to* tell stories. We *get to* speak in poetically rich and culturally unique ways; we don't *have to* speak in those ways. We *get to* offer our physical bodies as living sacrifices; we don't *have to,* and there is always a grace not to do so on certain

---

2. James K. A. Smith, *Imagining the Kingdom: How Worship Works* (Grand Rapids: Baker Academic, 2013), 187.

days, thank God. But inasmuch as art in worship is chiefly an opportunity and an invitation rather than a burdensome compulsion or an onerous obligation, there is still a sense in which perhaps we *need to* offer our sights and sounds, our bodies and our well-crafted words to God—for our life's sake.

When we fail to offer all our senses, all our affections, all our imaginations to God in worship, we may well be fighting against the grain of creation's praise. We may be harming our *own* humanity. We may be stunting our growth in Christ and the riches of his grace. Or we may simply be missing out on the fullness of life that Jesus offers us. More forcefully, perhaps, to the extent that our experiences of liturgical art form our sense of God, our sense of ourselves, and our sense of the world, what we do with the liturgical arts matters, and we may wish to engage certain practices of liturgical art intentionally, whether or not we feel like doing them, because they would form in our humanity a faithful sense of God, ourselves, and the world.

In God's economy there is room for both "festal muchness" and "cleansing simplicity."

Along these lines, in God's economy there is room for lavish beauty and simple beauty.[3] This is something we witness in God's creation (with its tropical and desert biomes) and in God's word (with the poetry that marks the books of Job and Isaiah). As it relates to the arts in worship, there is room, I might suggest, for both Catholic cathedrals and Amish benches. I would also like to believe that in God's economy there will always be room for both extravagant expenditures of time, money, and energy on works of art as well as extravagant expenditures of time, money, and energy on works of justice and mercy in service of the "least of these." To participate in God's economy of abundance and simplicity through the arts can become, I suggest, an act of eschatological faithfulness, as the people of

---

3. While beauty is not an uncontroversial idea, and while it is burdened by a complicated and contested history in the church's appropriation of the idea in service of corporate worship, it should not be summarily dismissed from a discussion of standards that might guide the practice of art in worship. Helpful resources on the topic include Daniel J. Treier, Mark Husbands, and Roger Lundin, eds., *The Beauty of God: Theology and the Arts* (Downers Grove, IL: IVP Academic, 2007); W. David O. Taylor, "Spirit and Beauty: A Reappraisal," *Christian Scholars Review* 44, no. 1 (Fall 2014): 45–59; Umberto Eco, *Art and Beauty in the Middle Ages* (New Haven: Yale University Press, 1986); Richard Viladesau, *Theological Aesthetics: God in Imagination, Beauty, and Art* (Oxford: Oxford University Press, 1999); Nicholas Wolterstorff, "What Happened to Beauty?," in *Art Rethought: The Social Practices of Art* (Oxford: Oxford University Press, 2015), ch. 19; and select chapters in W. David O. Taylor, *For the Beauty of the Church* (Grand Rapids: Baker, 2010).

God enact now a foretaste of what is to come. In Barth's words, "all artistic creation is futuristic."[4]

In other words, the liturgical arts can become a way for the body of Christ to participate, here and now, in the Spirit's life that marks the new creation. That might include both Lutheran cantatas and homemade songs, both the richness of sacred harp song and the luxurious polyphonic music of Giovanni Pierluigi da Palestrina (1525–1594), both multimedia pageants and multi-day retreats of silence and solitude.[5] Since no practice of art, moreover, can capture the whole range of human experience, nor exhaustively serve the faithful worship of God, it will require all of eternity for the people of God to offer to God a whole sacrifice of praise as it gives voice to the whole of creation's praise.[6]

Liturgical traditions generate inertias for the uses of art in worship.

The ecology of a liturgical tradition results in certain things becoming more likely, more easily, and more frequently generated in one's practice of art in worship. A given liturgical tradition will awaken and cultivate certain expectations for the liturgical arts over other expectations. It will involve both dominant and dormant genetic tendencies that identify boundary lines for what is desirable and doable with certain media of art. It will also result in a particular vision of faithful speaking or faithful seeing, which, in turn, forms a certain way of being in the world—how we see and speak to others. A liturgical tradition may also experience genetic changes that result in a fundamental disruption of its artistic ecology, such as those that took place in the Reformation and the postmodern eras. Such genetic changes will open up and close down other possibilities for the theory and practice of liturgical art.

---

4. "Artistic creation will always aim at the unheard of, at that which has never been, at giving shape to the impossible shaping. In principle all artistic creation is futuristic. It will always have to come back to reality ... the reality that was created by God and has been reconciled to him, but this as redeemed reality in its senses and anticipated perfection." Karl Barth, *Ethics* (Edinburgh: T&T Clark, 1981), 508.

5. See Stephen Proctor, *The Guidebook for Visual Worship: Basic Training for Visual Worship Leaders* (n.p.: Illuminate.Us, 2014), https://illuminate.us/learn/.

6. "[In the books of Hebrews and Revelation, we see how] our earthly song of praise is but the icon, the reflection—in the Pauline sense of *mysterion*, a visible appearance that is bearer of the reality it represents—of the heavenly liturgy of our eternal Lord before the throne of God, and, as such, is an ever-present, vibrant participation in the very eschatological, *ephapax*, once-and-for-all accomplished worship of his Son." Robert Taft, "What Does Liturgy Do? Toward a Soteriology of Liturgical Celebration: Some Theses," *Worship* 66, no. 23 (1992): 203.

In relation to the contents of this book, I might encourage readers not to neglect the riches of their own church tradition. Explore the details and the peculiar ways in which Christians in your particular tradition have worshiped through the arts. Study how they have worshiped across cultural and historical contexts. Tease out the possibilities for faithful worship that may be latent in previous centuries; learn, too, how they have developed the tradition. Seek always the wisdom of key figures in your tradition, but look out also for the wisdom that less prominent figures might offer, those who perhaps remain hidden or marginal to the standard chronicles. Discover in them the good gifts of "dead poets and artists."[7] Discover in them, in short, the "living faith of the dead," as Jaroslav Pelikan wonderfully put it.[8] And while you do these things, take full advantage of the "Great Tradition," that tradition of Christ's body that includes the wisdom of the eastern and western church, of the Global South and Global North, of both grassroots initiatives and institutional efforts, across time and space.[9]

Artistic minimalism is neither more nor less faithful than artistic maximalism.

Within certain ecclesial communities, the presumption is that artistic minimalism will protect the Christian from arousing wanton, destructive passions and preserve as "pure" the worship of a holy God. This presumption should be charitably questioned. The problem, according to this line of thought, is that the real danger for faithful worship lies in the aesthetic domain—that is, the domain of our senses, our emotions, and our imaginations—and that the powers that reside in these domains require not so much a harness as a muzzle. Against this presumption, I suggest a counterproposal: that these powers need to be trained rather than restrained. While it is true that Christians, for the sake of pastoral care, have felt the need to abstain from certain liturgical practices for a season (such is the case with Matt Redman's song "Heart of Worship")[10] or for a generation

---

7. T. S. Eliot, "Tradition and the Individual Talent," in *T. S. Eliot: Selected Essays* (New York: Harcourt, Brace and Co., 1932), 4.

8. Jaroslav Pelikan, *The Vindication of Tradition* (New Haven: Yale University Press, 1984), 65.

9. Cf. James S. Cutsinger, ed., *Reclaiming the Great Tradition: Evangelicals, Catholics and Orthodox in Dialogue* (Downers Grove, IL: IVP, 1997).

10. Jeremy Armstrong, "Song Story: Heart of Worship," *Worship Leader Magazine*, January 22, 2013, https://worshipleader.com/articles/song-story-heart-of-worship/.

or two (as with Catholic and Dutch Reformed approaches to the organ),[11] these decisions need not be regarded as absolute.

Against the consistent worry over the power of the arts to arouse errant passions, I offer that the liturgical arts can, at their best, contribute to the sanctification of the church in order to counter the idols of the mind, the forgetfulness of memories, a will that is bent against God, and the disorder of broken bodies and dysfunctional emotions. I suggest also that the liturgical arts, as sensory attestations of God's character, contribute to a distinctly Christian way of viewing the world. And as indispensable rather than dispensable material media that liturgically symbolize the new life in Christ, I suggest finally that the arts in worship form the church in a holy imagination, enabling the faithful to imagine their lives "in Christ," as Christ himself imagines their lives, and by the Spirit's power to live the whole of their lives with this view of the world, for the sake of a cosmos that is marked by God's shalom.[12]

The misuse and abuse of art in worship is always a real possibility.

The possibility for misuse and abuse of the arts in worship remains a constant danger for churches in all traditions and contexts. This includes, for instance, the possibility of idolatry (confusing Creator and creature), hypocrisy (engagement of body without heart and mind), superstition (confusing the Source of power), misappropriation (failing to respect other cultures), and the unnecessary multiplication or diminishment of liturgical art (aesthetic engorgement or aesthetic impoverishment). Humility and prudence will always be needed to guide and guard our employment of art in worship.

This task is best accomplished, I think, when we welcome other members of Christ's body to examine our own practices—to show us where we may have confused gospel and culture or to encourage us to take greater advantage of the wisdom of the global and historic church. This being said, I always find the advice of sixteenth-century Reformers helpful: *abusus non tollit usum,* "abuse does not take away use." In other words, the possibility of misuse of art in worship does not necessarily involve the abolishment of such art. The question for church leaders thus is not so much the goodness

---

11. See, for instance, Jonathan Gibson and Mark Earngey, eds., *Reformation Worship: Liturgies from the Past for the Present* (Greensboro, NC: New Growth, 2018); or this article from the American Guild of Organists: "Dutch Organ Culture During the Reformation," December 4, 2017, https://www.agohq.org/north-central-dutch-organ-culture-reformation/.

12. Leithart, "Embracing Ritual: Sacraments as Rites," 14–15.

of art per se but its specific use or misuse in particular contexts of worship, and it is for these misuses that we need to remain alert and discerning.

We ought not to underestimate the need for and power of silence.

Silence is essential to the experience of faithful worship. This may seem like a strange thing to say in a book on the arts, with its many encouragements to say and sound and move and show in worship. But it bears stressing nonetheless: silence is not opposite to acts of worship but intrinsic to them. Silence, of course, is not merely a negative thing: the absence of speech, the omission of sound, the refusal to act. It is also a positive thing.[13] Much like Mary's "Let it be," which she speaks in response to the divine word in Luke 1:38, silence is a kind of active passivity, opening up a space for God to speak and to transform us. If God is at work before we say or do anything in worship, and if Christ and the Spirit are continuously at work *during* our worship, then the proper human response is, first, to be silent, to listen, to wait, to watch, and not to rush in with our own words or to clog up the silence with busy activity. As Habakkuk 2:20 (NRSV) exhorts us: "the LORD is in his holy temple; let all the earth keep silence before him!"

It also needs to be stressed that silence plays a determinative role in the proper experience of art in worship. In music, as scholars and practitioners might remind us, silence represents a fullness rather than an emptiness. In the interstices of musical notes, silence swells and contracts, thereby generating meaning. For poets, speech lies hidden in silence, while language often finds its force in negative spaces. With the theater, at the end of an extraordinarily good play, an audience may sit sated and satisfied, unwilling just yet to break the silence with applause. A great play may also begin in silence—in a moment that invites anticipation. In dance, silence often creates particular moods and tensions, and with body language our silent gestures and movements often say everything. And unless we stand silently before a work of art and architecture, it will not yield its best insights to us or work its good powers on us.

So, for those of us who make art for worship and who make the decisions about which art to include or exclude, we do well to make plenty

---

13. Joseph Dougherty, "Silence in the Liturgy," *Worship* 69, no. 2 (1995): 143: "Silence is much more than the absence of sound, though when it occurs in a relatively quiet environment, silence wields great impact. Silence is the partner and foil of speech, and it is also the encompassing milieu, the envelope, in which all speech occurs."

of space for silence in our worship—in our songs, in our prayers, in our looking and showing, in our listening and narrating, and in our moving and resting. We do well, as C. S. Lewis imaginatively reminds us in *The Screwtape Letters*, to resist the demonic temptation to fill our lives and liturgies with more noise.[14]

The calling of liturgical artists is to be humble shepherds of the arts in worship.

The calling of liturgical artists is to be caretakers of the imagination, custodians of the emotional life, stewards of physical reality, and creators of life-giving metaphors that serve the various activities and purposes of corporate worship in a way that is attentive to the logic and powers of the arts but not on the terms of the arts. For artists who serve the church's worship, the terms of worship must always be central. Beyond this fundamental calling, the calling of liturgical artists is to offer "articulate" voice to creation's praise while never seeking to replace creation's own praise.[15] Their calling is to invite the church to delight in creation's "endlessly remarkable quiddity" for God's sake, rather than to take creation's own praise onto some "higher plane."[16]

Their calling is less a matter of "How can I do my art right?" and more a matter of "How can I love this people well?" When the latter question is answered properly, the former question, I suggest, usually takes care of itself. The honing of one's craft matters, yes; it too is a work of love. And the aim to provide a congregation with excellent art also constitutes a form of love. But anything that risks distracting artists from the fundamental vocation to love God and to love the people of God requires careful scrutiny. In love, finally, artists are freed to serve God, regardless of particular outcomes, to serve the people of God who have been entrusted to them in their congregation rather than the people who they *wish* were there, to learn everything they can from those who have gone before them and to

---

14. C. S. Lewis, in *The Screwtape Letters* (New York: HarperOne, 2015), 119–20, has the devil Screwtape say: "Music and silence—how I detest them both! . . . [Hell] has been occupied by Noise—Noise, the grand dynamism, the audible expression of all that is exultant, ruthless, and virile—Noise which alone defends us from silly qualms, despairing scruples and impossible desires. We will make the whole universe a noise in the end. . . . The melodies and silences of Heaven will be shouted down in the end."

15. Cf. Jeremy Begbie, "Christ, Creation, and Creativity," in *Voicing Creation's Praise: Towards a Theology of the Arts* (Edinburgh: T&T Clark, 1991), 169–85.

16. Richard Bauckham, "Joining Creation's Praise of God," *Ecotheology* 7 (2002): 52.

serve generously the generations that will follow them, and to discover in this manifold service a freedom that sets them fully free.[17]

Let love always be our guide.

In the end, when the love that characterizes the life of the Trinity marks all our practices of art in worship, it is then that they will serve the purposes of God in the church's liturgical life. This means that to love the Father as Jesus by the Spirit loves the Father is a way for us to love the things that the Trinity loves. It means that to love creation, and in particular the aesthetic and artistic aspects of creation, as Jesus by the Spirit loves creation for the sake of the Father's glory, is a way for us rightly to love creation. It means that the liturgical arts become good gifts of God when they enable the people of God to love Jesus and therefore, by the love that the Spirit sheds abroad in our hearts, to love our neighbors, whoever they may be, wholeheartedly.[18]

It means that pastors, worship leaders, and artists love God's people well by becoming more care-filled in their practices of liturgical art. They do so by encouraging a more thoughtful, contextually sensitive engagement of the arts in worship. They do so by discerning the way in which a specific practice of art in worship might be most appropriate at a given time and place. They do so by an engagement of the processes and products of liturgical art in a manner that is marked by Christ's self-sacrificial love.[19] And they do so for the sake of a transformative encounter with God that

17. I write at greater length about the calling of artists in the appendix, "Advice to Artists."

18. In chapter 12, "Liturgical Love," of his book, *Acting Liturgically: Philosophical Reflections on Religious Practice* (Oxford: Oxford University Press, 2018), Nicholas Wolterstorff writes about the two loves that ought to characterize all faithful experiences of worship: Christ-like friendship love and neighbor love. As an example of the former, he says: "Tolerating what one doesn't like is a form of love" (257). This might include the songs that are sung or the manner of dress. As an instance of the latter, he suggests that the "prayers of the people" fulfill God's command to love our neighbors. "In participating in such prayers," he writes, "one is manifesting one's love for one's neighbors by giving voice to that love. One is declaring that one is *for* one's neighbors. One is standing in solidarity with them" (269, emphasis original).

19. "Contemplation sees the hand stamp of the artist, the honesty and care that went into an object's making, the pleasing form and color and texture. Quality means love and care in the making of something, honesty and genuineness with any materials used, and the artist's special gift in producing a harmonious whole, a well-crafted work. This applies to music, architecture, sculpture, painting, pottery making, furniture making, as well as to dance, mime or drama—in other words, to any art form that might be employed in the liturgical environment or action." National Conference of Catholic Bishops, *Environment and Art in Catholic Worship* (Washington, DC: United States Catholic Conference, 1977), 10–11.

would enable God's people to live more faithfully in the actual contexts and conditions of their lives, however easy or difficult those may be.[20]

Blessed, then, is the church that learns to love the Trinity in this way. Blessed is the church that learns to love creation as God loves creation. Blessed is the church that loves the world as God so loves it. Blessed is the church whose practices of art in worship enable people to become whole and holy. Blessed is the church whose practices of art in worship enable human beings to become "aflame with the present glory of the Lord."[21] And blessed is the church that, with the glorious end in mind of God's purposes for the new creation, enables the faithful to become true children of God who "waste time for the sake of God" by delighting in God and in the bounty of God's goodness in creation.[22]

20. The Calvin Institute of Christian Worship has produced a host of excellent resources on the relation between worship and disability. This article in particular includes a variety of links to essays, books, and practical helps on the issue: "Each Ability and Disability Reveals God," February 25, 2014, https://worship.calvin.edu/resources/resource-library /each-ability-and-disability-reveals-god/. For a good list of books, see here: https://worship .calvin.edu/resources/resource-library/disability-within-faith-communities/. For helps specifically related to the arts in worship, see here: https://worship.calvin.edu/resources /resource-library/universal-design-vertical-habits-and-inclusive-worship/.

21. Jürgen Moltmann, *The Source of Life: The Holy Spirit and the Theology of Life* (London: SCM, 1997), 134.

22. Romano Guardini, *The Spirit of the Liturgy*, trans. Ada Lane (New York: Aeterna, 2015), 40.

Young people carrying a float during the Procession of James the Apostle, Patron Saint of Antigua, Guatemala (Photograph by author)

The Videographic Arts: Questions for Discernment

Technology allows us to amplify our worship to larger-than-life pro-
portions, so we can hear a whispered melody across a ten-thousand-
seat auditorium, but perhaps what we really need is worship that is
human-sized.

Greg Scheer, *Essential Worship*

11.9 percent of American congregations used video projection equipment in 1998, 26.5 percent in 2006–2007, and 35.3 percent by 2012.

Swee Hong Lim and Lester Ruth, *Lovin' on Jesus*

The job of media artists is attending to the "palette" of image and
color, movement and rhythm, sound quality and sound effect that
will best support and convey the message.

Marcia McFee, *Think Like a Filmmaker*

Just as the musical worship leader leads the congregation through
song, the visual worship leader leads the congregation through image.

Stephen Proctor, *The Guidebook for Visual Worship*

On the Promethean Powers of Electricity

With the introduction of electricity during the early decades of the twentieth century, the way that Christians worshiped together would never be
the same. Among other things, it allowed congregations to explore a whole
new territory of art—chief among them, media of art that took advantage
of the amplification of sound and the projection of images. Whether it
improved or marred the liturgical experience was a matter of perspective.

In all cases, the introduction of electricity to corporate worship has been a matter of context. And as it relates to the specific use of video in a context of public worship, it opens up a host of questions that require careful discernment. The purpose of this appendix is to provide a bit of context for the videographic arts in corporate worship and to suggest some questions that might be helpful for church and worship leaders to ask relating to the inclusion of screens, short films, environmental projection, or multimedia projectors in a liturgical space.[1]

How did electricity change worship? With the aid of electricity, artificial light could illuminate the worship leader and reduce ambient distractions for the worshiper by focusing attention on the leader. Film reels could replace the unpredictability of in-person testimony, while climate-control machines could enable the faithful to attend to the events of worship without the distractions of inclement weather. Lighting systems could also be installed to simulate both the theater and the concert stage. This might be done, as the case may be, to accent the drama of worship or to foreground the missional dimension of public praise. With the help of electricity, overhead projectors could be employed to eliminate the need to hold a songbook in hand. Hands could be freed up and the line of eyesight could be raised—from "down" to "up," from "near me" to "out to others." Within certain liturgical contexts, it could also liberate the hands to gesture freely, so that head, heart, and hand might move in concert to the praise of God.

It is also the case, for instance, that the loss of songbooks includes a lost opportunity to teach people how to read music. The inclusion of spotlights—by which mood can be modulated, visibility restricted, the perception of worship leaders altered, and a videographic scenery superimposed on the worship leaders—might, in certain contexts, stimulate theater-like desires that are at odds with the intentions of specific liturgical activities. The replacement of in-person testimonies with videoed testimonies might

1. "Media in worship can comprise any combination of nineteenth- and twentieth-century media forms: photography; cinematography; overhead projectors and transparencies; multimedia presentations with multiple active screens and audio tracks; audio recording and playback technologies including magnetic tape, CD, CD-ROM, DVD; music and computer-related forms of music and other sounds; video technologies, cameras, games, and video art; computer technologies and computer art; integrative digital multimedia technologies and digital art; and interactive performance and installation arts." Eileen Crowley, *Liturgical Art for a Media Culture* (Collegeville, MN: Liturgical Press, 2007), 15.

keep the worship on time, but it can also increase a sense of inadequacy in parishioners who witness these edited, prefabricated testimonies, set to a particularly evocative soundtrack, and find that their own nonedited, "natural," inarticulate, unscored lives cannot measure up to the lives of their brothers and sisters played out on the silver screen. Every use of artificial power in service of the arts in worship has opened up and closed down possibilities to form a congregation.

At the very least, electricity has enabled churches to do more and to do it longer. No longer bound by the physical limitations of the human body, the church is now able to amplify the powers of the body: a soft voice can become loud, a distant face can become near, and a large space in which parishioners are unequally positioned to the center of liturgical action can become small by virtue of high-definition speakers and high-resolution screens.[2] No longer limited by the rhythms of the natural world, the church can extend the hours of the day and bend the powers of the physical world in order to accomplish what, to early generations, might have felt like signs and wonders. What electricity has enabled, in short, is the obviation of the rhythms of nature, a triumph over the limitations of nature, and an enhancement of the powers of nature—for better and for worse.[3] With the videographic arts, human beings can be digitized, time can be manipulated, and sound can be matched to image in uncommonly powerful ways.

Equal parts undiluted enthusiasm and visceral antipathy mark the church's relation to the videographic arts. Events like the Worship Technology Conference or the SALT conference, for example, represent the enthusiastic embrace of all tech media that enhance both worship and mission.[4]

---

2. Cf. Swee Hong Lim and Lester Ruth, *Lovin' on Jesus: A Concise History of Contemporary Worship* (Nashville: Abingdon, 2017), 54.

3. Greg Scheer asks an important question on this account: "Have our sound systems dulled our ability to 'be still and know that I am God' (Ps. 46:10), taken away the intimacy of blending our voices with that of our neighbor, and made us forget the unabashed joy of singing a cappella so loudly that the room reverberates with praise? And as a practical matter, are the thousands of dollars we invest in sound equipment going to yield benefits if volunteers aren't trained to run it?" *Essential Worship: A Handbook for Leaders* (Grand Rapids: Baker Books, 2016), 214.

4. See https://www.worshiptechva.com ("This is the conference to attend to ask questions about audio, lighting, video, graphic design, Pro-Presenter, livestreaming, and more!") and https://saltcommunity.com ("Every Movement has a name, and every name has a meaning. For us, SALT is a reminder of the role creativity plays in the context of the local

Robb Redman speaks for many in this camp: "The arts and multimedia technology are not optional extras that add glossy slickness to their services. Rather they are a crucial element of the service because of the way that postmodern, post-Christian North Americans view their world."[5] On the other side stand those who worry that the inclusion of such media represents a distortion or distraction to faithful worship. Assuming that the TV, when placed at the center of a home, is detrimental to the formation of humans, a Twitter user asked Andy Crouch what it might mean for video venues at church. Crouch answered by tweeting a passage from Scripture: "When you see the abomination of desolation in the place it ought not to be . . . let the reader understand."[6]

What's needed, then, for those inclined to include the videographic arts in corporate worship, is a clear understanding of their peculiar powers and the wisdom to employ them well within a liturgical context. A brief exposition of their powers may be helpful here.

The Powers of the Videographic Arts

"A film is not a mere aggregate of various cinematic elements," writes Kutter Callaway. "It is a wholly new synthesis that issues from the dynamic interaction between the images we see and the sounds we hear."[7] Much like the visual arts, but in a far more totalizing, all-consuming fashion, with film or video the image is everything. Deriving from the Latin verb *video*, "I see," the art of video is a fundamentally visual medium, driven by the construction and juxtaposition of moving images. The power of a videographic work of art lies as much in what it shows as in what it hides. As Elijah Davidson puts it, "The movement in question is both that of the things contained within the image—the characters and objects—and the frame of the image itself."[8]

---

church. We believe that creativity is a seasoning, it's not the main course or a substantive side dish because creativity has no nutritional value").

5. Robb Redman, "Welcome to the Worship Awakening," *Theology Today* 58, no. 3 (2001): 372. Cf. Crowley, *Liturgical Art for a Media Culture*, 32.

6. Cf. Routley, *Twentieth Century Church Music* (New York: Oxford University Press, 1964), 156.

7. Kutter Callaway, *Scoring Transcendence: Contemporary Film Music as Religious Experience* (Waco, TX: Baylor University Press, 2013), 67.

8. Elijah Lynn Davidson, *How to Talk to a Movie: Movie-Watching as a Spiritual Exercise* (Eugene OR: Cascade, 2017), 38–39.

An additional power of video is its capacity to totally absorb our senses. With a videographic work of art, we enter into an intensely multimedia, multisensory experience. As Joe Kickasola explains, a video "so immerses us and engages us that it sparks our imaginative capacities for *simulation*. Some psychologists believe that dreams work the same way, which is why so many theorists have compared film to dreams."[9] Closely related to this power is the power to manipulate time. Famed Russian filmmaker Andrei Tarkovsky believed that the essence of cinema was its ability to capture moments and "to roll them and to unroll them forever."[10] Unlike the experience of a theater play, which unfolds in a consecutive timeline, a video may take the viewer into any number of experiences of time. And unlike a painting, which "embalms time," as André Bazin says it, a video cannot be properly experienced apart from an immersion in its "time frame," as one image succeeds another and so on and so forth.[11]

In contrast to the experience of a painting on a canvas, the power of storytelling in video resides in the images that move across a screen. "When film tells stories," observes Kickasola, "it is doubling its powers." In juxtaposing images and sounds, furthermore, an editor creates meaning for the viewer, while close-ups or establishing shots often function as emotional cues. And unlike the experience of reading of a poem, watching a video involves an experience of sights and sounds that have been juxtaposed in expected and unexpected ways. Finally, unlike musical theater, the sights and sounds are concentrated on a flat surface rather than in a three-dimensional, physical space. As Kickasola again explains, with a video, "we are often seduced into treating it as if it were real." Like Plato long ago, Christians have often worried about this particular power of video.

The Videographic Arts in Corporate Worship

With this brief exposition of the powers of the videographic arts in mind, what are the different ways that they might enter a context of corporate worship? As it is practiced today, the medium of video might be utilized to enhance the announcements; to support the giving of

9. Shared with me in email correspondence. November 3, 2015.

10. Davidson, *How to Talk to a Movie*, 41.

11. André Bazin, *What Is Cinema?*, vol. 1, trans. Hugh Gray (Berkeley: University of California Press, 2004), 14.

a testimony; to substitute for a sermon illustration; to function as a backdrop to the projection of lyrics on a screen; to generate a visual environment; to complement the confession of faith; to generate enthusiasm for service, evangelism, or mission; to serve as a visual parable; or to meet the needs of multicampus projection.[12] As the case may be, they may also serve to accent visual silence. As Stephen Proctor sees it, even "with the best intentions, our creative and technical efforts subtly take the focus off Jesus, and we deprive our congregations of the indescribable expressions of worship that can be found in an atmosphere of simplicity and silence."[13]

Questions for Discernment

What sorts of questions, then, might be worth asking as we discern the manner in which we incorporate the videographic arts into corporate worship? Here are a few questions that might jumpstart that conversation. Each set of questions is placed under a specific category.[14]

---

12. Cf. Marcia McFee, *Think Like a Filmmaker: Sensory-Rich Worship Design for Unforgettable Messages* (Truckee, CA: Trokay Press, 2016). For examples, see https://www.worshiphousemedia.com; https://www.theworkofthepeople.com; https://fullerstudio.fuller.edu/series/liturgical-meditations/; https://www.life.church; https://illuminate.us/faq/. TripleWide defines environmental projection as "the act of creating a visually immersive worship environment that ushers the intimate and powerful role of visuals, art & media back into our modern worship spaces," https://triplewidemedia.com/what-is-environmental-projection/.

13. Stephen Proctor, *The Guidebook for Visual Worship: Basic Training for Visual Worship Leaders* (n.p.: Illuminate.Us, 2014), 8; https://illuminate.us/learn/.

14. Sincere thanks to Steven Vredenburgh, a PhD student at Fuller Theological Seminary, for his insights and suggestions here. Thanks also to Greg Scheer, whose wisdom in his book *Essential Worship* (esp. pp. 220–23) has proved immensely helpful.

1. Liturgical

a . Is the use of videographic art there to be "cool" or "just because," or is it clearly serving a specific activity or purpose of worship? Is it clear to the congregation what action it is serving—for example, prayer, preaching, confession, Lord's Supper, testimony, and so on?

b . Is it serving that liturgical action in a manner that fits well? Do any kind of introductory remarks or words afterward need to be offered to put the videographic art in context?

c . How might a work of videographic art introduce a sense of awe into our worship? How might it help deepen a congregation's love of God?

d . Asked bluntly: do we really need animated graphics or video in our corporate worship? Just because we can doesn't mean we should.

e . Will projectors and screens become too jarring for the space and therefore become a perpetual distraction in worship rather than an aid to it?

f . Are the background, animated graphics to lyric projection really necessary? Are they tacky or are they tasteful? Do they overstimulate the eye or do they enable the eye and the ear—and the mouth—to worship fulsomely?

2. Cultural

a . How might the regular experience of video in the rest of our lives (at home, in the theater, on mobile devices, etc.) support or undermine the faithful practice of video in corporate worship?

b . In what ways might a film/video/TV-savvy people become spectators or consumers in the context of corporate worship rather than more faithful worshipers?

c. How might the predominant entertainment culture that absorbs most of Western society prove challenging to the faithful use of this medium of art?

d. What kind of teaching or instruction might a congregation need in order to respond well (effectively and faithfully) to graphic arts, short films, video installations, or projections?

3. Aesthetic and Technical

a. How important is the kind and quality of the work of videographic art?

b. Does the space support the use of videographic art well—for image and sound projection? If not, how can the space be redesigned to include videographic art in a manner that serves rather than detracts, by being ugly or clunky, from the given purposes of worship?

c. What is an economically prudent expenditure of money on the instruments and contents of videographic art?

d. Are there skilled people to run it well?

e. What does it mean to be a faithful steward of our resources? Are we spending too much or too little on technical equipment? Does a short-term investment in good-quality equipment become a long-term benefit or detriment to our worship together?

4. Ethical and Missional

a. In what ways might this medium serve the deaf, the elderly, the children, the young people, the homebound, the sick, caregivers, the persecuted church, people without transportation or on vacation, the severely disabled, or those with a variety of learning styles?

b. How might the videographic arts deepen relationships rather than perpetuate individualistic tendencies?

c. How might the videographic arts forge connections and kinships with members of the global church?

d. What environmental questions should a congregation be asking itself? How might our use of videographic art represent a way to care for God's creation?

Fate of the Earth, by Peter Gourfain, Cathedral of Saint John the Divine, New York City (Photograph by author)

Seven Affirmations on Context and the Worship Arts

1. All practices and experiences of art in corporate worship are fully meaningful only in context. Terms like "universal" and "timeless" to describe a work of liturgical art, for example, should not be used without qualification.

2. Contextuality is a complex rather than a singular thing. The following are specific elements that characterize contextuality, and they combine with each other to generate specific contextual intensities.

- Where a work of liturgical art is made/conceived/originated
- The local/geographic place in which it is experienced
- The ethnic/social/psychological culture of the congregation that experiences it
- The liturgical/theological culture of the congregation that experiences it
- The expectations that a congregation brings to a particular practice of art in worship
- The cultural associations evoked by a practice of art in worship
- Where it occurs within the order of worship and how it underscores or subverts the expectations of the particular liturgical activity to which it is matched
- The artistic tradition to which a practice of liturgical art belongs

3. For a work of liturgical art to effectively serve a particular activity of corporate worship, and in this way become faithful and fruitful for the particular congregation that experiences it, the context in which it is experienced must be understood and respected.

4. Artistic excellence is contextually relative.

5. Faithful, responsible artists will make every effort to understand and to respect the artistic tradition and therefore the larger art-historical and church-historical context within which they generate their work. This involves, among other things, attending to the history of the medium of art, honing their craft of art, and remaining informed of and involved in the contemporary conversation around the given medium of art.

6. A congregation's ability to enter deeply and appreciatively into a work of art in worship is, in many ways, determined by its understanding of the place within which the work exists in church history and contemporary cultural context.

7. In the spirit of the Nairobi Statement on Worship and Culture, the following things will always be true:

- Art in the context of corporate worship will always in some sense be transcultural.
- Art in the context of corporate worship will always in some sense be contextual.
- Art in the context of corporate worship will always in some sense be countercultural.
- Art in the context of corporate worship will always in some sense be cross-cultural.

Crucifix, St. George's Episcopal Church, Nashville, Tennessee (Photograph by author)

Exercises for Discernment

The following are a series of exercises that I give to my students in order to help them discover how the arts might form a particular congregation in a particular fashion. In asking them to choose among the possible variables, with respect to each exercise, I help them to discern the ways in which a specific practice of art in worship forms a congregation in contextually specific and intensive ways. I include these exercises here to offer readers an opportunity to discover with others how different media of art might form a specific community, depending on the variables chosen. Plenty of similar exercises could be done using other media of art in connection to specific activities of corporate worship.

Exercise 1: The musical arts and the liturgical activity of the confession of the church's unity.

Task 1: Choose a specific song related to the church's unity in Christ.

Task 2: Taking the confession of church unity as your liturgical activity, choose one item from the lists that follow.

Task 3: What does your choice open up and close down for the formation of a given congregation?

Body Posture

1. Walking
2. Bowing
3. Kneeling
4. Sitting
5. Standing
6. Hands raised
7. Holding hands

Participants

1. Instrument(s) only
2. An individual
3. A choir
4. All together (harmonized)
5. All together (melody only)
6. A canon/round
7. Call and response

Musical Style

1. A cappella
2. Chant
3. Folk
4. Pop-rock
5. Gospel/R&B/hip-hop
6. Global music
7. Classical

A Variable

1. Architecture
2. Seating arrangement
3. Ethnic makeup
4. Socioeconomic
5. Urban, rural, suburban
6. Ecclesial tradition
7. Other

Exercise 2: Visual art and prayer.

Task 1: Choose one from each category to explore the use of visual art in service of prayer.

Task 2: What does your choice open up or close down for the formation of this congregation?

Visual Media

1. A painting
2. A banner
3. A live painting
4. A sculpture
5. A digital projection
6. A stained glass window
7. A typographic art

Type of Prayer

1. Adoration
2. Confession
3. Thanksgiving
4. Petition
5. Intercession
6. Contemplation
7. Examination

Musical Accompaniment

1. Silence
2. A cappella
3. Instrumental
4. Folk/pop-rock
5. Gospel/R&B/hip-hop
6. Global music
7. Classical

Variables

1. Architecture
2. Seating arrangement
3. Ethnic makeup
4. Socioeconomic

5. Urban, rural, suburban
6. Ecclesial tradition
7. Other

Exercise 3: Church architecture and the liturgical activity of the Lord's Supper.

Task 1: Choose one from each category to create a combination of church architecture in service of the distribution of the Lord's Supper.

Task 2: What does your choice open up or close down for the formation of a congregation?

Building Design

1. Longitudinal
2. Central
3. Meetinghouse
4. Theater ("fan")

Image of Christ

1. King
2. Teacher
3. Friend
4. Prophet
5. Suffering Servant

Image of the Church

1. Family of God
2. Body of Christ
3. Temple of the Spirit
4. Ark of salvation
5. A pilgrim people

Variables

1. Socioeconomic/ethnic culture
2. Ecclesial/theological culture
3. Urban/rural/suburban setting
4. Architectural style
5. Other

Exercise 4: The kinetic arts and the liturgical activity of benediction.

Task 1: Choose one from each category to explore the use of the physical body in service of the benediction.

Task 2: What does your choice open up or close down for the formation of this congregation?

Physical Posture

1. Sitting
2. Kneeling
3. Standing with hands raised at waist level
4. Standing with hands raised above head
5. Holding hands
6. Dancing

Text

1. None (use instrumental music instead)
2. Numbers 6:24–26
3. Jude 24–25
4. Psalm 121:7–8
5. Second Corinthians 13:14
6. First Thessalonians 3:11–13

Ecclesial Identity

1. Nondenominational megachurch in suburbs
2. Rural Baptist with twenty-five elderly members
3. Presbyterian in Cairo, Egypt
4. Inner-city multiethnic
5. Conservative Anglican in San Francisco
6. Charismatic church plant in New York City

Contextual Variables

1. The communal culture of the congregation
2. The liturgical-theological culture of the congregation
3. The expectations of the congregation
4. The cultural associations evoked
5. Other?

Exercise 5: The theater and videographic arts and the liturgical activity of testimony.

Task 1: Choose one from each category to explore narrative art (spoken or filmed) in service of a testimony.

Task 2: What does your choice open up or close down for the formation of this congregation?

Task 3: What's one thing you could do to mitigate the losses involved in what your choice "closes down"?

Art Medium

1. A live testimony by person standing in front of congregation
2. A filmed testimony, edited and shown to the congregation on a screen

Topic

1. Story of God's rescue
2. Story of God at my job
3. Story of God in the world
4. Story of God's goodness
5. Story of God's neighborly love

Ecclesial Identity

1. Nondenominational megachurch in suburbs
2. Rural Baptist with twenty-five elderly members
3. Presbyterian in Cairo, Egypt
4. Inner-city multiethnic
5. Charismatic church plant in New York City
6. Conservative church in San Francisco

Contextual Variables

1. Who exactly is giving this testimony?
2. What is the communal culture of the church?
3. What's the theological culture of the church?
4. What are its expectations?
5. Other?

The Peace Fountain, bronze sculpture, Cathedral of Saint John the Divine, New York City
(Photograph by author)

APPENDIX D

Advice to Artists

Holiness is not something hazy and elusive that we know apart from earth but something that we can know only as it wells up out of the earth, out of people even as clay-footed as Jacob. . . . In spite of every-thing . . . Jacob reeks holiness.

Frederick Buechner, *Now and Then*

We have to be braver than we think we can be, because God is con-stantly calling us to be more than we are, to see through plastic sham to living, breathing reality, and to break down our defenses of self-protection in order to be free to receive and give love.

Madeleine L'Engle, *Walking on Water*

Failure taught me things about myself that I could have learned no other way.

J. K. Rowling, *Very Good Lives*

For those of you who participate in a regular or in an occasional way to serve the worship of the church as artists, a heartfelt thank you. Here are a few words of advice that I might offer to you as you think about your calling as an artist and about your work in service of the church. At the end of each point I pose a corresponding question that could be explored individually or with a small group.

1. Living deeply into your identity as the beloved of God, like Christ Jesus himself, is the ground upon which you will flourish in your calling as an artist. Living into your true identity, as God's beloved, does not happen automatically or naturally. It happens through hard-won, God-graced effort; it happens, as it did for Jesus in his earthly ministry, by the power of the Spirit. It requires also that you embed yourself in genuine community; that you cultivate deep friendship; that you seek the help of those who are more skilled than you and the wisdom of those who have gone before you; that you become a good student of tradition; that you pray; that you rest well and not just work hard; and that you trust that God will be faithful to bring to completion that which was begun in you. Living in this way, with this deeply rooted sense of your identity, enables you to take risks and to be okay if you fail. It enables you to plunge into life with a confident contentment rather than a fear-based, performance orientation. It enables you to face difficult conflict with other people because you know that you will not be undone by it. Living as God's beloved enables you to be always generous with others, because you know that God will ultimately take care of you by being *with* you, *for* you, above and below you, behind and before you, in quiet and in danger, to comfort and restore you, to borrow from the words of Saint Patrick's hymn. QUESTION: What is one way this year that you wish to live more fully as God's beloved?

2. **Think of your work as a way to participate in the prophetic vocation of Christ.** This means, among other things, that your work seeks to bear witness to the Word of God, both the Word made flesh in Christ Jesus and the Word written in Holy Scripture. Your work seeks to bear such witness to the church, to the world, and, chiefly, to yourself. This prophetic calling involves a proclamation and enactment of all that, by God's grace, is right in the world; of all that, by dint of human sin, is wrong in the world; and of all that, by the power of the Spirit, needs to be mended in the world and is in fact already being mended. This prophetic vocation includes naming and enacting justice and mercy, grace and truth. It includes hospitality to both friend and stranger. It also includes naming the complicated lot of human beings in the world in truthful, honest fashion. Participating in the prophetic vocation of Christ does not give you permission to be a bossypants or to stand on the margins of community, over against the community. It involves instead an invitation to true humility and to stand with and among, and even under, the community. QUESTION: What is one way that your work might bear prophetic witness to Christ's kingdom?

3. **Think of your work as a way to participate in the priestly vocation of Christ.** This means, among other things, that your calling through the work that you do for the church's worship is to offer the things of God to the world and, likewise, to offer the things of our world back to God. Your calling is to offer the life of God—the good, true, merciful, comforting, forgiving, hopeful, encouraging, redemptive, holy life of God—to the people of God. Your calling is also to offer the lives of the people—the confident and humble, whole and broken, heartfelt and half-hearted, faith-

ful and faithless lives—back to God in love. This calling involves sympathizing with people, not just for them. It involves interceding for your community, not just doing things for them. It involves vulnerability and transparency, not just courage and boldness. QUESTION: What is one way that your work might offer the life of God to your community?

4. Think of your work as a way to participate in the kingly vocation of Christ. In the Gospels we see Jesus the maker. As a maker, he fulfills the royal calling of Adam, to exercise dominion over the earth, to steward it, to make something of it and thereby to make sense of it. Jesus makes bread and fish, he makes wine out of water, he makes blind eyes see, he makes justice visible. Jesus also makes sense of things—of a world that is broken but not abandoned by God, and of a divine kingdom that is present yet hidden. In this light, your calling as an artist is to take the stuffs of creation and to make something of them in whatever context you may find yourself. You do so in order to make sense of the world that God so loves. You do so as witnesses to both the woundedness and wholeness of the world. QUESTION: What is one way that your work might enable your community to see the wounded yet beloved nature of the world?

5. Think of your work as a way to help us to become at home in our physical bodies. In many ways what you do as an artist is to enable us yet again to perceive our bodies as God in Christ perceives them and to trust that the Spirit is in the business of healing them. Look for ways to invite us to inhabit our senses and to discover the beloved world of God through our senses. See your work as a way to help us to become re-sensitized to the things that matter, above all to become more acutely sensitive to God. View your work as a way to nourish the eye, the ear, the nose, the tongue, and the skin and bones that God has given us, so that we might become instruments of God's healing of other people's bodies, too. QUESTION: How is your work helping people to connect to their physical bodies?

6. Think of your work as a way to help us to imagine the world as God imagines it. As scholars often remind us, we become what we repeatedly imagine. And it is the very stuff of our lives that constitutes our imaginative life. Our family systems, our personal experiences (now engrained in our memories), our daily and weekly customs, the media we regularly imbibe, the friends we gather around us, the spaces we frequently inhabit, the sources of our instruction, the authority figures we choose to admire, the art and entertainment we enjoy, the living conditions that mark our lives—all of these affect what we imagine possible or impossible, probable or improbable, desirable or undesirable. And because we do not rightly imagine the world by doing what comes most "easily" or "naturally" to us, we need help. That's where you come in as artists. You help us to imagine our lives as God imagines them, through the lens of the kingdom of heaven as Jesus describes it. QUESTION: How is your work enabling people to see the world as Jesus sees it?

7. **Think of your work as a way to help people, including yourself, to become emotionally mature.** See your art as a way to reflect and shape an emotional life that is attuned to the heart of God. Make work that gives edited language to our un-edited emotions. Because of the particular ways that the arts bring us into intentional and intensive experience of our emotions, think of your art as an aid to becoming emotionally in-tuned with others, too. Look also for ways to help all of us—and yourself as well—to cultivate "faithful feelings," feelings that have been healed by the Spirit and conformed to the desires of Jesus for this world. In this vein, the "true" version of you, remade in the image of Christ and refashioned by the Spirit, rather than the "false" version of you, marred by sin and the brokenness of this world, is one of the most powerful testimonies to the church and the world. QUESTION: How is your work making it possible for people to become emotionally whole?

8. **An insight is not a muscle.** Knowing a thing does not automatically result in doing a thing well. Reading a great book does not a great artist make—nor does attending a conference or a retreat, or getting struck by the Muse, or talking to smart people. Hard work is needed. Muscles must be exercised. Virtues should be cultivated, such as the virtues of humility, courage, diligence, and generosity. Nor can excellence in your craft be achieved apart from a measure of sacrifice, commitment to a rich community life, immersion in the practices that define your medium of art, and repeated exposure to the great works that characterize your art-historical tradition. As I tell my artist-daughter often, remember the 3 P's: perseverance, patience, and practice. And beyond that: *practice, practice, practice.* Keep making things, keep doing things, keep trying things, whether they're good or not, because the point is as much the process as it is the product. QUESTION: Which virtue do you most wish to cultivate in this season of life: humility, courage, diligence, or generosity?

9. **Something begets something.** If you make something with your art, that something will generate a *something* that leads to other *somethings*. Conversely, as I often told the artists under my care at our church in Austin, Texas: nothing begets nothing. Doing nothing, thinking nothing,

imagining nothing, feeling nothing, trying nothing—this is guaranteed to generate nothing. Sometimes all that's needed, then, in order to discover the way forward, is to make *something*. That something, that small beginning—that crummy, dodgy, rough, messy, embarrassing, awful, half-baked beginning—may require a great deal of faith and courage, but it will be worth the doing and it will beget something more. QUESTION: What is one *something* that you can do this week to make art?

10. **A disciple of Jesus is one who keeps disciplines.** The disciplines that we adopt in order to grow as an artist are God's instruments of grace. They are our way of reverently co-operating with God. The consequence of living an undisciplined life, or as Eugene Peterson puts it, an "unscripted life," is that we become governed by our base (or dysfunctional) passions and inordinate appetites. A good disciple, however, does not acquire disciplines overnight. A good disciple acquires them slowly but surely, usually best within a community of friends. While such a community is often hard to come by, it is what we must pray for continually. QUESTION: What is one discipline that you would like to cultivate in this season of life?

11. **Your calling is to be faithful to what God has entrusted to you, no more, no less.** What God has entrusted to you will be accompanied by the necessary graces to fulfill that calling. Or as Calvin Seerveld put it more generally, "Christ's body does not need to finish its cultural task in a given generation: it only needs to be faithful with what it is entrusted." This is easier said than done, of course, but it is still important to remember. You don't have to do everything. You don't have to do what your neighbor is doing. And just because you can doesn't mean you should. And while you may feel tempted to believe that this life is your only opportunity to fulfill God's calling in your life—to accomplish all your heart's desires—you must resist that temptation by God's grace and the regular encouragement of friends. The New Creation awaits you, and there will be an eternity to explore all the things you ran out of time to explore in this earthly pilgrimage. Be at rest. All will be well. QUESTION: How might you describe in one short paragraph what God has entrusted to you?

12. **To serve is to be free.** One of the prayers from the Book of Common Prayer says that to serve God is "perfect freedom." While this may seem counterintuitive in our contemporary age, we see its truth beautifully played out in the life of Jesus, who came among us as a servant. In his generous and glad service to the world, which he performed in equally generous and glad service to his Father, Jesus was perfectly free. It is his example that we must follow. Remember, then, that your work is a service chiefly

to God, who sees all that you have done and will honor your service. Your service is also to the people of God who have been entrusted to you in your congregation, not the people whom you *wish* were there. Your service is to your craft. Your service is to those who have gone before you. Your service is to those who will follow after you. Your service by the Spirit's power is a freedom that sets you free (Gal. 5:1). QUESTION: Whom are you being called primarily to serve in this season of your life?

13. The question for you as an artist is not only, "What is my calling?" but also and equally much, "With whom am I called to walk?" In the end we return to our beginning: a deep fellowship with others that arises out of our deep fellowship with the Triune God. As many of you have learned over the years, the discernment of your vocation is not a static thing. It is a dynamic thing, something you discover rather than determine; it is a thing that unfolds through time, not despite time, and it unfolds gradually, with fits and starts, rather than falling into your lap ready-made. A calling might be discerned early in life, but it is only truly lived into its depth, into its full richness, over the course of time. And if there is a coherent trajectory to your calling, it will be something that you will be able to trace only at the end of your life—and perhaps to make sense of fully only in the New Creation. The best condition for you to discover and to live into your calling, then, is in the company of kindred friends and in the community of those who share a common love and a common mission. May God grant you the grace to discern your calling and give you the gift of a community in which to flourish in your calling. QUESTION: Whom has God called you to walk with in this season of your life?

For Further Reading

The following list is far from comprehensive, but my hope is that these resources might serve as starting points for further reading, research, and informed uses of the arts in worship.

Chapter 1: The Meanings of Worship

On the general topic of sound worship leadership, I recommend Constance M. Cherry's book, *The Worship Architect: A Blueprint for Designing Culturally Relevant and Biblically Faithful Services* (Grand Rapids: Baker Academic, 2010). Also helpful are Ruth C. Duck, *Worship for the Whole People of God: Vital Worship for the 21st Century* (Louisville: Westminster John Knox, 2013); Zac Hicks, *The Worship Pastor: A Call to Ministry for Worship Leaders and Teams* (Grand Rapids: Zondervan, 2016); and Greg Scheer, *Essential Worship: A Handbook for Leaders* (Grand Rapids: Baker Books, 2016).

For those who wish to read an entry-level introduction to so-called liturgical worship, see Mark Galli, *Beyond Smells and Bells: The Wonder and Power of Christian Liturgy* (Brewster, MA: Paraclete Press, 2008). On the formative power of such liturgical worship, I recommend Jonathan Linman, *Holy Conversation: Spirituality for Worship* (Minneapolis: Fortress, 2010); Byron Anderson and Bruce T. Morrill, editors, *Liturgy and the Moral Self: Humanity at Full Stretch Before God* (Collegeville, MN: Liturgical Press, 1998); and Susan J. White, *The Spirit of Worship: The Liturgical Tradition* (Maryknoll, NY: Orbis, 1999). On the opposite end of the liturgical spectrum, I recommend Swee Hong Lim and Lester Ruth, *Lovin' on Jesus: A Concise History of Contemporary Worship* (Nashville: Abingdon, 2017); and Robert Woods and Brian Walrath, editors, *The Message in the Music: Studying Contemporary Praise and Worship* (Nashville: Abingdon, 2007).

For a clear-headed, cogent exposition of Trinitarian worship, see James B. Torrance, *Worship, Community and the Triune God of Grace* (Downers

Grove, IL: IVP Academic, 1996); I make it required reading in all my courses. For a more concentrated study of the Trinity in musical worship, I recommend Robin A. Parry, *Worshipping Trinity: Coming Back to the Heart of Worship* (Eugene, OR: Cascade, 2012). Also good is Simon Chan, *Liturgical Theology: The Church as Worshipping Community* (Downers Grove, IL: IVP Academic, 2006), and James J. Buckley and David S. Yeago, editors, *Knowing the Triune God: The Work of the Spirit in the Practices of the Church* (Grand Rapids: Eerdmans, 2001). Online resources include: https://worship.calvin.edu; https://cardiphonia.org; https://hymnary.org; http://www.brehmcenter.com/initia tives/fredbock/; http://www.brehmcenter.com/initiatives/globalworship/.

Though it's a collection of essays rather than a monograph, Frank Burch Brown's book, *Inclusive Yet Discerning: Navigating Worship Artfully* (Grand Rapids: Eerdmans, 2009), addresses important topics such as "Is Good Art Good for Christian Worship?" and "Enjoyment and Discernment in the Music of Worship" in an accessible manner. Similarly wise and generous-spirited is Harold M. Best, *Unceasing Worship: Biblical Perspectives on Worship and the Arts* (Downers Grove, IL: IVP, 2003). Both theoretically and practically helpful are Nicholas Wolterstorff's essays in *Hearing the Call: Liturgy, Justice, Church, and World*, edited by Mark R. Gornik and Gregory Thompson (Grand Rapids: Eerdmans, 2011), which put his considerable philosophical powers to the service of the church. Especially helpful are Wolterstorff's three essays specifically geared to the worship arts: "Thinking about Church Music," "Trumpets, Ashes, and Tears," and "The Theological Significance of Going to Church and Leaving and the Architectural Expression of That Significance."

Chapter 2: The Meanings of Art

For readers in search of the "Encyclopedia Britannica of the Arts in Worship," see Robert E. Webber's near-exhaustive book, *The Complete Library of Christian Worship*, volume 4: *Music and the Arts in Christian Worship, Book 2* (Nashville: Star Song, 1994). While it's a bit hodgepodge at times, it's still extraordinary what Webber collects here as an editor: essays on music and the arts among Messianic Christians, Independent Fundamentalist Churches, Reformed Episcopal, and the Women's Aglow Fellowship; essays on the history of jubilation and music leadership; articles on secondary visual arts resources; examples of drama, dance, and mime in worship; and so much more.

Resources that were particularly helpful to me in this second chapter include George Lakoff and Mark Johnson, *Metaphors We Live By* (Chicago: University of Chicago Press, 1980); Mark Johnson, *The Meaning of the Body: Aesthetics of Human Understanding* (Chicago: University of Chicago Press, 2007); Iain McGilchrist, *The Master and His Emissary: The Divided Brain and the Making of the Western World* (New Haven: Yale University Press, 2009); Morris Berman, *Coming to Our Senses: Body and Spirit in the Hidden History of the West* (New York: Simon and Schuster, 1989); Howard Gardner, *Frames of Mind: The Theory of Multiple Intelligences* (New York: Basic Books, 2011); and James K. A. Smith's first two entries in his Cultural Liturgies series, *Desiring the Kingdom: Worship, Worldview, and Cultural Formation* (Grand Rapids: Baker Academic, 2009) and *Imagining the Kingdom: How Worship Works* (Grand Rapids: Baker Academic, 2013).

Chapter 3: The Theological Meanings of Art in Worship

My book *The Theater of God's Glory: Calvin, Creation, and the Liturgical Arts* (Grand Rapids: Eerdmans, 2017) served as the theological backbone for much of what I write in this third chapter. Using John Calvin as a primary conversation partner, I show how the arts in worship arise out of the Trinity's good purposes for creation and culture making. Teasing out these good purposes of God for the arts, both Jeremy Begbie and Trevor Hart advance arguments along Trinitarian lines: with Begbie's two books, *Voicing Creation's Praise: Towards a Theology of the Arts* (Edinburgh: T&T Clark, 1991) and *A Peculiar Orthodoxy: Reflections on Theology and the Arts* (Grand Rapids: Baker Academic, 2018); and with Hart's two books, *Between the Image and the Word: Theological Engagements with Imagination, Language and Literature* (Surrey: Ashgate, 2013) and *Making Good: Creation, Creativity, and Artistry* (Waco, TX: Baylor University Press, 2014). Another book that I assign in my art and faith classes is Andy Crouch, *Culture Making: Recovering Our Creative Calling* (Downers Grove, IL: InterVarsity, 2013); it's both thoughtful and accessible.

Chapter 4: Worship and the Musical Arts

Jeremy Begbie's book *Resounding Truth: Christian Wisdom in the World of Music* (Grand Rapids: Baker Academic, 2007) involves a focused and substantive theological treatment of music, not just as it appears in worship, but as it shapes and participates in nearly every sector of human society. Along similar lines, I would recommend the multi-author volume *Resonant Witness: Conversations between Music and Theology*, edited by Jeremy S. Begbie and Steven R. Guthrie (Grand Rapids: Eerdmans, 2011), which includes categories such as "Music and Cosmos," "Music and Culture," "Music and Theology," and "Music and Worship." For a more narrowly focused christological investigation of music in the New Testament, I suggest starting with Matthew E. Gordley, *New Testament Christological Hymns: Exploring Texts, Contexts, and Significance* (Downers Grove, IL: IVP Academic, 2018).

Whereas Begbie's book is chiefly theological in nature, Tim Dowley's book *Christian Music: A Global History* (Minneapolis: Fortress, 2011) offers an excellent historical review of music in the church's life. For a more thematically organized review of church music, see Paul Westermeyer, *Te Deum: The Church and Music* (Minneapolis: Fortress, 1998). Also helpful are Ralph P. Martin, *Worship in the Early Church* (Grand Rapids: Eerdmans, 1975); and Calvin Stapert, *A New Song for an Old World: Musical Thought in the Early Church* (Grand Rapids: Eerdmans, 2007). Constance Cherry's book, *The Music Architect: Blueprints for Engaging Worshipers in Song* (Grand Rapids: Baker Academic, 2016), offers concrete and practically sound advice to pastors, worship leaders, and music directors. Similarly helpful is Reggie Kidd, *With One Voice: Discovering Christ's Song in Our Worship* (Grand Rapids: Baker Books, 2005); Roberta King, with Jean Ngoya Kidula et al., *Music in the Life of the African Church* (Waco, TX: Baylor University Press, 2008); Ned Bustard, editor, *It Was Good: Music to the Glory of God* (Baltimore: Square Halo Books, 2013); James Abbington, editor, *Readings in African American Church Music and Worship*, volumes 1 and 2 (Chicago: GIA Publications, 2014).

For a fascinating study of music in global Pentecostalism, see Monique M. Ingalls and Amos Yong, editors, *The Spirit of Praise: Music and Worship in Global Pentecostal-Charismatic Christianity* (University Park: Pennsylvania State University Press, 2015); also helpful is Monique Ingalls, Carolyn Landau, and Tom Wagner, editors, *Christian Congregational Music: Performance, Identity and Experience* (New York: Routledge, 2016).

Chapter 5: Worship and the Visual and Architectural Arts

Robin M. Jensen's book *The Substance of Things Seen: Art, Faith, and the Christian Community* (Grand Rapids: Eerdmans, 2004), occupies the same basic territory as William Dyrness, *Visual Faith: Art, Theology, and Worship in Dia-*

logue (Grand Rapids: Baker Academic, 2001). Both books introduce readers to the visual arts in Christian faith and worship in a way that is suitable to both classroom use and lay audiences. For a more focused investigation of the contemporary arts in worship, see W. David O. Taylor and Taylor Worley, editors, *Contemporary Art and the Church: A Conversation between Two Worlds* (Downers Grove, IL: IVP Academic, 2017).

I recommend both of Mark Torgerson's books on church architecture: *An Architecture of Immanence: Architecture for Worship and Ministry Today* (Grand Rapids: Eerdmans, 2007) and *Greening Spaces for Worship and Ministry: Congregations, Their Buildings, and Creation Care* (Herndon, VA: The Alban Institute, 2012). Both offer accessible, substantial, practical insights into the meaning of architecture for congregational life. More "hefty" books on church architecture, but still helpful, include the works of Allan Doig, *Liturgy and Architecture: From the Early Church to the Middle Ages* (London: Routledge, 2008), and Nigel Yates, *Liturgical Space: Christian Worship and Church Buildings in Western Europe 1500–2000* (London: Routledge, 2008).

Patricia S. Klein's book, *Worship without Words: The Signs and Symbols of Our Faith* (Brewster, MA: Paraclete, 2007), is a perfectly compact introduction to the meaning of signs, symbols, gestures, vestments, calendar, colors, feasts, saints, and architectural and sacramental elements of the church's historic liturgical worship. More focused on the church's use of images throughout history—such as images related to the stories and miracles of Jesus, angels, the afterlife, Old and New Testament figures, flowers and plants, real and mythic animals, shapes, letters and numbers, and so on—is Judith Couchman's book *The Art of Faith: A Guide to Understanding Christian Images* (Brewster, MA: Paraclete, 2012). Concentrated exclusively on liturgical vestments is David Philppart, editor, *Clothing in Glory: Vesting the Church* (Chicago: Archdiocese of Chicago, Liturgy Training Resources, 1997).

Those who wish to learn about the history, use, manufacture, theological significance, and effect of stained glass on the church's worship should read Virginia Chieffo Raguin's book *Stained Glass: From Its Origin to the Present* (New York: Harry N. Abrams, 2003). It's difficult to find a one-stop-shop book on the use of electronic, videographic, and digital arts in corporate worship, but Eileen D. Crowley's book *Liturgical Art for a Media Culture* (Collegeville, MN: Liturgical Press, 2007) does the job sufficiently well. Similarly helpful in this vein is Stephen Proctor's e-book, *The Guidebook for Visual Worship: Basic Training for Visual Worship Leaders*, which can be accessed online here: https://illuminate.us/learn/. Also helpful is this online resource: http://www.artway.eu/artway.php?lang=en.

I cannot more highly recommend the following online resource to pastors, worship leaders, artists, teachers, and scholars: The Visual Commentary on Scripture (https://thevcs.org). In the words of its director, Ben Quash, professor of Christianity and the Arts and director of the Centre for Arts and the Sacred at King's College London: "The Visual Commentary on Scripture (VCS) is a freely accessible online publication that provides theological commentary on the Bible in dialogue with works of art. It helps its users to (re)discover the Bible in new ways through the illuminating interaction of artworks, scriptural texts, and commissioned commentaries. Each section of the VCS is a virtual exhibition comprising a biblical passage, three art works, and their associated commentaries. The curators of each exhibition select artworks that they consider will open up the biblical texts for interpretation, and/or offer new perspectives on themes the texts address. The commentaries explain and interpret the relationships between the works of art and the scriptural text."

Chapter 6: Worship and the Poetic Arts

The unique gift that Malcolm Guite brings to the topic of poetry is his twin capacity as theologian-pastor and poet. In *Faith, Hope and Poetry: Theology and the Poetic Imagination* (New York: Routledge, 2010), Guite examines poetry from a theological perspective, while in *Sounding the Seasons: Seventy Sonnets for the Christian Year* (Norwich: Canterbury, 2012) he shows the reader what such a theologically informed understanding of poetry might look like in the service of the church's worship.

Similarly helpful are the following resources: Robert Atwan and Laurance Wieder, editors, *Chapters into Verse: A Selection of Poetry in English Inspired by the Bible from Genesis through Revelation* (Oxford: Oxford University Press, 2000); Eugene Peterson, *Holy Luck* (Grand Rapids: Eerdmans, 2013); Jeanne Murray Walker, "On Poets and Poetry," in *The Christian Imagination: The Practice of Faith in Literature and Writing* (Colorado Springs: Shaw Books, 2002); Robert Alter, *The Art of Biblical Poetry* (New York: Basic Books, 2011); Andrew Rumsey, "Through Poetry: Particularity and the Call to Attention," in *Beholding the Glory: Incarnation through the Arts*, edited by Jeremy S. Begbie (Grand Rapids: Baker Academic, 2001); E. C. Lucas, "Terminology of Poetry," in *Dictionary of the Old Testament: Wisdom, Poetry and Writings*, edited by Tremper Longman III and Peter Enns (Downers Grove, IL: IVP Academic, 2008); "Worship Resources,"

The African American Lectionary (http://www.theafricanamericanlection ary.org/PopupWorshipAid.asp?LRID=70); and the poetry section of https://imagejournal.org.

Chapter 7: Worship and the Narrative Arts

While the general idea of narrative in Scripture and of the story-telling shape of Christian faith is relatively uncontroversial for Christians, the particular idea of story as fundamental to the way we do theology, or the way we think philosophically about what it means to be human, or the way we conceive of the macro and micro elements of worship is less easily embraced.

Resources that have helped me think these things through theologically and philosophically include Kendall F. Haven, *Story Proof: The Science Behind the Startling Power of Story* (Westport, CT: Libraries Unlimited, 2007); Robert Alter, *The Art of Biblical Narrative* (New York: Basic Books, 2011); Garrett Green, editor, *Scriptural Authority and Narrative Interpretation* (Eugene, OR: Wipf & Stock, 2000); Robert McKee, *Story: Substance, Structure, Style, and the Principles of Screenwriting* (New York: Regan Books, 1997); C. S. Lewis, "On Stories," in *Of Other Worlds: Essays and Stories* (London: Geoffrey Bles, 1966); Frederick Buechner, *Telling the Truth: The Gospel as Tragedy, Comedy, and Fairy Tale* (New York: Harper & Row, 1988); James K. A. Smith, *Imagining the Kingdom: How Worship Works* (Grand Rapids: Baker Academic, 2013); N. T. Wright, "How Can the Bible Be Authoritative?," *Vox Evangelica* 21 (1991): 7–32; Paul M. Blowers, "The *Regula Fidei* and the Narrative Character of Early Christian Faith," *Pro Ecclesia* 6 (1997): 199–228.

More specifically worship-related resources include Eugene H. Peterson, "Novelists, Pastors, and Poets," in *Subversive Spirituality* (Grand Rapids: Eerdmans, 1997); Robbie F. Castleman, *Story-Shaped Worship: Following Patterns from the Bible and History* (Downers Grove, IL: IVP Academic, 2013); Jeff Barker, *The Storytelling Church: Adventures in Reclaiming the Role of Story in Worship* (n.p.: Parson's Porch Books, 2011); John W. Wright, *Telling God's Story: Narrative Preaching for Christian Formation* (Downers Grove, IL: IVP Academic, 2007); Herbert Anderson and Edward Foley, *Mighty Stories, Dangerous Rituals: Weaving Together the Human and the Divine* (San Francisco: Jossey-Bass, 1998); Anna Carter Florence, *Preaching as Testimony* (Louisville: Westminster John Knox, 2007); Eugene Lowry, *How to Preach a Parable* (Nashville: Abingdon, 1989).

Chapter 8: Worship and the Theater Arts

Interest in the role of the theater arts in worship surged in the 1980s and 1990s, but then, with the advent of affordable video equipment, began to wane in the early 2000s and to the present day. While there's no substitute for the potency of a live performance, congregations have found film and video to be cheaper and easier to pull off than works of theater. That being said, I would recommend several resources for churches that wish to take advantage of the medium of theater for worship.

Max Harris's book *Theater and Incarnation* (Grand Rapids: Eerdmans, 1990) isn't widely known, but I've found it to be one of the most useful books to think about theater theologically. While Dale Savidge and Todd Johnson, in *Performing the Sacred: Theology and Theatre in Dialogue* (Grand Rapids: Baker Academic, 2009), bring two perspectives to the table, that of a scholar and a practitioner, and while Wesley Vander Lugt and Trevor Hart introduce readers to a range of scholarly perspectives, in *Theatrical Theology: Explorations in Performing the Faith* (Eugene, OR: Cascade, 2014), Harris's book has the advantage of developing a single idea through to the end, namely, how the flesh-and-blood world of the theater is intimately related to the Word become flesh in Jesus of Nazareth. In Samuel Wells, *Improvisation: The Drama of Christian Ethics* (Grand Rapids: Brazos, 2004), the disciplines of theater and theological ethics, with a glance at worship, are brought together.

More practically helpful books include Max McLean and Warren Bird, *Unleashing the Word: Rediscovering the Public Reading of Scripture* (Grand Rapids: Zondervan, 2009); Michael Perry, editor, *The Dramatized New Testament: New International Version* (Grand Rapids: Baker, 1993); Alison Siewert, *Drama Team Handbook* (Downers Grove, IL: IVP, 2003); Jerusha Matsen Neal, *Blessed: Monologues for Mary* (Eugene, OR: Cascade, 2013); Jana Childers, *Performing the Word: Preaching as Theater* (Nashville: Abingdon, 1998); and Anna Carter Florence, *Preaching as Testimony* (Louisville: Westminster John Knox, 2007).

Chapter 9: Worship and the Kinetic Arts

Like the theater arts, the kinetic arts, or more particularly the dance arts, suffer from a paucity of material related to corporate worship. So much good work still needs to be done in this field, not just by practitioners and worship leaders but by theologians, too. One of the books that I assign in my classes is Ronald Gagne, Thomas Kane, and Robert VerEecke, *Introducing Dance in Christian Worship* (Portland, OR: Pastoral Press, 1984). Like so many books in this field, however, it's an older publication. It seems that the 1970s and 1980s were the heyday of liturgical dance for mainline congregations.

I had the privilege of hearing Celeste Snowber Schroeder speak in one of my seminary classes. Her book *Embodied Prayer: Harmonizing Body and Soul* (Liguori, MO: Triumph Books, 1995) is a thoughtful treatment of dance as a vehicle for spiritual formation. Similarly helpful is Sara Savage's essay, "Through Dance: Fully Human, Fully Alive," in *Beholding the Glory: Incarnation through the Arts*, edited by Jeremy S. Begbie (Grand Rapids: Baker Academic, 2001).

Other helpful resources include Angela Yarber, *Dance in Scripture: How Biblical Dancers Can Revolutionize Worship Today* (Eugene, OR: Cascade, 2013); Carolyn Deitering, *The Liturgy as Dance and the Liturgical Dancer* (New York: Crossroad, 1984); Kimberly Bracken Long, *The Worshiping Body: The Art of Leading Worship* (Louisville: Westminster John Knox, 2009); Sarah Pack, "How Lifting My Hands in Worship Became My Protest to God," *Christianity Today*, January 16, 2007, http://www.christianitytoday.com/ct/2017/january-web-only/how-lifting-my-hands-in-worship-became-my-protest-to-god.html; James Abbington, editor, *Readings in African American Church Music and Worship*, volumes 1 and 2 (Chicago: GIA Publications, 2014); and Steven Guthrie, "Temples of the Spirit: Worship as Embodied Performance," in *Faithful Performances: Enacting Christian Tradition* (New York: Routledge, 2007).

Online resources include: "Cultural Resources" via *The African American Lectionary*, http://www.theafricanamericanlectionary.org/PopupCulturalAid.asp?LRID=426; http://sacreddanceguild.org; https://hillsong.com/worship/hillsong-creative-new-campus-package/welcome-to-dance/; https://www.reformedworship.org/article/march-2005/praise-him-dance-its-time-consider-use-dance-worship; http://breakfree2024.com; http://www.balletmagnificat.com.

Chapter 10: Mother Tongues and Adjectival Tongues

The one resource that proved most helpful to me in this section was Colin Gunton, *The One, the Three and the Many: God, Creation and the Culture of Modernity* (Cambridge: Cambridge University Press, 1993). Additionally helpful were Nigel Love and Umberto Ansaldo, "The Native Speaker and the Mother Tongue," *Language Sciences* 32 (2010): 589–93; M. Paul Lewis and Gary F. Simons, *Sustaining Language Use: Perspectives on Community-Based Language Development* (Dallas: SIL International, 2016); Lamin Sanneh, *Translating the Message: The Missionary Impact on Culture* (Maryknoll, NY: Orbis Books, 1989); Alan Aldridge, "In Their Mother Tongue," *Modern Churchman* 29, no. 2 (1987): 12–18; Andrew Walls, *The Missionary Movement in Christian History* (Maryknoll, NY: Orbis Books, 2002); and Anna Carter Florence, *Preaching as Testimony* (Louisville: Westminster John Knox, 2007), ch. 4, "True Speech in the Mother Tongue."

Chapter 11: The Worship Arts and the Mission of the Church

Ruth A. Meyers, in *Missional Worship, Worshipful Mission: Gathering as God's People, Going Out in God's Name* (Grand Rapids: Eerdmans, 2014), has written the definitive book on the mutual relation between worship and mission. Similar in nature, though of an older vintage and from a different liturgical-theological context, is Sally Morgenthaler, *Worship Evangelism: Inviting Unbelievers into the Presence of God* (Grand Rapids: Zondervan, 1995).

On the question of multicultural, multiethnic, and global church worship, I recommend Sandra Maria Van Opstal, *The Next Worship: Glorifying God in a Diverse World* (Downers Grove, IL: InterVarsity, 2016); Gerardo Marti, *Worship across the Racial Divide: Religious Music and the Multiracial Congregation* (Oxford: Oxford University Press, 2012); Patrick R. Keifert, *Welcoming the Stranger: A Public Theology of Worship and Evangelism* (Minneapolis: Fortress, 1992); Josh Davis and Nikki Lerner, *Worship Together: In Your Church as in Heaven* (Nashville: Abingdon, 2015); and James R. Krabill, editor, *Worship and Mission for the Global Church: An Ethnodoxology Handbook* (Pasadena, CA: William Carey Library, 2013).

On the ethical implications of our corporate worship, I suggest starting with Mark Labberton, *The Dangerous Act of Worship: Living God's Call to Justice* (Downers Grove, IL: InterVarsity, 2007), and Paul Westermeyer, *Let Justice Sing: Hymnody and Justice* (Collegeville, MN: Liturgical Press, 1998). I also heartily recommend the work of Arrabon (https://arrabon.com) and Urban Doxology (http://www.urbandoxology.com).

Equally helpful are these online resources: https://worship.calvin.edu/resources/resource-library/bilingual-worship-three-lessons-i-learned/; https://worship.calvin.edu/resources/resource-library/universal-de

sign-vertical-habits-and-inclusive-worship/; http://globalworship.tumblr
.com; https://www.diu.edu/world-arts-center/; https://www.worldofwor
ship.org; http://heart-sounds.org; http://www.ethnodrama.com; https://
proskuneo.org.

For help with worship resources in ethnic and cultural perspective, I
recommend James Abbington, editor, *Readings in African-American Church
Music and Worship*, volumes 1 and 2 (Chicago: GIA Publications, 2014). This is
a wide-ranging, richly suggestive collection of essays exploring topics such
as "Perspectives on Praise and Worship," "Hip Hop and/in the Church,"
and "Hymnody: Sound and Sense." I also recommend Roberta King with
Jean Ngoya Kidula et al., *Music in the Life of the African Church* (Waco, TX:
Baylor University Press, 2008); Gláucia Vasconcelos Wilkey, editor, *Worship
and Culture: Foreign Country or Homeland?* (Grand Rapids: Eerdmans, 2014);
C. Michael Hawn, *One Bread, One Body: Exploring Cultural Diversity in Worship*
(Herndon, VA: The Alban Institute, 2003); and Charles E. Farhadian, editor,
Christian Worship Worldwide: Expanding Horizons, Deepening Practices (Grand
Rapids: Eerdmans, 2007).

Index